The Social Construction of Communities

Studies of Urban Society

Gerald D. Suttles

The Social Construction of Communities

The University of Chicago Press
Chicago and London

The University of Chicago Press, Chicago 60637
The University of Chicago Press, Ltd., London

© 1972 by The University of Chicago Press
All rights reserved. Published 1972. Fourth Impression 1974
Printed in the United States of America

International Standard Book Number: 0–226–78189–5
Library of Congress Catalog Card Number: 74–177310

For Kirsten

Contents

Acknowledgments

The papers included in this volume were written over a considerable period, and I am more than usually indebted to a number of people who have helped along the way. Morris Janowitz was the first to encourage me to produce the volume, and throughout its preparation he gave me thoughtful comments and criticism. At the outset, David Street urged me along with the work and later performed the painstaking job of a critic who read every sentence and aided me in necessary revisions. Much of the merit and clarity of the volume are due to his careful reviews. The discussions we have had in preparing the book have been an additional pleasure.

Wives are usually thanked last for their extreme patience. I would like to thank mine for her critical review of each chapter and her good humor when she gave me her telling reactions.

Throughout the preparation of this volume I was aided greatly by the Center for Social Organization Studies at the University of Chicago and funds provided by the Russell Sage and Ford Foundations. Aid was also provided by the Human Side of Poverty Project at the University of Chicago and the Rockefeller Foundation.

Some of the papers included here were first presented elsewhere and profited from revisions suggested by those who heard them. "The Defended Neighborhood" was presented first to the Faculty Seminar at the University of Chicago, and I would like to thank Morris Janowitz, David Street, Robert Hodge, Edward Shils, Donald Levine, and Terry Clark, all fellow members of the seminar, for their comments. "The Contrived Community" was presented at a seminar at the State University of New York and profited from the comments of Charles Perrow. The papers "Territoriality and Aggression" and "Territoriality and Distancing" were prepared for a seminar at the University of Chicago, and I am indebted to all the students in this seminar, especially Steven Barsky, Mosche Schwartz and Galen Cranz.

I would like to thank Julie Streich, who typed the manuscript, showed great tolerance toward my changes in mind, and exercised wise editorial judgment.

Part 1

Introduction

1. The Natural Community:
Its Followers and Revisionists

Practical and ideological issues tend so to overshadow our attention to urban residential groups that it is hard to gain any general perspective on them for explanatory purposes. There is a loud call for "local community control," for "all power to the people," for the "neighborhood school," and even for a sociology which seeks to serve only local populations.[1] There are also those who say that local urban communities have never had it so good or who recommend a kind of benign neglect to avoid hasty intervention before the self-healing effects of the unregulated marketplace have their rightful chance.[2] These policy proposals have both their conservative and their radical exponents. Some draw on the imagery of the local urban residential area to retrieve political power from the elites of national or large-scale economic and political organizations. Others draw on this same imagery to foreclose the possibility of developing higher-order social communities and to equate a kind of provincial conservatism with the "biological urge to territoriality."[3] All points of view seem to reify residential groups or "the community" into a social category whose reality is to be forced upon the urban metropolis rather than seeing the community as a social category to be used solely for purposes of description and analysis.

One of the purposes of this book is to pick a way through these competing images of urban residential groups while representing them authentically and pointing up their sociological significance.

1. Henry Etzkowitz and Gerald M. Schaflander, *Ghetto Crises* (Boston: Little, Brown and Co., 1969); and William W. Ellis, *White Ethics and Black Power* (Chicago: Aldine Press, 1969).

2. Edward Banfield, *The Unheavenly City* (Boston: Little, Brown and Co., 1968).

3. Robert Ardrey, *The Territorial Imperative* (New York: Atheneum, 1966); Konrad Lorenz, *On Aggression* (New York: Harcourt, Brace and World, 1966); and Desmond Morris, *The Naked Ape* (New York: McGraw-Hill, 1967).

Both folk models and social science images of the local community have an importance which goes beyond their representational accuracy. These simplified images serve us well by reducing the complexity of the urban landscape to a range of discrete and contrastively defined ecological units despite the general continuity, gray areas, and constant changes in any section of the city. They help us to decide where to live, where to walk at night, and when to start worrying about our children's absence; they help us make a welter of day-to-day decisions in which what we do depends heavily on where we think we are. Above all, these cognitive maps show our preoccupation with personal safety and the need to get a quick fix on the relative trustworthiness of fellow pedestrians, residents, and "trespassers." In the absence of a very discrete and simple ecological pattern to urban life, the images developed by social scientists or other observers become especially essential to decision making of this type. Where these cognitive models may not be correct, they are at least determinate. Sometimes the actual ecological pattern of a city is so inchoate or gradually changing that a direct, or literal, description, if that were possible, could only confuse and lead to indecision. A cognitive map of our urban environs is useful for precisely the reason that it simplifies to the point of exaggerating the sharpness of boundaries, population composition, and neighborhood identity.

Such images, however, are seldom only gratuitous fictions which people resort to in the absence of clear guidelines, self-evident from an inspection of the urban environment itself. To a large extent the folk models we have for urban communities have become the operating bases for both the urban planner and the citizen selecting a place to live. Our technical, sociological models of the urban community are drawn largely from these folk images and have added to their diffusion and acceptance as realistic or "scientific" portraits. Both kinds of cognitive maps can become self-fulfilling prophecies which help tailor the urban landscape into a more discrete and stereotypic pattern. But sociological models of the urban community have not just made more explicit the preexisting folk models which persist. Sociological studies of the urban community have also been especially powerful in raising doubt about the accuracy of folk models and tend to supplant them as authoritative accounts of where people live, how they live, and what the possible functional relationship is between ecological areas.

Doubtless, this role for sociological models of urban communities was unanticipated. But the authoritative character of sociological models based on a broad selection of empirical materials has made them advantaged competitors in developing our images of the urban community. The extraordinary complexity of the city and the partiality of individual experience make necessary some concerted and self-conscious attempt to represent the urban landscape for its residents. Often then, sociological models have been appealed to because of their relative accuracy and generality. In turn, these models are on their way to being reincorporated into our folk images and to a self-fulfilling pattern of urban distribution. Nowhere is this more evident than in Chicago, where urban sociology had its start and has left its imprint in the city's seventy-five "authoritative" community areas. These community areas do not wholly coincide with popular collective representations nor are they solely the contrivance of Burgess and his students.[4] Over time, however, they seem to have emerged as the most durable and widely used bases for describing the community life of the city and for devising a number of territorially based programs, businesses, and administrative units.[5]

This role of sociological mapping of urban communities is not something we must deplore or try to avoid lest it make research more difficult. As I hope to show in the following chapters, urban life requires a differentiated model of its community areas and places a premium on those models which are accurate and have the most potential for becoming a guide for future urban development. To the extent that sociological descriptions of the urban

4. Vivian Palmer, *Field Studies in Sociology* (Chicago: University of Chicago Press, 1928). Also see Albert J. Hunter, "Local Urban Communities: Persistence and Change" (Ph.D. dissertation, University of Chicago, 1970).

5. See a forthcoming study by Steven Barsky, "The Consolidation and Fragmentation of Local Communities" (Ph.D. dissertation, University of Chicago).

community are accurate, they provide people with their most authoritative way of choosing a home, of guiding the daily movements of their children, and of adjusting present ecological and administrative structures to form a coherent system. As sociologists aspire to a scientific representation of the urban community, they cannot avoid providing also an authoritative model which people accept as true as well as useful for future planning.

The ecological facts of urban existence do not of course disappear because people have oversimplified or misrepresented them. The physical plant of a city, its transportation lines, and the distribution of population characteristics are not just facts which people must pick and choose from in constructing cognitive models; they are stubborn conditions which residents must sometimes strain to conceptualize lest their behavior become irrational and unfulfilling. Much of the research carried out by hard-data ecologists assumes a sort of persistent aggregate rationality in the way residents, businessmen, public officials, and criminals come to grips with their physical environments.[6] This sort of calculating behavior is possible only if it is guided by a model of community areas along with some notion of the ways they develop, become recognizable, and persist. Behind the "rational" activities of the realtor or the burglar, for instance, there stands an intricate structure of assumptions about how the city is carved into separate pieces and why these spatial units persist, change, or become different from one another. An immediate inspection of the urban landscape leads to little more than confusion. Doubtless most of the city's ecological patterns are present and often they are insusceptible to easy alteration. But these stubborn features of the urban metropolis do not immediately make themselves known to its residents. In the United States millions of immigrants and migrants have persistently demonstrated that they are only confused in their first encounter with the naked facts of urban distribution and the functional relationships between its spatial fixtures.

---

6. Brian J. L. Berry and Phillip H. Ries, "The Factorial Ecology of Calcutta," *American Journal of Sociology* 74 (March 1969): 445–91; and Calvin Schmidt, "Urban Crime Areas," *American Sociological Review* 25, pt. 1 (August 1960): 527–42, pt. 2 (October 1960): 655–78.

A reasonable or rational approach to urban life depends on a mental template of its structure and the way some natural and man-made features of the environment help determine that structure. Inevitably sociologists contribute to these models of the urban community and the way in which some parts of it are brought into conformance with the models.

The purpose here, then, is to provide a more differentiated perspective on urban residential or territorial groups, one which preserves the distinction between our cultural and ecological models while also viewing these localized groups as portions of a much more complex society. Essentially, there are two aims. One is to show how people use territory, residence, distance, space, and movement to build up collective representations which have communicative value. The other is to show how residential groups and locality groups are inevitably partial structures whose very existence and character depend on their relationship to a wider society. Before we confront these problems in the next chapter, it is worthwhile to pause and look at the prevailing sociological model of the urban community and the ways in which it has limited or foreshortened our collective representations.

Original Ingredients of the Natural Community

Universality

Many of the conflicting claims for or against the autonomy of residential groups could be dismissed as a value conflict were it not for the way in which factual and sociological accounts get drawn into the fray. A large part of the confusion derives from the equivocal and partial accounts of sociologists who have framed questions and answers which have been dragged into policy statements whether or not their authors wished them there. The way in which these policy statements seem to abuse or misuse sociological materials is an index to our lack of clarity and our tendency to formulate concepts and alternatives which get reified past our data. A long-time culprit in this regard is the idea of the "natural community," introduced early in the development of

sociology by Park and Burgess.[7] As I read Park and Burgess, they
meant to emphasize the way in which urban residential groups are
not the planned or artificial contrivance of anyone but develop out
of many independent personal decisions based on moral, political,
ecological, and economic considerations. Their views were closely
tied to the American urban community, and they may have meant
only to distinguish American residential groups from those which
were more nearly the brainchild of European monarchs or governments. Nonetheless, the term *natural* was apparently picked up
and taken to mean a type of residential solidarity which was universal because it was uninfluenced by culture or administration.
Some observers were quick to point out the restricted occurrence
of the natural community, the variety of other residential groups,
and the way in which communities fit into broader social structures.[8] The natural community was, nonetheless, eventually productive of a series of false starts, one of which was the controversy
over whether or not the local community still existed. The word
natural seems to have left the impression of a primordial social
solidarity which existed apart from social convention in somewhat
the same way as the social categories of male and female, young
and old, are presently defined in popular discussion. Cast against
this set of presumptions, practically no local urban neighborhood
or community seemed to achieve the appropriate degree of consensus on membership and a sufficiently close identification of its
members. A large number of people seemed unaware of the community in which they lived and some seemed not to identify with
it in any case. The local community, some said, was disappearing.[9]

   Such a judgment was wrong on two counts. First it assumed
that there was some golden age during which the local community

   7. Robert E. Park, Ernest W. Burgess, and Roderick D. McKenzie,
The City, 4th ed. (Chicago: University of Chicago Press, 1967).
   8. Milla Aissa Alihan, *Social Ecology: A Critical Analysis* (New York:
Columbia University Press, 1938); James A. Quinn, "The Burgess Zonal
Hypothesis," *American Sociological Review* 5 (April 1940): 210–18; and
Walter Firey, "Sentiment and Symbolism as Ecological Variables," *Ameri-
can Sociological Review* 10 (April 1945): 140–48.
   9. Maurice R. Stein, *The Eclipse of Community* (New York: Harper
and Row, 1960); and Robert A. Nisbet, *The Quest for Community* (New
York: Oxford University Press, 1953).

had achieved almost total consensus on its membership and a personal identification on the part of its residents. Second, it assumed that the local community needed the allegiance or recognition of all or most of its members to continue as an influential social unit. Janowitz's study of the community press addressed the latter issue, and his concept of the community of limited liability was partially responsible for drawing attention to the specialized role of the community and the limited number of people who act as its custodian.[10] The image of the local community as a planless outgrowth of ecological segregation has persisted, nonetheless, and along with it the view that homogeneity and stability were at least once characteristic of local residential groups.

Planless Stability

People seem willing enough to accept the community of limited liability as an appropriate contemporary formulation, but the assumption of a golden age when the local community was supreme has remained even less contested in sociology.[11] This romantic image has endured as a poignant fixture in the public statements of those interested in deriding the present to negotiate for either a different future or a return to the past. The concept of the natural community seemed to lend itself to this usage because it suggested a process in which communities were more nearly the products of personal and human nature than the contrivances of planners, bureaucracies, and depersonalized institutions. There is evidence, however, that local communities have varied enormously in their stability and autonomy over the last two hundred years.[12] Some of the early mill towns of New England were composed almost wholly of female migrants who nonetheless seemed to have

10. Morris Janowitz, *The Community Press in an Urban Setting: The Social Elements of Urbanism,* 2d ed. (Chicago: University of Chicago Press, 1967).

11. Louis Wirth, "Urbanism as a Way of Life," *American Journal of Sociology* 44 (July 1938): 1–24; and Nisbet, *Quest for Community,* pp. 3–74.

12. William Parrish, "Migration and Modernization: The Impact on Social Participation" (unpublished manuscript, 1970).

formed a quiet and orderly community.[13] The early company towns in the textile and coal-mining regions of the South were certainly not autonomous and belie any assumption that the intervention of government and big business is a recent phenomenon.[14] Reports on mining towns and those which grew up around the lumber industry make some of our inner city slums sound like orderly places to live.[15]

Even as Park and Burgess wrote, the visible hands of the builder, the booster, and the developer were probably as active as they are today. Chicago, like many cities in the United States, was partially a contrived city with the Burnham plan, the grid pattern, and the construction of adjacent areas under the control of a small number of developers. In emphasizing the planless character of the city, Wirth only pointed to the absence of a single plan and governmental controls.[16] But the city did not really grow like Topsy: its designers were not a single group, but to a large extent they were of a single mind. By comparison, the great urban centers of today may lack comparable directing forces to give them pattern and stability.

Alternatively, some of the most disruptive and unforeseen events that have made urbanization difficult to plan for may be declining at the present time. The great migrations initiated by the discovery of the New World and those set off by industrialization may have slacked off some in recent decades. Banfield may be right in saying that these long-term sources of residential instability have declined, without, however, being correct in the assumption that urban communities are more stable and agreeable

13. Hannah Josephson, *The Golden Threads* (New York: Russel and Russel, 1949).

14. Harry M. Caudill, *Night Comes to the Cumberlands* (Boston: Little, Brown and Co., 1963); John Kenneth Moreland, *The Millways of Kent* (New Haven: College and University Press, 1965); Lester Pope, *Millhands and Preachers* (New Haven: Yale University Press, 1965); and Morton Rubin, *Plantation County* (Chapel Hill: University of North Carolina Press, 1951).

15. Theodore Dreiser, et al., *Harlan Miners Speak: Report on Terrorism in the Kentucky Coal Fields* (New York: Harcourt, Brace and Co., 1932).

16. Louis Wirth, "A Bibliography of the Urban Community," in Park, Burgess, and McKenzie, *City*.

places to live.[17] The stability and loyalty of residential groups are features that the residents can only partially achieve on their own. More than ever, the local community must juggle an increasing range of exchanges and communications with other residential groups and organizations in the wider society. In some ways the company town has an advantage because its adversaries and benefactors are consolidated into one or a few organizations. It is in a weak bargaining position, but it knows with whom it must bargain. Today the local community in an urban metropolis must often try to negotiate with several federal and state authorities and as many as one hundred city bureaucracies.[18] Finding a way of formulating these relationships may be far more crucial in the future of residential areas than the disruptions due to transiency, ethnic conflict, or anonymity. The growth of megalopolis is in large part a man-made problem caused by the inflexibility of city boundaries, administrative fragmentation, and our failure to find administrative channels by which communities can identify themselves to either their opponents or potential benefactors. Rather than benign neglect, this situation probably requires a more centralized attempt to define local communities and relate them directly to the public and private agencies supposed to serve them.

Sentiments

For the entire length of its widespread usage into the 1940s, the natural community was not seen as primarily an intentional or instrumental collectivity, and subsequent explanations of its solidarity were heavily weighted toward the development of sentimental ties among coresidents.[19] This had a number of consequences,

17. Banfield, *Unheavenly City.*
18. I have been told that members of the Hyde Park-Kenwood Neighborhood Council attribute part of their success to having learned of and established contact with over 130 municipal bureaucracies.
19. Norton Long, for example, seems to take sentiments as being crucial to neighborhood organization in an otherwise unsentimental account of the local community, "Political Science and the City," in L. Schnore and H. Fagin, eds., *Urban Research and Policy Planning* (Beverly Hills: Sage Publications, 1967), pp. 243–62. Even in his criticism of Park and Burgess, Firey tended to support the large role of sentiments in community formation (Firey, "Sentiment and Symbolism").

the first of which was to direct attention to shared social characteristics as a basis for shared feelings and values. Although this was often a correct description of current urban neighborhoods in the United States, it overemphasized the role of loyalty as the single most important claim which coresidents could make on one another.[20] Where researchers found that the loyalties of coresidents were weak, they went on to assume that the local community was insignficant in their lives. This left us unprepared for communities, like those created by public-housing projects, where the residents are very homogeneous in their social characteristics but may still lack any strong loyalties to one another. Correspondingly, such an outlook deflected our attention from the circumstantial definitions which do affect coresidents irrespective of their loyalty to each other. The most extreme example of this may be Rainwater's study of the Pruitt-Igoe housing project, in which a very homogeneous population is almost totally lacking in loyalty among coresidents but, because of their residence, cast in the public mind as a group of losers.[21] Whether or not residents identify with their neighborhood or feel very positive about it, it is something with which they must live.

This emphasis on sentimental ties also tended to focus research on interactional networks, shopping practices, and local usage patterns as a way of accounting for the progressive development of a localized web of interpersonal relations and intimacy.[22] The local community, then, could be seen as a sort of gradual, aggregate by-product of individual action. This has never struck me as a very likely line of argument, for there seems no reason for such unbounded networks to eventuate into a corporate identity and any sharp sense of neighborhood boundaries. There is simply no reason why people should try to simplify and condense this cobweb of relationships into a cognitive model that vastly distorts them. Most likely, local communities and neighborhoods, like

20. Long, "Political Science."
21. Lee Rainwater, *Behind Ghetto Walls* (Chicago: Aldine Press, 1970).
22. Harvey Warren Zorbaugh, *The Gold Coast and the Slum* (Chicago: University of Chicago Press, 1929).

other groups, acquire a corporate identity because they are held jointly responsible by other communities and external organizations. Thus, I suggest, it is in their "foreign relations" that communities come into existence and have to settle on an identity and a set of boundaries which oversimplify their reality. It will be useful, then, for us to reexamine the more instrumental and external demands placed on the local community and to balance them against a long-term stress on the growth of sentiment and the indigenous development of communal groups.

Primordial Solidarities

Part of the attraction to the term *natural community* was the analogy it drew to plant communities and to the processes of competition and segregation. In communities in the United States this analogy was especially compelling both because of the country's unregulated forms of competition and because of the wide range of ethnic and racial groups sorting themselves out in its large cities. The ethnic, economic, religious, or socioeconomic enclave and the local community, then, became almost parallel descriptions of the same thing. In turn, the further usage of the "natural categories" of race, ethnicity, and native ability seemed to round out the picture and keep it within the same framework.

Such a starting point was rich in further implications and lines of departure. One of the first was to point out the preexistence of cultural unity among such groups as a continuing basis of local solidarity.[23] Another was to emphasize traditional forms of affiliation through marriage, religion, and ethnic associations as the avenues along which the local community developed its internal order and a mounting conceptualization of itself as a corporate group. As a result of both these approaches, the local urban community could be thought of as a sort of crescive by-product in which its broader identity was only a summary statement for many social groupings. Thus, the summary identity was not an essential element but only a kind of epiphenomenon or oversim-

23. Louis Wirth, *The Ghetto* (Chicago: University of Chicago Press, 1928).

plification. In turn, some demographers and ecologists felt entirely justified in reducing the community back into its separate elements —ethnicity, race, income, and the like—in a quantitative study of available data on individual characteristics.[24]

Unfortunately, this style of research failed to capture what some thought essential to communities, particularly their reputational content and the ethos of local culture.[25] Such an approach also prejudged what was an important research question: How are varying proportions of racial, ethnic, and income groups selectively highlighted in the reputation of local communities? Finally, it excluded from consideration the relationships between communities and their broader social environments. One of the aims of this book is to reopen these questions and reexamine the problem of how aggregate population characteristics along with more structural features are included into community reputation and help determine its relationship to its environment.

Taken together, the separate elements of the natural community fell together to form a single gestalt in which every piece of the puzzle suggested the others. The presumed universality of the local community pointed toward its grass roots construction on the basis of such durable differences as race, ethnicity, and income. The primordial ties of its residents and their reliance on traditional forms of affiliation implied the strong play of sentiments and the crucial role of loyalty or clannishness in community formation. The planlessness of the community gave full range to the play of sentiment and the exercise of noninstrumental prejudices developed through the crescive growth of interpersonal networks. All these elements were in tune with one another and

24. For example see Maurice R. Davie, "The Pattern of Urban Growth," in George P. Murdock, ed., *Studies in the Science of Society* (New Haven: Yale University Press, 1937), pp. 131–61.

25. Anselm L. Strauss, *Images of the American City* (New York: The Free Press of Glencoe, 1961); Georg Simmel, "The Metropolis and Mental Life," in K. Wolff, ed., H. H. Gerth and C. Wright Mills, trans., *The Sociology of Georg Simmel* (Glencoe, Ill.: Free Press, 1950); and Robert E. Park, *On Social Control and Collective Behavior* (Chicago: University of Chicago Press, 1967), pp. 3–18, 55–84.

seemed to conjure up an almost inevitable reality in which sentiment, nature, primordialism, universality, and unplanned clannishness combined in a particular social configuration which we
could scarcely doubt existed.

Unfortunately, this vision of the community in the United States
left us with the impression that it was a sort of survival, like the
appendix or a second-order abstraction from more basal elements
of social morphology.[26] With the decline of ethnic differentiation
and segregation, some communities should have disappeared. Heterogeneity, when and if it occurred in some populations, should
have removed any sense of community or any attempt to strive
toward a community. The nucleated shopping center should have
produced an equally centripetal sense of community and made
some suburbs our strongest candidates for the label *community*.

During the 1960s and early 1970s nothing like this has quite
taken place. Despite the forecast of community decline, whole
social movements have aroused themselves around the issue of
local control. Some of the most heterogeneous residential groups
have been among the most vociferous in demanding their recognition and their right to be acknowledged as a social group.
Well-planned suburbs with their central shopping districts and
segregation from cross-traffic seem to be among our most atomized communities and the least able to develop a corporate body
of representatives and a native identity apart from the one developers have given them. At times the community seems to force
itself on the attention of administrators when they are least prepared to expect it. At other times, the community is least able to
mobilize itself when most expected to.

This book suggests a way of dealing with these questions and
of going past the concept of the natural community without wholly
abandoning the contributions promoted by so suggestive a concept. One starting point is to view residential aggregates as essentially artificial or imposed forms of residential segregation in
which the residents themselves and their shared characteristics
are also distinctive earmarks which the residents, outsiders, and

26. Stein, *Eclipse of Community.*

external organizations seize upon to sort one another out for selective treatment and the extension of areally defined policies.
Another starting point is to recognize that residential aggregation
inevitably produces proximity and the necessity of establishing
discrete areas as the basis for extending trust, for sharing guilt by
association, for swapping gossip or private knowledge, and for
mobilizing to meet both the symbolic and material challenges
brought on by the environment.

Territoriality as Social Principle

While the natural community receives continued critical attention
from sociologists, a new intellectual movement developing from
the sidelines threatens to reduce it to an even more primitive formulation. The harbingers of this movement are not numerous, but
they have behind them the accumulated research of ethologists
on nonhuman communities, and they are reluctant to wait for
contemporary sociologists to find analogies as Park and Burgess
drew theirs from the ecologists Warming and Clement. In the view
of Ardrey, Lorenz, and Morris, the natural community is not
merely a suggestive and powerful analogy, but a literal and universal form which humans share with other animals because their
instincts and genes drive them toward "territoriality."[27] Recast as
a "territory," the local urban community can be reduced even
further from the influence of human planning, choice, and external influence.

Such a view of the human community has little evidence to
warrant it except for the powerful suggestibility of a vocabulary
in which sociologists and ethologists have freely adapted each
other's terms to suit their own purposes. Indeed, one can see in
the overriding analogies of Ardrey, Lorenz, and Morris the diffusion of sociological terms adopted by ethologists which are now
returning to haunt sociologists. There are, I think, two ways of
viewing this peripheral movement. First, such analogies include
a strong ideological component which attempts to give such re-

27. Ardrey, *Territorial Imperative;* Lorenz, *Aggression;* and Morris,
Naked Ape.

ceived social forms as the family and the community uncontested places in society. Deriving from this is a view that small-scale, local groups are fundamentally antagonistic to one another and that almost all attempts to combine them into larger, cooperative groups can only be regarded as ineffective idealism. This parochial conservatism is a defensive posture and one among many aiming to stave off the effects of further integration and consolidation of local groups into national systems. Such a movement and its imagery are understandable at a time when many local groups feel especially powerless or unable to reach the distant organizational levels at which decisions seem to be made.

Second, it seems that ethologists have raised an important question for sociologists by the way in which the former have directly incorporated "territory" as an organizational principle into their descriptions of animal societies. Sociologists have persistently attempted to explain territorial groups as something else: as the result of ethnic clannishness, or associational networks, or of attempts to segregate income groups and the like. What ethologists have done is to take territorial distinctions themselves as a basis for associational selection and to demonstrate in study after study the utility of this forthright approach.

Looking over a number of sociological works, I find that there is a great deal to be gained from the ethologists on this count. Although sociologists seem uncomfortable with such a principle of organization as territoriality, their skepticism is scarcely warranted by what seems an implicit judgment of the arbitrariness of territorial selection. In retrospect such selective principles as age, sex, kinship, race, or ethnicity are similarly arbitrary in the sense that they involve a human choice rather than a subsocial pattern. More positively, however, such a forthright inclusion of territoriality needs to be initiated because we are surrounded by examples of it that will go unstudied unless they are frankly approached as social facts. The proliferation of administrative districts, the rigidity of the corporate city limits, the defined boundaries of the local housing development, and the "federal experimental site" are all instances of this type, and we understand little of their origin and impact. Obviously these examples are not, as some ethologists might claim, derived from some generic drive toward territoriality and parochial defensiveness. Rather, they are preeminently human constructions and, judging from the examples given above, often imposed in an intentional way by organizations which are quite remote from the local community. This points us, not toward a study of generic human drives, but toward a fuller examination of what Warren has called the vertical and horizontal axis in the study of territorial groups.[28]

28. Roland L. Warren, *The Community in America* (Chicago: Rand McNally, 1963), pp. 237–302.

Part 2

Contemporary Urban Communities

2. The Defended Neighborhood

The residential group which seals itself off through the efforts of delinquent gangs, by restrictive covenants, by sharp boundaries, or by a forbidding reputation—what I will call the defended neighborhood—was for a time a major category in sociological analysis. In their efforts to analyze the territorial configuration of the city, Park and Burgess and their followers left a wealth of descriptive and analytical material on this sort of residential group.[1] Most of this analysis, however, attempted to resolve the defended neighborhood into a manifestation of other social categories thought to be of prior importance: ethnicity, income, race, and the like.[2] In due course the defended neighborhood was frequently dismissed as a sort of epiphenomenon because it was thought only to reflect more substantive social differences.

It is my intent to resurrect the concept of the defended neighborhood and show that it still may be usefully applied to urban areas if we keep in mind two different levels of analysis.

First, there is the physical structure of the city; the location of its facilities, residential groups, transportation, and communication lines; and its specialized activities. These are the items which urban ecologists have discussed in greatest detail and which have formed the empirical basis on which theories of urban structure have risen or fallen.[3]

1. Robert E. Park, Ernest W. Burgess, and Roderick D. McKenzie, *The City,* 4th ed. (Chicago: University of Chicago Press, 1967), provides the classical essays on this topic and a bibliography tracing much of the subsequent work.
2. David Reisman, *The Lonely Crowd* (New Haven: Yale University Press, 1950); and Donald L. Foley, "Neighbors or Urbanites," in *The University of Rochester Studies of Metropolitan Rochester* (Rochester: University of Rochester Press, 1952).
3. See Beverly Duncan, "Variables in Urban Morphology," in Ernest W. Burgess and Donald J. Bogue, eds., *Contributions in Urban Sociology* (Chicago: University of Chicago Press, 1963), pp. 17–30.

Second, there is the cognitive map which residents have for describing, not only what their city is like, but what they think it ought to be like. This cognitive map of the city need not necessarily correspond closely with the actual physical structure.[4] The discrepancy is often quite apparent when residents give very discrete boundaries for a neighborhood or area of usage despite there being no sharp disparities between such adjacent spaces. Similar departures are even more apparent when we compare the actual physical structure of the city with the structure its residents think it ought to have.

These two levels for analyzing urban structure are not wholly independent, for people do seize upon actual markers in the physical makeup of the city to draw up their cognitive maps no matter how unrealistic they are otherwise. Also, within broad and shifting limits, the ideas that people have about where things belong do carry some weight. The problem, however, is not simply to correlate or draw some causal chain between the city's physical structure and the cognitive maps which residents use to describe urban areas. It is of equal or greater importance to find what function these cognitive maps of the city serve and why people should bother with such reifications in the first place.

The principal point of view expressed here is that these cognitive maps are part of the social control apparatus of urban areas and are of special importance in regulating spatial movement to avoid conflict between antagonistic groups. In this respect, such cognitive maps provide a set of social categories for differentiating between those people with whom one can or cannot safely associate and for defining the concrete groupings within which certain levels of social contact and social cohesion obtain. These cognitive maps, then, are a creative imposition on the city and useful because they provide a final solution to decision making where there are often no other clear cutoff points for determining how far social contacts should go. The actual structure of most cities is best described as a series of gradients, and there are very few

4. For a discussion of this issue see Morris Janowitz, *The Community Press in an Urban Setting: The Social Elements of Urbanism,* 2d ed. (Chicago: University of Chicago Press, 1967).

clear boundaries or sharp junctures which cannot be crossed by a simple decision to do so. In order to regulate one's spatial movement and locational possibilities, then, one needs a simpler model, because in the final analysis most decisions must be answered "yes" or "no." The utility of a more qualitative map of the city is that it permits this type of decision making, whereas the physical structure of the city leaves one in an eternal state of ambiguity.[5]

Continuous Physical Structure of the City

Although Park and Burgess were the main proponents of the defended neighborhood and a discrete internal structure of the city, one can also find in their work the undoing of these concepts. As originally spelled out, the most dynamic element in their theory of urban growth was an unplanned economic process by which many independent units competed in an open market for land and location.[6] The fundamental considerations in this argument were adapted from economics, with land values and transportational costs determining the major lineaments of urban growth. Louis Wirth, and other followers of Park and Burgess, picked up this element of their argument and thoroughly exploited it to explain the physical structure of the city.[7]

5. The same observation is made by Milla Aissa Alihan, *Social Ecology: A Critical Analysis* (New York: Columbia University Press, 1938). James A. Quinn has attempted to reply to this criticism by saying: "The contention by Alihan that a gradual gradient makes impossible the existence of zones does not seem valid. In the field of physics, for example, the gradual change in the length of light rays throughout a rainbow spectrum may be taken as an example of a gradient. Nevertheless, distinct zones of red, yellow, and blue appear in the rainbow even though no sharp line of demarcation can be drawn between them. It seems possible, therefore, for distinct zones to appear even when gradients unquestionably exist." What Quinn fails to point out, however, is that the distinct zones of the rainbow are imposed by the viewer rather than being self-evident in the light spectrum itself. ("The Burgess Zonal Hypothesis and Its Critics," *American Sociological Review* 5 [April 1940]: pp. 210–18.)
6. Park, Burgess, and McKenzie, *City*.
7. See particularly Wirth's emphasis on the "unplanned" structure of the city, ibid., pp. 175–82.

This view of the city turned out to be rather profitable. In large part one could explain the locations chosen by various businesses, residential groups, and individuals by the position of each in the open market and the ability of each to bid on a location whose desirability was determined largely by transportational costs. Since transportational costs are a continuous variable, they generally produced a gradient from the inner city outward without any sharp breaks or neat boundaries.

Naturally there were problems in such an analysis because transportational costs were only one of the expenses which went into the pricing of land. In addition, one had to consider the lay of the land, its height during floodtime, and the proximity of adjacent activities.[8] All of these considerations, however, seemed to be costs which could be entered on the same balance sheet with transportational costs, and although they might complicate the picture, they did not take our view of the city outside a basically economic model. One rather stubborn problem was that Park and Burgess had initially settled on the costs due to the shipment of materials rather than those due to labor as the decisive expenditure in the pricing of locations. As both the levels of skill that were demanded and the price of labor rose, nearness to labor pools became an increasingly important consideration in land values. Accordingly, many industries, businesses, and dependent institutions moved away from what had previously been their ideal economic locations to ones where they would have ready access to what had become their most expensive import—skilled labor.[9]

These new considerations in the competition for location were, however, rather like transportational costs because they could be represented in monetary values. They introduced new costs into the accounting process, but together they simply formed a new gradient of prices without sharp boundaries. Obviously, such a determination of land usage was antithetical to a view of the city

8. E. Frederick Schietinger, "Racial Succession and Changing Property Values in Residential Chicago," in Burgess and Bogue, *Urban Sociology*, pp. 86–99; and Vera Miller, "The Areal Distribution of Tax Delinquency," in ibid., pp. 100–111.

9. Brian Berry, Personal communication, 1969.

as a discrete set of natural areas or defended neighborhoods. If urban growth is essentially a gradual and continuous process, then sharp breaks between areas ought not exist and insular sectors become an anomaly. The central business district will merge into the zone in transition, the zone in transition will gradually fade into the zone of workingmen's homes, and so forth.

Economic View of the City

The economic view of the city took hold in the work of urban ecologists and for good reason. By and large, it was a rather adequate way of analyzing the city, and within manageable limits of error it could account for the major contours of urban growth. So far as it went, such a model could do rather well at assigning locations to bidders in the open market. What it did not do was provide the citizens of the city itself with a set of manageable guidelines or a cognitive map which they could use to regulate their own spatial movement, residential cohesion, and definitions of one another. For these purposes a more simple and qualitative description of the city was required. Like Park and Burgess, the residents of the city had to divide the city into zones, areas of usage, neighborhoods, and the like in order to represent the city to themselves and to one another.

Seen in this light, it is not surprising that the description of the city held by its residents did not closely conform to the city's physical structure or play any major role in regulating the pattern of urban growth. The importance of these cognitive maps lay elsewhere, as did their consequences.

The Ethnic Neighborhood

Despite the general utility of the economic model for urban growth, there were always some stubborn exceptions which resisted this sort of analysis. One such exception was the ethnic neighborhood where residents recognized sharp boundaries between themselves and adjacent residential groups, and a general antipathy obtained between neighborhoods. The second problem arose from a few areas of usage such as the red-light district, skid row, and the bright-lights area. Often these were also areas which were sharply delimited in space, occupying a single street or series of streets.[10] They did not always fade off gradually into other areas of the city as did transportational costs and further considerations which could be represented by monetary values.

For Park and Burgess the ethnic neighborhood was not much of a problem because to them the market system of evaluating urban locations was part of our culture and the defended neighborhood was simply an additional fixture to be included as a countervailing set of considerations in locational choice. Some groups in the city chose to live near one another and as a result experienced certain economic losses. For the most part, Park and Burgess argued, these were recent immigrants among whom propinquity was more valued than residential location alone. For Park and Burgess, the city was still a "state of mind, a body of customs and traditions."[11] Cost accounting was one element included in this body of customs, but it did not weigh any heavier than the propinquity which recent immigrants so valued.

For the followers of Park and Burgess, the immigrant neighborhood presented a more serious problem. By this time monetary considerations in the location of residential groups had achieved a sort of hegemony of thought and were juxtaposed against other considerations as if the latter were cultural and the former were rational. Choices based on monetary calculations were somehow reasonable, whereas those based on any other attribute were considered to have been based on prejudice. Park and Burgess had themselves laid the foundation for this division. First, they had contrasted the immigrant's desire for propinquity with the American valuation of cost accounting. This led to the conclusion that these immigrant neighborhoods were a temporary fixture and would gradually disappear as people became acquainted with American culture.[12] Followers of Park and Burgess, then, regarded these immigrant neighborhoods as only a sort of atavism which

10. Park, Burgess, and McKenzie, *City*.
11. Ibid., p. 1.
12. Ibid., p. 191.

would soon disappear given time for the working of our melting pot.

Second, Park and Burgess laid great weight on the cultural homogeneity of these immigrant neighborhoods as their internal basis for the attraction of people to one another. On this point they badly misled their followers, because most of what they said was only half-truth. Very few of the defended neighborhoods in Chicago which Park, Burgess, and their followers described seem now to have been exclusively or almost exclusively occupied by a single ethnic group. Moreover, many of the defended neighborhoods reported by Park and Burgess retained their identities and their boundaries despite continuous shifts in ethnic composition. On the Near West Side of Chicago, for example, the neighborhood known as Taylor Street has retained its identity for at least forty years, despite the fact that it was never ethnically homogeneous until about five years ago when urban renewal removed practically everyone but the Italians from the area. For thirty-five years, successive and continuous invasions characterized the area.[13]

Similar descriptions can be drawn for a large number of the defended neighborhoods of Chicago, and although they are often identified with a single ethnic group, their identities and boundaries seem to have persisted during periods of transiency and invasion as well as during the heights of ethnic homogeneity.[14] Indeed, it appears that the most persistent characteristic of these defended neighborhoods is their boundaries and the necessity of anyone who lives within these boundaries to assume a common residential identity.

14. For example, the areas called Jew Town, Bucktown, the Casbah, and Bridgeport. One of these areas has even retained its original ethnic label despite a complete change in the race of its residents. All of the other areas have retained their labels despite drastic changes in the ethnic background of their residents. Practically none of the community areas which Burgess identified ever were occupied by only one ethnic group; all remain ethnically heterogeneous except a few which have been totally occupied by blacks since the time of his original work. (Ernest W. Burgess and Charles Newcomb, eds., *Census Data of the City of Chicago* [Chicago: University of Chicago Press, 1920].)

13. Gerald D. Suttles, *The Social Order of the Slum* (Chicago: University of Chicago Press, 1968).

The view of the defended neighborhood as only a reflection of
ethnic conflict and cohesion suffers further when we notice that
there are large residential areas in most cities which are ethnically
homogeneous but nonetheless internally divided into several conflicting or defended neighborhoods. Large portions of the Black
Belt in Chicago, for instance, are homogeneous in terms of race,
income, and general background. This area, however, is honey-
combed with small neighborhoods, each defended by its adolescent
gangs, community groups, and forbidding reputation. Perhaps the
most striking example of this sort is a large block of public housing consisting of a series of high-rise buildings. Almost all the
residents are black and have low incomes and similar backgrounds.
About the only discernible difference in the area is the color of
the buildings. One portion of the sequence of buildings is red and
the other is white. Arbitrary as this difference seems, it is a major
cleavage in the area, and there is mutual opposition between the
residents in the red buildings and those in the white.

The arbitrariness of this particular distinction points up the
way in which the defended neighborhood is indeed a creative
imposition on the city. Although this may be a limiting case, it
nonetheless shows the futility of trying to explain the defended
neighborhood as no more than a shorthand description of some
other social distinction, such as ethnicity or social class. The presence of strong boundaries around neighborhoods which are not
ethnically homogeneous, the persistence of neighborhood boundaries during periods of ethnic transition, and the absence of abrupt
differences between adjacent populations support the same conclusion. The defended neighborhood creates a new mosaic in the
city which crosscuts rather than reflects only those distinctions
already present in such items as race, ethnicity, income, and
social background. In this sense the defended neighborhood is a
social reality in its own right because it provides an additional
basis for social differentiation and social cohesion. The necessity
for this additional basis for the social organization of cities lies in
their very nature, since cities inevitably bring together populations that are too large and composed of too many conflicting
elements for their residents to find cultural solutions to the prob-

lems of social control. The result seems to be a partitioning of the
city into several villagelike areas where the actual groupings of
people are of more manageable proportions.

The Problem of Social Control in Urban Areas

In their own analysis, Park, Burgess, and Wirth frequently made
use of a rural imagery and implied that the urban neighborhood
was a sort of atavistic survival from a rural past rather than an
integral part of the city.[15] This imagery is unfortunate because,
with rare exception, rural areas do not seem to have defended
neighborhoods of the type present in the city. The delinquent gang,
restrictive covenants, private guards, and doormen seem to be
almost entirely urban phenomena. Even the term *neighborhood*
seems to be uncommon in rural areas. In sections of the country
such as Kansas and Nebraska where there are no major physical
barriers to communication, neighboring relations tend to trace
out a vast network without any clear boundaries.[16] The defended
neighborhood, then, seems to be very much an urban product, and
it is in the nature of cities that we must find its origins.[17]

The roots of the defended neighborhood appear to lie in what
Wirth saw as the defining characteristics of the city: its large
population, its density, its diversity, its tolerance for individual
variability, and the declining significance of primary control along
with the increasing significance of formal procedures of social
control.[18] Implicit in Wirth's statement was the view that the city

15. Ibid.

16. Ibid., pp. 190–91.

17. Weber notes that the eastern city was and remained for centuries a
segmented structure composed of villagelike settlements, whereas the western city was a more integrated structure because it provided the common
role of citizen to every resident. What Weber fails to remind us of is that
the role citizen does not define all one's relations but only sets aside a
small realm of participation in which one neglects one's local area. In the
early city which Weber is discussing, this realm of life concerns chiefly a
voice in political affairs and economic participation (Max Weber, *The
City* [Riverside, New Jersey: Collier Books, 1958].)

18. Louis Wirth, "Urbanism as a Way of Life," *American Journal of
Sociology* 44 (July 1938): 1–24.

is too variegated and heterogeneous to provide a single normative order which is shared consensually and is sufficient to maintain order. Primary ties are weakened and in any case cannot be extended to so large a group of people. A heterogeneity of attitudes, values, appetites, and activities is not only tolerated but cultivated by the city. Depersonalization and rationality become the only way of handling large numbers of people and are institutionalized in some urban roles. Taken together, Wirth pointed out, these conditions require formal procedures of control.

Going a bit further, one can add that formal social controls are by themselves inadequate to cope with the heterogeneity and potential for conflict and exploitation that exist in a large city. It is obvious that major disturbances occur in cities and get out of hand despite existing formal procedures for control. Yet formal social controls are themselves limited in their scope and the realms of life within which they can pry. First, there are practical limits: how many people can be drawn out of productive roles to specialize as policeman, social worker, judge, juror, and so forth. Not all situations can be observed unless there are personnel to appoint to each, and the demands of each situation are highly variable and require an equally variable allocation of personnel.[19]

Second, there are also normative limits to formal procedures of social control; the imposition of formal procedures of control into the family and other primary groups would itself vitiate their integrative function. A thorough and enduring attachment to tradition or an exchange of sentiment seems impossible in the presence of a policeman or some other coercive authority. Such private and integrative groupings seem an essential element of an urban society, but they cannot prosper under the surveillance or guidance of an inspector. They are intimate and thus primary groupings essentially because they are not pervious to impersonal supervision. And taking into account such findings as we have on the subject, there is every reason to assume that primary relations

19. For a discussion of this issue see Janowitz, *Community Press,* pp. 5–7.

are the mainstay of social control in both the city and the most formal organizations.[20]

Also there are important lapses of information exchange in the city. It is exceedingly difficult for policemen, social workers, precinct captains, and even psychiatrists always to be in touch with a situation that will condition another person's behavior. As Wirth points out, one of the characteristics of urban areas is the segmentalization of life and the partial range of information that each person has about the other. Even granting that it is possible to thoroughly supervise all social relations, it is doubtful that supervisors can obtain or coordinate the information they need to attune their behavior to situational exigencies. What a boy's schoolteacher, mother, father, employer, and peers know is not immediately known to a youth officer. In varying degrees each must exercise social control without a full accounting of what has gone before. Such information exchanges may be facilitated by computer technology, but frequently urban residents must evaluate each other's behavior without any more information than they would have about an utter stranger. Formal procedures of control, then, must be inacted on the basis of "face" evidence that neglects all other evidence because it is unavailable through formal channels of communication.

Granted the inability of formal procedures of social control to detect and forestall all or even most forms of urban disorder, some additional mechanisms seem necessary for the maintenance of order. Among the available mechanisms, a set of rules governing and restricting spatial movement seems a likely and highly effective means of preserving order. Such a set of rules has some fairly obvious advantages: it segregates groups that are otherwise likely to come into conflict; it restricts the range of association and decreases anonymity; it thrusts people together into a common

20. See, for example, George C. Homans, *The Human Group* (New York: Harcourt, Brace and Co., 1950); and Edward A. Shils, "Primary Groups in the American Army," in R. Merton and P. Lazarsfeld, eds., *Continuities in Social Research: Studies in the Scope and Method of "The American Soldier,"* (Glencoe, Ill.: Free Press, 1950), pp. 16–39.

network of social relations that overlap rather than diverge from one another.

In most instances the qualitative map thus produced cannot match exactly or even closely the physical structure of the city. Usually, ecological distributions merge or shade into one another with no obvious break. For example, people may describe three adjacent areas as "white," "black," and "mixed," although in fact each racial group simply shades off into the other. In this sense, one's taxonomy of the city represents a creative imposition on the real world. It is not unrelated to the real world but translates it to another scale. One must be highly selective of the information that is to be considered relevant, and one must be able to lump together or separate items in a way that cannot be derived directly from observation. The primary question one must ask, then, is, not whether such shared maps are "correct," but whether or not they will work, that is, whether they provide an internally consistent set of directives, a collection of consensually shared understandings about what one's spatial location means, and a separation between persons apt to fall into conflict.

On the whole, a cognitive map composed of defended neighborhoods will work in this sense. It helps to tell a person where his enemies and friends are and how to find them. And if a person has no friends, the defended neighborhood lets a person know where he had best cultivate them. Above all, the defended neighborhood simplifies many of the choices of spatial movement to where they can be made as most decisions must be made: among a set of qualitative alternatives. It is possible that a cognitive map which does not consist of a series of contiguous, defended neighborhoods would also work, but the functional merits of the defended neighborhood are considerable, as I will try to point out in the succeeding pages.

Distribution of Defended Neighborhoods

The imperative for a set of rules to govern one's spatial movement does not fall equally on all people or on all areas of the city. The inadequacies of formal procedures of social control are most striking where there are sharp cleavages between people, where anonymity is great, and where people have little assurance that everyone will observe legal or customary norms. Historically in the United States these sources of deviance and conflict have tended to be concentrated in the inner city. This is where ethnic and racial cleavages are still most apparent, undiluted, and irreconcilable. It is also that part of the city where population density and transiency are highest and together promote high levels of anonymity.

In addition to containing these cleavages and anonymity, the inner city is typically the residential area relegated to people with little or no income. In the United States financial insecurity and failure in the job market have always been taken as signs of an individual's character indicating that he is shiftless in the first place or desperate in the second. In either case the poor, and thus the majority of the residents in the inner city, are expected to be rather unruly, predatory, and unprincipled.

These apprehensions about the poor, of course, are shared by the poor themselves. Indeed, there is at least some evidence that the poor are the most likely to assume a simple connection between poverty and unprincipled greed.[21] Since the poor generally live near one another, it is among them that there is the greatest need for a set of rules by which people can safely navigate within their own residential areas.

The coincidence of poverty, anonymity, and social cleavages compounded within the inner city, then, dictate a highly differentiated cognitive map among its residents. It is here that the defended neighborhood should have its greatest appeal and serve best to mollify the imagined or real dangers which exist in the inner city.

Judging from the fragmentary evidence available, the empirical pattern, at least in Chicago, seems to support this conclusion. Zorbaugh's study, *The Gold Coast and the Slum*, as well as prac-

21. Shils, "Primary Groups."

tically all similar studies done under Park and Burgess,[22] shows the inner city to be finely differentiated into many relatively small defended neighborhoods. My own study of the Near West Side and Thrasher's more extensive account of gangland report a similar pattern with a high incidence of defended neighborhoods toward the inner city and many fewer toward the periphery of the city.[23] Even Park and Burgess's classic mapping of the gross outlines of Chicago show the zone in transition to be divided into a greater number of small defended areas than the zones farther out.[24] In at least one recent study of the outer city there is a striking lack of spatial differentiation, boundaries, and defensive arrangements.[25]

The inner city is also the area where one finds most of the other obvious earmarks of the defended neighborhood. It is here that street-corner gangs claim a "turf" and ward off strangers or anyone else not a proper member of the neighborhood. It is here that one finds vigilante community groups, militant conservation groups, a high incidence of uniformed doormen, and frequent use of door buzzers and TV monitors. Not all of these defensive tactics are equally available to all residents of the inner city, and in many instances one may replace the other. What they indicate is the general apprehensiveness of inner city dwellers, rich and poor alike, and the necessity for each of them to bound off discrete areas within which he can feel safe and secure.

Social Cohesion of Defended Neighborhoods

Although the defended neighborhood does not always seem to arise from preexisting cohesive groupings, it may itself create cohesive groupings. The defensive measures of these neighbor-

22. Harvey Warren Zorbaugh, *The Gold Coast and the Slum* (Chicago: University of Chicago Press, 1929); Roderick D. McKenzie, *The Neighborhood: A Study of Neighborhood Life in the City of Columbus, Ohio* (Chicago: University of Chicago Press, 1923); and Burgess and Bogue, *Urban Sociology.*

23. Suttles, *Social Order*; and Frederick Thrasher, *The Gang* (Chicago: University of Chicago Press, 1927).

24. Park, Burgess, and McKenzie, *City.*

25. Harvey Molotch, "Intervention for Integration: A Community Competes for Whites" (Ph.D. dissertation, University of Chicago, 1967).

hoods, of course, generally call for some level of concerted action
and thus a certain degree of cohesion. This cohesion is most apparent in street-corner gangs, vigilantelike citizens' groups, and
restrictive covenants. All of these measures require joint action
and produce at least traces of cohesion that endure for purposes
other than defense.

By far the most common type of cohesion said to exist in all
types of neighborhoods is a positive and sentimental attachment
to neighbors, local establishments, and local traditions to the exclusion of other persons, establishments, and traditions. No doubt
such warm attachments to neighborhoods do exist, but they are
too narrow and special a case to characterize fully the range and
forms which neighborhood cohesion can take. Indeed, it is because
of such a narrow focus on positive and exclusive sentimental
attachments to the neighborhood that some researchers may have
simply discounted the very existence of the neighborhood. Similar
reasoning, however, would discount the existence of the family
since there also not all members are always firmly and positively
attached to one another.

Like the family, the neighborhood is largely an ascribed grouping and its members are joined in a common plight whether or
not they like it. The preeminent characteristics of the defended
neighborhood, then, are structural rather than sentimental or
associational. Perhaps the most important of these structural elements is the identity of the neighborhood itself. A neighborhood
may be known as snobbish, trashy, tough, exclusive, dangerous,
mixed, or any number of other things. Some neighborhoods may
simply be unknown, and reference to one's residence may arouse
only puzzlement and necessitate one's explaining one's guilt or
virtue by residential association. In any case, neighborhood identity remains a stable judgmental reference against which people
are assessed, and although some may be able to evade the allegations thrown their way, they nonetheless find such evasions
necessary.

A second structural characteristic of the defended neighborhood
is that its coresidents often share a common fate at the hands of
city planners, realtors, politicians, and industry. Like the residents
of the city itself, these initiators of change often must selectively

apply their resources to distinct areas of the city rather than dis-
tribute their impact generally over a metropolitan region. In the
end, a factory or high school must be placed somewhere, political
jurisdictions must be drawn, and social welfare programs must
have distinct target areas. The boundaries drawn by these intru-
sive and exogenous institutions may or may not coincide with
those already accepted by coresidents. The net result is a continuous shifting of boundaries and foci of concern by residential groupings. Protest groups, conservation committees, landowners' groups,
and realty associations spring into existence, thrive, and then decline, as the issue which brought them into existence waxes and
wanes. All this tends to give the defended neighborhood an ephem-
eral and transient appearance, as if it were a social artifact. But
these social forms are real enough, and they leave at least a residue
of a formula for subsequent cohesion.

Perhaps the most subtle structural feature of the defended
neighborhood is its shared knowledge or what might be called its
underlife. People who share a residential identity are privy to a
variety of secrets which range from the assured truths of gossip
to the collective myths of rumor. These bits and pieces of knowledge touch intimately on the lives of those who share a residential
area because they add to the collective guilt or pride of coresidents.
But they are also some of the surest markers which separate in-
siders from outsiders. And at the same time these local half-truths
are much valued because they provide at least an omen of what
one's neighbors are really like. Thus, while persons who share a
common residential identity may collude at impression management, they are also apt to pry into one another's business and
jointly move farther and farther away from an official version of
what people are supposed to be like. Taken to their full extreme,
these local truths may add up to a sort of subculture where a private existential world takes hold and overshadows that provided
by an equally undependable version of truth available through
official sources.[26] More often the subterranean bits and pieces of

26. Lee Rainwater, "The Problems of Lower Class Culture" (Paper
prepared for the Department of Sociology Colloquium, University of
Wisconsin, September 23, 1966).

information available to coresidents are received as gossip pure and simple. Persons who share a residential identity, however, have a special right to such knowledge, and this inside "dope" may lead them to what seem aberrant or provincial ways of behaving.

Yet another structural characteristic of the defended neighborhood is the fact that it may be divided into levels or orbits which radiate from an egocentric to a sociocentric frame of reference. When a person speaks of "my neighborhood," he may be referring to a small area which centers on himself and is different for any two individuals. "Our neighborhood," on the other hand, tends to refer to some localized group which can also be identified by other structural boundaries such as ethnicity or income. "The neighborhood," however, has a more fixed referent and usually possesses a name and some sort of reputation known to persons other than the residents.

All of these structural characteristics give the defended neighborhood an amorphous and indistinct appearance so long as we look for only a single bounded unit persisting through time. The defended neighborhood can expand or contract boundaries; it's activation is episodic; and the cohesion of its members is always qualified by alternative loyalties. This does not mean that the defended neighborhood is unimportant but calls for a specification of that realm of life over which it exercises its special influence.

Specialization of Neighborhood Functions

The segmental character of urban life leaves only some people free some of the time to invest their energy and interests into the defended neighborhood. This introduces into the maintenance of neighborhood life a qualified involvement and a certain specialization.

The extent to which persons can or must concern themselves with the defended neighborhood is especially likely to vary with the life cycle. Of all those who reside in a neighborhood, children seem to be most nearly contained in its boundaries. Most of the groups to which they can belong—school groups, church groups, athletic teams, and the scouts—remain territorially defined. These groups may not coincide very closely in the boundaries they select, but together they greatly narrow the range of childhood movement and association. Children must, more often than adults, walk to most of the places they frequent, and this gives them a rather obvious interest in their personal safety and the routes and places where they are welcome or unwelcome. Age restrictions on certain places of entertainment, the child labor laws, and curfews sharply delimit their participation in the wider society.

The dangers of the city are especially relevant to children because they are generally thought rather defenseless. One major reason for selecting a particular residential area, in fact, is that it is a safe or agreeable place to raise children.[27] Indeed, perhaps the best way to discern the spatial orbits which make up a neighborhood is to listen to how parents allow or restrict the movements of their children.

Because they are so restricted to their neighborhood or its immediate vicinity, children may be the major producers and carriers of neighborhood life: its local stereotypes, its named boundaries, its known hangouts, its assumed dangers, and its informal groupings. Certainly there are a number of studies and observations which suggest as much.[28] In many inner city areas, the adults may remain rather atomized while their children quickly coalesce into local street-corner gangs. Seemingly it is only children—or teenagers—who persistently organize to defend a local turf, name themselves after some shabby street corner, and regard their betters elsewhere with contempt. Adults, in turn, complaining about their present neighborhood, frequently engage in a good deal of nostalgia that mixes references to their youth and "the old neighborhood."

27. Peter Rossi, *Why Families Move: A Study in the Social Psychology of Urban Residential Mobility,* conducted under the joint sponsorship of the Bureau of Applied Social Research and the Institute for Urban Land Use and Housing Studies of Columbia University (Glencoe, Ill.: Free Press, 1955).

28. Roger G. Barker and Herbert F. Wright, *The Midwest and Its Children: The Psychological Ecology of an American Town* (Evanston, Ill.: Row, Peterson, 1954); and William Foote Whyte, *Street Corner Society* (Chicago: University of Chicago Press, 1943), pp. 5–6, 104–8.

Perhaps the most telling index to the connection between children and the defended neighborhood is the continuing importance of residential segregation compared with segregation in most other areas of life. A long line of research shows that Americans are less willing to desegregate their residential areas than almost any other public realm of life.[29] This resistence to residential desegregation seems to grow directly from the fears which surround childhood contacts and the basic safeguards which the defended neighborhood erects in the first place. The defended neighborhood is largely, although not entirely, a way of assuming that children will have "safe associates."

There may be good reason for this resistance to residential integration so long as equalitarian or casual interracial relations are seen as a source of conflict and danger. Within the workplace and most public establishments, formal procedures of social control can be fairly adequate. On the streets, on playgrounds, and in alleys, formal procedures of social control are, at best, imperfect. These, however, are often the avenues that children take to enjoy their most personal moments.

Moreover, there is at least some reason to think that this sort of territorial configuration is essential to the personality development of children. Full access to all areas of the city permits a highly segmentalized style of life where role playing need not go beyond impression management. To avoid this sort of chameleonlike behavior and personal development, individuals must be encompassed in a smaller and more nearly closed framework of social relations where they have to "keep their stories straight." Presumably, this type of closed informational system is especially crucial to the development of children who are still in the process of acquiring a holistic personality.[30] By allowing for close proximity among those who handle youth (parents, schoolteachers, store owners, youth officers, the parents of peers), the defended

29. Herbert H. Hyman and Paul B. Sheatsley, "Attitudes toward Desegregation," *Scientific American* 211 (July 1964): 14.

30. James S. Plant, *The Envelope: A Study of the Impact of the World upon the Child* (New York: Commonwealth Fund, 1950).

neighborhood acts as a sort of container which helps keep together an informational network surrounding each child.

Next to children, mothers with young children are probably the most confined and involved in the defended neighborhood. At minimum, they have an interest in knowing enough of the neighborhood to advise and direct the movement and associations of their children. Like children and like other women, mothers are likely to have to walk to various local facilities and to be concerned especially with their personal safety. The defended neighborhood, then, is particularly relevant to these women, and they are apt to have a considerable investment in its defenses and a clear view of its internal structure.

One can extend this analysis to other age groups, income groups, and various stages in the family life-cycle. The point, however, is that neighborhood participation and the maintenance of neighborhood life may be rather specialized responsibilities.[31] Children and their mothers may continue the more traditional forms of neighborhood life: primary relations, information exchange, and affective attachments. Old people may unwittingly provide a certain measure of surveillance and social control. Formal neighborhood associations and other means of competing for municipal services may fall largely into the hands of those who have political connections, an ideological commitment to neighborhood work, or some reputation for expertise in this area. The remaining residents, particularly those who are young and single, may cooperate only to the extent that they remain detached from neighborhood affairs and do not impose their cosmopolitan interests on the locals.

Such a differentiated and specialized participation in the defended neighborhood means that its content and structure must be obtained by a selective inquiry from those segments of the population which transmit and defend its traditions, informal relations, and distinct identity. To evaluate the viability and vigor of a neighborhood, then, it is not enough to find out the proportion of all residents who are appreciably involved in "neighboring" or

31. Frank L. Sweetser, Jr., *Neighborhood Acquaintance and Association: A Study of Personal Neighborhoods* (New York, 1941).

local voluntary organizations. A far more pressing problem is the extent to which certain select groups, no matter how few in number, are able to keep intact neighborhood boundaries, to provide a general knowledge of its internal structure, and to keep alive their myth of unity and cohesion.

Emerging "Artificial" Neighborhoods

In the past, the physical structure of most American cities and the cognitive maps which people imposed on these cities have tended to follow rather independent courses. The physical structure was determined largely by an economic process with locational possibilities being worked out through an unplanned market system. The cognitive maps which people imposed on the city were largely retrospective and a way of coping with a reality out of their control. These cognitive maps and the defended neighborhood had their own consequences, but these did not include much influence on the city's physical structure.

Now, with the advent of urban planning the physical structure of the city is no longer subject only to an economic process but involves politics and some cultural image of what the city ought to be like. Many of the new, planned residential areas, particularly those in the inner city, seem to be incorporating at least three elements of the defended neighborhood into the physical structure of the city itself. First, each new residential development seems to have extremely distinct boundaries laid out by through streets but also reinforced by a unified architectural design and a single source of ownership.

Second, each of these new developments possesses a ready-made name and an image or identity even before it is occupied. For private developments this identity is usually manufactured by owners and advertising men. Nonetheless, the residents seem to fully accept their somewhat contrived identity, and it is as much a source of pride or shame as one homegrown. For public-housing developments, governmental bodies provide a name and at least enough of an official line to allow people to elaborate a rather obvious stereotype since most of the eligible residents are black or poor or both. The ready-made identity provided the residents in public housing is probably not very agreeable to them, but nonetheless it is a social fact with which they must contend.

The cultural homogeneity of these new residential developments is a third characteristic of the defended neighborhood which is being incorporated into their physical structure. The old defended neighborhood attempted to maintain its ethnic, racial, and economic purity, and although this attempt was not very successful, its residents often pretended they were alike and created their own cultural unity. The cultural unity of most of these new residential developments seems to be in better hands because the screening of new residents is centralized in the hands of a single realtor.

In many of these recent residential developments, traditional indices to cultural unity seem to be observed, and in Chicago, at least, some of these new residential enclaves are far more segregated than any defended neighborhood. In some of the private developments, however, ethnic and racial considerations have been subordinated to more subtle indices of cultural uniformity. Sometimes the size of the dwelling unit is the determining factor, and in some developments the two-bedroom rental assures that only young couples with one or two young children, old people, and singles will live there. More often the policy of realtors intervenes to assure that the people in these residential aggregates will get along. In Chicago, for example, one can find entire developments which are reserved primarily for family types, for young singles, or for retired couples. There is even one new development which aims to appeal to people who want the maximum mix in terms of income, sex, age, familialism, and ethnicity so long as they can pay their rent.

These new residential developments may seem scarcely comparable to what I have called the defended neighborhood. Despite many structural alterations, however, they continue many of the same functions as the defended neighborhood. Their boundaries are in most cases more sharply drawn and as closely guarded as those of any ethnic neighborhood. The identity of each development is well cultivated and well publicized by central management and advertising men. Even the myth of cultural unity in the defended neighborhood is perpetuated through screening policies and the selection of compatible residents.

Judged against our image of the defended neighborhood as an emergent and sentimental union of similar people, these new residential developments may seem rather foreign. This image of the defended neighborhood, however, was always partial. Its cultural unity and the sentimental attachment of coresidents was sometimes a myth and sometimes a secondary development. The basic functions of defense, the segregation of conflicting populations, and the provision of a residential identity were always somewhat specialized activities. The new and inclusive urban residential developments take this specialization to an extreme. This specialization may eliminate from many new residential areas those characteristics we thought most commonly associated with the defended neighborhood.

This, however, does not mean that the local residential group is going to lose all importance. What is happening to the defended neighborhood seems analogous to what happened to the nuclear family during the early part of this century when the domestic group lost most of its economic functions and became more exclusively a child-rearing group. A parallel pattern of specialization and differentiation may be appearing in the defended neighborhood. The new residential development with physically distinct boundaries and a single source of management does not imply the decline of the defended neighborhood but brings into greater relief its basic functions.

Albert J. Hunter and
Gerald D. Suttles

3. The Expanding Community of Limited Liability

In the late 1960s the topic of residential groups drew tangent with a number of controversial issues in the United States. The most directly related of these issues was that of community control, which included a number of popular demands for a greater local voice in the schools, housing, and the parks. Closely allied demands grew out of the controversy surrounding the model cities program, urban renewal, and public housing. The civil rights movement and racial segregation were long-term issues which had frequently moved with or against the claims of autonomy voiced by the community-based groups.[1] The issues of pollution, urban sprawl, and poverty were more remote, yet continued to be associated with our notions of the rights and responsibilities of the local community or neighborhood.

The positive slogans of this ill-defined malaise were community control, decentralization, or simply, the people. A great deal of wrath was spent on the establishment, centralization, and expatriate do-gooders or agitators. Yet, for those who attempted to respond to or loyally interpret these slogans, the situation seemed hopelessly confused. Rarely did the corporate community coincide with what different groups called the community. In most instances local communities seemed impossible to find so long as one thought of them as neatly bounded areas whose residents were of a single mind. At one and the same time, a community group would insist on its own autonomy and agitate for open housing in adjacent communities. Those who claimed to represent "the community" were often badly divided and could not settle on the same constituency or boundaries. And, although there was a loud outcry for the individuated treatment of local communities, there was an equally loud outcry when they were treated unequally.

1. Some of the highlights of this controversy are included in Patrick Moynihan, *Maximal Feasible Misunderstanding* (New York: The Free Press of Glencoe, 1969); and Martin Mayer, *The Teachers' Strike: New York, 1968* (New York: Harper and Row, 1969).

It is too early to prognosticate the long-term direction of this
public outcry, but two things seem clear. First, we have no well-
defined and widely shared model of the local urban community
or neighborhood which is so compelling that it can be applied
authoritatively to current residential groupings in the United
States. Second, the absence of such a compelling model of the
local urban community or neighborhood makes it difficult for us
to distinguish between those rights and responsibilities which
belong to local groups and those which belong to broader collectivities or administrative units.

These are problems which face an entire nation, but they are
also intellectual and sociological problems. The question of how
residential solidarities are keyed into other social arrangements
bears on almost all the problems of societal integration. Thus, the
imperfections of sociological models of the local community are
symptomatic of a general attempt to grasp at representations
which are faulty, limited, unreal, or artifactual. Were our sociological representations of the local community and the wider
society more satisfactory, they might provide collective representations which would point a way out of this puzzling maze of
conflicting claims, demands, and confrontations. The inadequacy
of sociological representations to give both an appealing and
balanced account of the role of residential groups reopens the
question of what the local urban community is and what its place
is among an increasing number of broader collectivities.

In the present account it is argued that our folk and sociological
representations of the urban community are especially likely to
underestimate the role of external organizations and populations
in the definition and solidarity of residential groups. This underestimate applies especially to governmental units and the way in
which they must create the local groups to which government
itself must respond. Furthermore, it is suggested that the contemporary local urban community need not be seen as a detached
and primordial solidarity but is best conceived of as a pyramid of
progressively more inclusive groupings, in which each level of
sociocultural integration parallels the hierarchy of "adversaries"
or "advocates" who face residential groups. In this sense there is

no unique urban community, but instead a pyramid of residential collectivities which receive their recognition by common consent and whose expansion depends on the expansion of a hierarchy external to the community itself.

Folk and Sociological Representations of the Local Urban Community

Our simplest folk model of the local metropolitan community is that of a contiguous plane divided into several adjacent neighborhoods or community areas. Burgess's model of the community areas of Chicago was essentially of this order and presumably derived from a shared folk model (see map 1). Such a model can be extended, as Burgess extended it, to include a shared or dominant downtown area and several specialized areas (skid row, brightlights area, tenderloin, etc.) which serve the entire city or metropolitan area.[2] Such a model can also be used to construct concentric zones or sectors, since areas lying along a line extending from the center of the city or those areas lying along a circle enclosing the city center are apt to share certain characteristics. Basically, however, this folk and sociological model is one which emphasizes the comparability of community areas, their independent internal order, and the parallel development of each: "A mosaic of little worlds which touch but do not interpenetrate."[3]

Underlying this model of the metropolitan community were the assumed processes of growth, competition, segregation, invasion, and succession.[4] Competition gave rise to differences among people and their styles of life. These differences led to residential segregation, not only in terms of achieved life styles, but also those ascribed on the basis of race and ethnicity as well. With urban growth, however, all the segregated residential groups were unstable because they were bound to burst their boundaries and

2. Robert E. Park, Ernest W. Burgess, and Roderick D. McKenzie, *The City*, 4th ed. (Chicago: University of Chicago Press, 1967).

3. Ibid., p. 40.

4. Ibid.; and Robert E. Park and Ernest W. Burgess, *Introduction to the Science of Sociology* (Chicago: University of Chicago Press, 1921).

allow those with a less prestigious style of life to invade adjacent community areas occupied by those with a more prestigious style of life. In the aftermath of succession, the community areas were supposed to achieve a stable form, with a different style of life, but with roughly the same boundaries and internal unity.

Running parallel with this model of residential differentiation was a distinctive notion of how residential groups developed their own internal order and cohesion. Essentially this was a developmental sequence in which primordial solidarities gradually expanded through the extension of neighboring, marriage, and voluntary associations until all these social bonds drew together everyone in a single community area to the point that they shared a common residential identity, sense of solidarity, and willingness to cooperate. This process was visualized somewhat the same way as astronomers depict the gradual adhesion of separate particles into planets. The personal sentiments derived from ethnicity, friendship, kinship, and personal communication were seen as the basic adhesive bonds which could gradually weld people into residential collectivities mindful of their common identity and their separation from other groups. The expansion of these personal bonds was interrupted only by physical barriers to communication or ascribed divisions such as those of race or ethnicity. The general tendency, then, was to view residential groups as the product of congealed sentiments which could not expand past the obstructions to social communication posed by physical or primordial barriers.

This overview was considerably revised by Janowitz's concept of the community of limited liability.[5] The concept of the community of limited liability emphasized the intentional, voluntary, and especially, the partial and differentiated involvement of residents in their local communities. On the one hand, it pointed to the importance of local voluntary associations as a response to issues broader than those particular to an isolated community area. On the other hand, the community of limited liability pro-

5. Morris Janowitz, *The Community Press in an Urban Setting: The Social Elements of Urbanism*, 2d ed. (Chicago: University of Chicago Press, 1952).

vided a way of understanding the partial or incomplete involvement of people in their residential areas as it hinged, for example,
on phases in the family life cycle. Above all, Janowitz's work
showed how an external agent, such as the community press,
could act as a custodian in maintaining a community's sense of
integrity, its boundaries, and its responsibilities. Janowitz's work
came at a crucial juncture in the controversy over whether or not
the urban neighborhood still existed in modern urban society. As
his work showed, the urban neighborhood was becoming a more
specialized, a more voluntaristic, and a more partial institution.
The local neighborhood, then, could be understood within a general
intellectual framework which applied also to changes in other
institutions such as the family, the firm, or the church.[6] The local
urban community was not disappearing but being subjected to a
wider range of external influences while also undergoing internal
differentiation.

In an earlier work, one of the authors has pointed out how
grossly identified community areas are further subdivided into
smaller spatial units which combine in a definite order into temporary but enlarged alliances.[7] This ordered segmentation goes
past the view that neighborhoods are discrete and uncoordinated
collectivities, but it does not go far enough. Above all, it does not
consider the consolidation of still larger residential solidarities as
residential groups attempt to develop constituencies which parallel
the administrative levels and policy decisions of governmental
agencies. Conversely, this emphasis on the defended neighborhood
left unexplored the question of how an unconsolidated structure of
federal, state, or local governmental districts tends to diffuse or
impede the development of a pyramid of progressively inclusive
residential groups able to mobilize themselves to a level which
parallels the spatial districting at which administrative discretion
exists.[8] Beyond the expansion of the defended neighborhood, then,

6. For a conceptualization of this process in terms of levels of sociocultural integration, see Julian H. Steward, *Theory of Cultural Change*
(Urbana: University of Illinois Press, 1955).
7. Gerald D. Suttles, *The Social Order of the Slum* (Chicago: University
of Chicago Press, 1968).
8. For a discussion of the defended neighborhood see chapter 2.

one can visualize counteracting forces where either the consolidation or relative independence of governmental districts tends to make clear or obscure the necessity for residential solidarity. As already suggested, then, the basic problem here is to make clear the way in which residential groups larger than the defended community are also a response to their environment and especially the districting carried out by governmental bodies.

There are secondary reasons for undertaking this analysis. The prevailing model of how residential groups develop is one where grass roots or primordial sentiments expand to the point that they reach physical obstructions or a major social cleavage such as that posed by race, ethnicity, or income. This point of view does not do justice to the wider differentiation of residential groups where these social distinctions are not problematic. Nor does this same point of view bring into explicit consideration the very utilitarian and purposeful approach which some issue-oriented community groups adopt when confronting governmental bodies.

In addition, it is a matter of historical record that residential solidarity is very unevenly developed, despite the homogeneity and longevity of some residential groups.[9] Variations in the consolidation of governmental districts may provide a way of explaining this lack of residential solidarity even when other conditions seem especially propitious. Certainly the theory which emphasizes the crescive expansion of primordial sentiments does not help us much here.

Finally, there is the question of how ongoing patterns in the remainder of American society affect residential solidarities. The general trajectory of American society has been toward large-scale and specialized organizations which make extreme demands on consensus and the collaboration of groups previously unrelated to one another. The nation and its components seem to be drawing together—or apart—into a system which requires greater coordination, a more immediate responsiveness between institutions, and a widened scope for collective responsibility. Residential groups must fit themselves into this pattern since they continue to bear an

9. Suzanne Keller, *The Urban Neighborhood* (New York: Random House, 1968).

unavoidable social responsibility. People who share residential areas simply cannot ignore each other, because they are vulnerable to one another. Their personal safety and sense of security are dependent on a collective image of each other's character which carries some assurances of mutual trustworthiness.

Collective Determination of Neighborhood Boundaries and Identity

Much of the wind behind the sails of those who argue for strong local community control is propelled by the assumption that the local community grows from the ground up, that it is self-generating and potentially self-governing. Sometimes, as in de Tocqueville's works or those of his followers, the local community is seen as uniquely American, but there is also a broader school of thought which argues both the wisdom and actuality of such grass roots communities. The assumptions behind these positions have remained unexamined although they seem at best debatable. The following discussion reviews some of the residential collectivities which have appeared in the literature and finds that all of them have come into existence with the aid of adversaries and advocates. Sometimes these adversaries and advocates are built into the structure of urban life and require no planful or intentional activity on the part of government or business. At other times, residential identities seem to have depended very much on either the current or past activities of very intentional and self-conscious efforts to create a sense of community. In either case, however, there is little reason to draw a direct correspondence between the isolated residential group developing through its own indigenous powers and the urban community originating in a larger context.

The most elementary features of the urban community area or neighborhood are its identity and its boundaries. The former consists of a widely understood term which bears many connotations. Areas are known to be safe or unsafe, to be interesting or dull, to be risqué or square, or to be beautiful or ugly. The dimensions along which residential areas may differentiate are numerous, but they seem to devolve around a single cultural principle: residential groups are defined in contradistinction to one another. In other words, residential groups gain their identity by their most apparent differences from one another. A more or less black area is distinguished from a more or less white area. Neither area need be homogeneous in the characteristics or background of its residents, and studies which have emphasized social homogeneity as the basis for neighborhood solidarity have seldom shown such extreme homogeneity to exist.[10] Affluent and respectable areas often achieve their singularity by being only slightly different from less affluent and respectable areas. Areas closely identified with a particular ethnic group need not contain a majority of a single ethnic group but only a relative concentration when compared to other areas.[11] Residential identities, then, are embedded in a contrastive structure in which each neighborhood is known primarily as a counterpart to some of the others, and relative differences are probably more important than any single and widely shared social characteristic.

The presence of such a contrastive structure of neighborhood identities suggests quite a different origin for the identity and reputation of neighborhood areas than the crescive growth of primordial loyalties. As counterparts to one another, neighborhoods seem to acquire their identity through an ongoing commentary between themselves and outsiders. This commentary includes the imputations and allegations of adjacent residential groups as well as the coverage given by the mass media. It includes also the claims of boosters, of developers, of realtors, and of city officials. The residents themselves, of course, are not debarred from this commentary, but their role is less that of the typification of what is representative of their community than the expression of what is distinctive of it. Community identification, then, can be conceived of as a broad dialogue that gravitates toward collective represen-

10. For a general discussion see Donald J. Bogue, "Nodal versus Homogeneous Regions and Statistical Techniques for Measuring the Influence of Each," *Proceedings of the Conference of the International Statistical Institute* (Rio de Janeiro, 1955), pp. 377–92. For a general review see Keller, *Urban Neighborhood*, pp. 80–85. For specific findings on ethnic homogeneity see Harold M. Mayer and Richard C. Wade, *Chicago: Growth of a Metropolis* (Chicago: University of Chicago Press, 1969).

11. Mayer and Wade, *Chicago.*

tations which have credence to both residents and nonresidents alike.

There are numerous observations which seem to bear out this interpretation. First, the history of many named communities shows that the terms which identify them were coined by some outsider: a government surveyor, a developer, realtor, founding father, booster, or newspaper man, for example.[12] In Chicago, many of the local community areas represent the fragments of jurisdictionally distinct towns, named by their developers or founders before being incorporated into the city.[13] As Caroline Ware fully documents, the reputation of Greenwich Village was much more the product of eager real estate men than of the local bohemians.[14] Apparently, many of the community areas in Chicago scarcely had any identity until Ernest Burgess gave them one.[15]

Second, it is difficult to believe that many of the more humiliating identities for community areas in the United States were homemade by the local residents. Throughout the United States, the "Nigger Towns," "Jew Towns," "Little Sicilies," and "Back of the Yards" seem unlikely cognomens which the local residents would choose for themselves. Instead, they suggest the more likely

12. Evelyn M. Kitagawa and Karl E. Taeuber, eds., *Local Community Fact Book, Chicago Metropolitan Area* (Chicago: Chicago Community Inventory, 1963).

13. Ibid.

14. Caroline F. Ware, *Greenwich Village: 1920–30* (New York: Harper and Row, 1935).

15. One suspects that Burgess was only somewhat inaccurate in this respect and that what he often did was to designate areas which *should* be community areas rather than those which already were well-defined community areas. Certainly Burgess depended very heavily on physical obstruction's such as railroads, blocks of industry, and vacant spaces, to draw the line between community areas. Right or wrong in his claims, he may have been prescient in designating those areas which could become community areas if publicly recognized. Where he may have been more familiar with the local collective representations, he seems to have drawn much more refined and careful boundaries. For example, the four community areas surrounding the University of Chicago are among the smallest in the city and depend very little on boundaries which might be regarded as physical or natural barriers to communication. (Kitagawa and Taeuber, *Community Fact Book*.)

result of allegations coming from adjacent areas or unsympathetic outsiders.

There are even more general reasons for taking this stance on the development of community identities. As both Cooley and Mead argued, identities in general are often proposed to us rather than being self-produced. Community identities, no less than personal ones, should find their reflection in this looking-glass self. Tangentially, it should be noted that those primitive and isolated groups also lacked any term for themselves except that translated as "the people" or "mankind."[16] In order to be different, it is apparently necessary to have others to agree with you that you are different.

The terms which identify neighborhood or community areas are, of course, just vocabulary items which may change in what they denote or connote. It is at this point that the characteristics of the local residents figure in. As residential areas change in their composition, appearance, and distinction from comparative areas, their reputation changes to include new connotations, despite the frequent survival of a name. If the parvenu take over an area previously inhabited by the old rich, undoubtedly the area's image will change. But this change of identity is often less to the liking and sentimental attachments of the parvenu than to those who have moved elsewhere. The characteristics of the local residents, then, make their mark on the area in which they reside: it is just that outsiders help to tell local residents where they stand.

What we know about the development of boundaries for residential groups suggests a sequence in which outsiders play an equally fundamental role. Ordinarily the boundaries of residential groups are thought of as physical obstructions which are sufficient in their own right to reduce or eliminate any interaction between residents. Often these boundaries consist of railroad tracks, giant freeways, parks, or main streets. Physically these obstructions are real enough, but they also constitute no-man's-lands and impersonal domains which an individual is unlikely to trespass during

16. George Peter Murdock, *Our Primitive Contemporaries* (New York: Macmillan, 1934).

some hours of the day because they are unsupervised or draw to themselves the most uncertain collection of people.[17] Certainly such barriers reduce or eliminate communication. But it is the fears that people share about wider social differences that make these differences so ominous and unbreachable. It is difficult to cross an expressway; but, late at night, it is dangerous primarily because of the unselected group of people likely to be present. The same might be said of main streets which are available "to everyone" and frequently function as boundaries between neighborhoods. These boundaries, then, figure into troublesome societal divisions in which the fear of outsiders is central.

Thus, the identity and boundaries of community areas may rightfully be regarded as truly collective representations. They do not emerge solely from the crescive internal development of relations among coresidents, but also from the broader application of folk models about what can or should distinguish residential groups. The contiguous plane divided up into equivalent community areas, then, may only direct us toward artifactual representations of the urban neighborhood. The wider society surrounding communities is going through a number of changes in which what Hunter calls the principle of hierarchy is the most evident. This pyramid of districts and organizational units is especially evident among governmental bodies. To find the new urban community, we may have to be prepared to find a similar pyramid in which areas telescope into one another attempting, however unsuccessfully, to match their level of spatial consolidation with that developed by their counterparts.

Levels in the Sociocultural Integration of Residential Groups

The range of residential groups which have been referred to in the literature and in common discourse is quite wide. The block, district, neighborhood, area, project, and so on may be synonyms,

17. See Suttles, *Social Order,* pp. 35–38; and Harvey Warren Zorbaugh, *The Gold Coast and the Slum* (Chicago: University of Chicago Press, 1929).

but the presence of some residential areas with names inclusive of others suggests that people are grappling for more differentiated representations. In addition, the presence of partially overlapping official and unofficial community areas, as in Chicago, argues for the existence of more than one level in community differentiation. For reasons given below, it is argued that at least four levels can be discerned although they are incomplete and partial in their emergence.

Local Networks and the Face-Block

From the point of view of the local resident, the most elemental grouping of his coresidents is usually a network of acquaintances who have been selected primarily because they are known from shared conditions of residence and the common usage of local facilities. These are acquaintances who are recognized from face-to-face relations or encounters and seen regularly because they live on the same block, use the same bus station, shop at the same stores, and for any number of reasons continually cross one another's pathways. What distinguishes this association is not so much the common social background of its members but the assumption in the back of each person's mind that he knows each one primarily because he happens to live close by or use the same facilities.

Such a loose network does not constitute a neighborhood nor is it likely to have any residential identity. Usually it will differ for each person and in the urban United States it is unlikely to have any sharp boundaries or reach "closure."[18] Yet these loose networks are especially susceptible to the selective principles which early writers on the urban neighborhood felt essential to its origin. No doubt, people govern their progressive involvement on the basis of race, income, age, sex, kinship, and other primordial ties. But these loose networks do not constitute a residential identity, because they are egocentric, constantly changing, and different from the point of view of each member.

18. Elizabeth Bott, *Family and Social Network* (London: Tavistock, 1957).

Often such a network is concentrated within a single face-block, and this is one way of accounting for residents' sharing some identity with "their block." The face-block, however, has other properties which seem far more important in giving it a corporate identity. It is common for parents to use the face-block as an areal basis for confining the play of their children ("You can go out to play, but stay on your block"). For children, this makes the face-block a prescribed social world rather than something they gradually develop among themselves. It originates, in large part, from parental fears of having their children move out of their sight, where they can encounter strangers, and from a range of apprehensions which may accompany the block-by-block invasion characteristic of cities in the United States. Frequently, the children respond by making the face-block a basis for peer group activities or even gang recruitment. But the notion of the face-block as a prescribed social world anticipates these social solidarities rather than arising from them.

Even more responsive to the wider community is the block club, a common adult form of organization for acquiring better public services. In Chicago, such groups are common, especially in the black community.[19] Although these groups may arise at the initiative of two or three close friends living on the same face-block, their efforts at organization are constrained by two prescribed circumstances. First, the face-block itself seems to provide a fixture in their cognitive map of what constitutes an appropriate unit for mobilization; it is the smallest discrete areal unit other than the household which they can point to. Second, their mobilization as well as their demands hinge on the preexistence of precinct politics in which a local party man with a small area of responsibility is the first link to a larger political party controlling community services.[20] In other words, block clubs originate be-

19. Albert J. Hunter, "Local Urban Communities: Persistence and Change" (Ph.D. dissertation, University of Chicago, 1970).

20. For a different type of political pressure group organized in the absence of finely developed precinct politics see James Q. Wilson, *The Amateur Democrat* (Chicago: University of Chicago Press, 1962), pp. 96–125.

cause they can bargain within a political structure which is similarly divided into small spatial units.

The face-block, then, is often a social unit for both children and adults, yet it is not based mainly on the crescive growth of primordial solidarities. For children it is a prescribed social world carved out by parents and warranted by their fears of wider social relations for their children. For adults, the block club is a given fixture in their cognitive map of what is the appropriate bargaining agent to deal with a wider political organization broken down into similarly small units. In either case, the face-block is homogeneous only because its members treat it as such.

Interestingly enough, both the adolescent street-corner gang and the adult block club often become incorporated into larger confederations, the first as part of an alliance structure in opposition to similar gang alliances,[21] and the second as part of a political alliance to parallel the ward or precinct divisions of political parties.[22] In both instances, then, the areal consolidation of these groups depends on a correspondingly consolidated adversary or advocate. As we shall see, this seems to be a common principle in the further consolidation of territorial groups.

The Defended Neighborhood

The defended neighborhood is most commonly the smallest area which possesses a corporate identity known to both its members and outsiders. Functionally, the defended neighborhood can be conceived of as the smallest spatial unit within which coresidents assume a relative degree of security on the streets as compared to adjacent areas. The defended neighborhood, then, is an area within which people retreat to avoid a quantum jump in the risks of insult or injury they must take in moving about outside that area.

The defended neighborhood may be large or small although it undoubtedly has some upper limit in size. In populations where distrust is severe, as in low income areas of the inner city, the defended neighborhood may become so limited as to include only

21. Suttles, *Social Order.*
22. Hunter, "Local Urban Communities."

the residents of a single building. Or, in similar circumstances, the face-block itself may become a defended neighborhood. But generally these areas are simply too small for residents to carry out the practical business of shopping and pedestrian travel to work. Thus, the defended neighborhood is generally expansive enough to include a complement of establishments (grocery, liquor store, church, etc.) which people use in their daily round of local movements.

Since we have already discussed the defended neighborhood in the preceding chapter, it is unnecessary to do so here. What needs emphasizing is that the defended neighborhood is primarily a response to fears of invasion from adjacent community areas. It exists, then, within a structure of parallel residential solidarities which stand in mutual opposition. And it is this mutual opposition rather than primordial solidarity alone which gives the defended neighborhood its unity and sense of homogeneity.

The Community of Limited Liability

The defended neighborhood may or may not have an official identity honored by governmental acknowledgment. An official identity seems much more characteristic of and essential to the community of limited liability. Above all, the community of limited liability seems to have external adversaries or advocates who are anxious to claim a constituency or market and keep it intact. This requires a name and boundaries which are institutionally secured. The city and community press are among the obvious custodians in maintaining the identity of such residential groups.[23] In Chicago and doubtless in other large cities, there are numerous citywide or large-scale organizations which act to create or preserve the reputation and boundaries of some residential areas: the model cities program, the neighborhood phone directories, statistical reports on social problems, and an unknown number of business firms which pitch their advertisements and names in the direction of a local clientele.

23. Janowitz, *Community Press.*

Since the community of limited liability is so obviously a construct imposed by external commercial and governmental interests, it has been regarded by some as an artifact. Because it does not subscribe to the theory of indigenous community development, some writers prefer to ignore the community of limited liability rather than the theory which cannot account for it. The community of limited liability, however, is real enough and consists of an official identity and boundaries which are incorporated into the areal models of private and public organizations.

The community of limited liability is especially well represented in the familiar community areas of Chicago and a few other cities. But, with rare exception, cities are divided into a mosaic of noncoincident communities of limited liability and a range or organizations compete to construct an "authoritative mapping" of the city.[24] Thus, people tend to live in more than one community of limited liability and to have many different adversaries or partners in maintaining more than one corporate identity.

It is this mosaic of overlapping boundaries which probably gives the community of limited liability its most distinctive features. Since there are often two or more competing communities of limited liability, a resident frequently finds his interests divided among several adversaries or advocates and sometimes ones that are different from those of nearby coresidents. Participation in the community of limited liability, then, is a voluntary choice among options rather than one prescribed on the basis of residence alone. The local community organizations, improvement associations, political interest groups, and other organizations attract only a portion of the local residents. In turn, action on behalf of the community of limited liability becomes specialized and self-consciously oriented toward limited issues (housing standards, pollution, tree removal, and so on). The residents' interests thus are only partially captured by narrowly localized community groups.

This image of a mosaic of partially overlapping communities is even more complex and fragmented if we include as communities

24. Hunter, "Local Urban Communities."

of limited liability the incredible number of districts designated by governmental and private service agencies. Obviously neither Janowitz nor Greer explicitly intended to include such a multiplicity of formally designated areas into their original model of the community of limited liability.[25] Yet, there seems to be little in their analysis which would exclude such a multiplicity of community areas, and explicit considerations along this line may help some to broaden their interpretations. The community press, after all, is only one external organization vying with others to define its market and membership. The coexistence of several organizations, particularly governmental ones, claiming the rightfulness of their own jurisdiction complicates the picture developed by Janowitz and Greer but does not materially change their theoretical direction.

In particular, a multiplicity of communities of limited liability helps us to understand the partial involvement and frequent ineffectiveness of community organizations attempting to achieve better community services or redress inequities in their distribution. Such a mosaic of overlapping districts means that the loyalties, interests, and demands of coresidents are quite fragmented because those who serve them or act as their advocates are equally fragmented. Residents who live in the same police district do not necessarily live in the same smog-control district and those who live in the same smog-control district need not live in the same school district or Catholic parish. Attempts to concert local community groups, then, must proceed on the basis of arguments which attempt to move a particular intersection of interests as they are defined by the intersection of several different governmental and private district boundaries. Since the residents in any single area are unlikely to have more than a few common adversaries or advocates, they can be aroused only temporarily and then on the basis of one or a few issues to be brought before one or a few public or private agencies (park district, sanitation department, housing board, and so on). And, indeed, the history of community organization seems substantially this: community organizations

25. Janowitz, *Community Press*; and Scott Greer, in Ibid., pp. 245–70.

arise to meet a particular issue; they address their complaints or demands to one or a few service organizations; and with success or failure they all, except possibly their leaders, lapse into relative obscurity.

With some exceptions, then, the community of limited liability is fragmented, and its outlines are obscured because of the absence of consolidation in its external adversaries or advocates. As with the face-block or the defended neighborhood, the community of limited liability is a response to the wider community, but in this instance, the response is fragmented because both advocates and adversaries are not consolidated along district lines. Community organization may rise to a fever pitch in search of a vague establishment, and government may attempt to develop beneficent decentralization. Either effort, however, is apt to go askew so long as community groups along with their adversaries are so fragmented that neither can locate the other in some common fashion.

The Expanded Community of Limited Liability

The fragmentation of the community of limited liability is minor compared to its more expanded versions. The expanded community of limited liability is here an almost hypothetical entity, something we can see attempting to grope to the surface but still not quite visible. Token representation of such a larger urban community can be seen in the references of the mass media to entire sectors of a city such as the East Side or South Side. Recognition sometimes comes in the form of government policies and programs carried out on a similar scale and equally equipped with new spatial terms of reference. Occasionally, community groups may attempt to organize by claiming such large constituencies, although their claims may be poorly justified by their membership. More solid recognition for such broad sectors comes in the form of sales and distributing districts defined by some commercial firms.

There is reason to think, however, that such large-scale residential solidarities are not only attempting to identify themselves, but that the conditions underlying their occasional appearance are similar to those giving rise to the community of limited liability.

As big business and big government expand, they characteristically introduce two new features into their organization. First, they add new administrative levels which are often intermediate between the national, state, or metropolitan centers and the local districts. These intermediate levels of administration create enlarged areas and new centers of decision making which affect residential areas heretofore relatively independent of one another. If residents are to negotiate with these new advocates or adversaries, they must mobilize on a much wider footing.

Second, as big business and big government expand, they also seem to push discretion upward in their organization or, as the current terminology runs, to centralize. In government, this is most apparent in the growth of the civil service, which removes from local control certain crucial decisions on the release or transfer of personnel. This form of centralization is all the more evident among some precinct captains who complain that the people who make the decisions are so far above them that they can no longer do anything. In private business one runs into somewhat the same thing when managers and supervisors explain that they "can't do anything because our hands are tied."

No doubt this centralization arises for numerous reasons: increases in the scale of operations, the expense and scarcity of computers, the generally increasing ability and accountability of higher administrators, and the advantages of standardization along with the enforcement of standards. Whatever its sources, however, this new level of centralization poses a dramatic problem to small-scale residential groups who are interested in adjustments in public services or in being better served by private businesses. In the main, local community organizations—block clubs, improvement associations, fraternal associations, church groups, and so on—are too small and so lacking in stature that they cannot approach the high administrative offices which now affect them. Furthermore, they can seldom claim a broad enough constituency to rightfully represent the people in negotiations with administrative offices above that of the local district.

With a narrow support base and limited access to higher administrators, many traditional local groups seem to be frozen out of regularized and orderly negotiations with big government and big business. Too small to represent all the people from the point of view of many higher administrators, these traditional community organizations are often ignored. Too local and too low in status, community organization leaders themselves sometimes retreat from attempts to establish orderly negotiations with high administrators. Two separate lines of development seem to be arising from this predicament. First, many small, local, and traditional community organizations seem to have resorted to more militant tactics in bringing themselves to the attention of higher administrators. Dumping garbage on the mayor's doorstep, shouting down public officials and sleep-ins at public buildings are recent examples which come to mind. Often the actions of these small community organizations seem absurd and forlorn, as in the case of Florence Scala's attempt to forestall the location of the new University of Illinois campus in Chicago. Given the smallness and provincialism of such groups, their militancy on behalf of people they do not necessarily represent highlights the impropriety and rudeness of their efforts. Like southern white bigots who cry for self-determination, there is a precious irony evident in their tactics. Yet, the inability of these groups to be heard in some more orderly procedure is also evident and arouses widespread sympathy.

The second line of development is the growth of large-scale community organizations. Often, but not necessarily, confederational in form, these organizations expand their membership to include a wide range of residents, develop a more professional and high-status leadership, and attempt to speak to all issues concerning a contiguous area of considerable size and certainly larger than the defended neighborhood or community of limited liability. In Chicago, examples of this type of organization are Jessie Jackson's Operation Breadbasket, the West Side Organization, the Lawndale Organization, and two other groups (The Woodlawn Organization and the Back of the Yards Council) started by the Industrial Areas Foundation.[26] All of these organizations lay claim to a

26. Saul Alinsky, *Reveille For Radicals* (Chicago: University of Chicago Press, 1946). Alinsky's militant rhetoric seems to have obscured in

broad constituency, recruit widely, are open to affiliation with smaller localized groups, resist specialization in the issues they attack, and possess a high-status professional leadership able to present itself to high-status administrators. Certainly these groups use a militant rhetoric and engage in disruptive tactics. Nonetheless, on many occasions they seem to have succeeded in getting high administrators to gather with them at the bargaining table and to acknowledge the legitimacy of the organizations' representational role. Unlike the provincial and traditional community organization, they do not seem absurd and ironic in their claims to represent the people or in their use of militant tactics. They do have a broad constituency, and they do have leaders of sufficient stature to be taken seriously in their claims.

Certainly such large-scale community organizations are a long way from being able to mobilize most of the residents in any one city or from routine acceptance of their representational role. High administrators still speak of them as obstructionists and try to account for their militancy by claiming they are influenced by outside agitators. Mostly such groups are located in the black community probably because the blacks are less internally divided by ethnic and religious differences. Yet where they have emerged, these community organizations at least have a foot in the door of big government and big business. Both in their scale and in their form, they parallel that of big government and big business and, as with other residential solidarities, seem to be counterparts to their opponents and advocates. What is remarkable about such groups, however, is not their limited success, but the resistance they have met and our continued inability to develop any regularized due process in which big government, big business, and big residential areas can consult with one another.

---

the eyes of his critics a point of view which calls more for a change in structure than one of ideology. The Industrial Areas Foundation seems consistently to have promoted the emergence of wide-scale community organizations rather than narrow and local ones. Such a group cannot appeal to limited and sectarian views but must act as a political jobber for a broad range of interests. Furthermore, such groups are not likely to subvert established powers because they have the stature and power to enter into orderly negotiations with established powers.

Fragmentation of Grass Roots Communities

The face-block, defended community, community of limited liability, and expanded community of limited liability have been described as if they were intact and persistent forms. In the face-block and the defended community, incompleteness, and instability of residential solidarity have been understressed. Obviously, most residential areas do not subscribe closely to these types, and where some residential areas do become intact communities, they may be short-lived. Block clubs and street-corner gangs are quite limited in their occurrence. The defended neighborhood regularly undergoes invasion, deterioration, and change in both its solidarity and identity. The fragmentation of the community of limited liability is evident, whereas the expanded community of limited liability is represented only in very nascent forms.

The purpose of this typology, however, is not to describe a universal form which fits all American communities but to show how the solidarity of each kind of residential group depends on the reactions of its adversaries or advocates. The block-based street-corner group develops in a larger context where a concern for personal safety is so high that children are very restricted in their spatial movement. Thus the street-corner group or gang is very much a creature of the inner city, where commonplace stereotypes along with ethnic and racial differences warrant an extreme in provincialism. The adult block club, on the other hand, seems to depend on a political party structure where community services are controlled by precinct politicians. With either a decline in the distrust among some inner city groups or a decline in the discretion of precinct politicians, one may expect a corresponding decline in the street-corner gang and adult block club.

The street-corner gang and the defended neighborhood have reasonably reliable adversaries and advocates in the sense that they are adversaries to one another and built into the social structure of the United States through its stereotypes of racial, ethnic, and income groups. Intra- and inter-group fears of invasion in one form or another are so general that the street-corner gang and defended neighborhood develop naturally, without any conscious or intentional effort on the part of anyone. The adult block club and community of limited liability, however, depend not only on a conscious effort to create them but on an awareness of their functions. Neither the advocates nor the adversaries of the community of limited liability or its expanded version seem to possess this level of awareness, and much of the militancy of such community groups can be seen as an attempt to force themselves on the attention of high administrators. The consequent abrasiveness and disorderliness of these groups has given rise to a loud outcry for local autonomy, but local autonomy would only deepen the problems of negotiation between big business, big government, and big residential areas. Short of sponsored community development, one may expect continued militancy on the part of community groups while public and private agencies continue to standardize their policies irrespective of the needs or desire of local groups.

The lack of sponsored community development in the United States seems to have its roots in a prior model of the local community for which sociologists are in part responsible. In an ideological climate which emphasized local and individual initiative, it was convenient and sometimes flattering to think of local communities as developing indigenously from the grass roots without the aid of either opponents or advocates. Since de Tocqueville, we have chosen to think of American communities and neighborhoods as self-generated and self-governing entities comparable to the private entrepreneur although collective in character. Communities, no less than individuals, were expected to pull themselves up by their bootstraps and enter into interest group politics as independent parties. Indeed, it was sometimes thought that government sponsorship would be equivalent to government domination.[27]

27. This ideology seems to have its firmest expression in the doctrine of the separation of powers and the arguments supporting this concept. The power of such an ideology seems evident in numerous cases where even the voting rights of citizens living in communities sponsored by the government have been suspended on the assumption that they are dominated by the state, e.g., Washington, D.C., and Indian reservations. The restriction of voting rights to people who own property or have enough money to pay a poll tax derives from much the same argument: i.e., their fiscal integrity presumably removes them from undue influence by the incumbent government.

In order to maintain the full independence of community opinion, it was thought necessary to leave communities to their own devices and resources.

In fact, few communities or neighborhoods were able to mobilize by their own efforts, and the history of community organization in the United States is one of many small successes and several large failures. Where communities and neighborhoods did unify themselves to some degree, their efforts were largely defensive and their successes measured largely by how well they withstood various forms of invasion from adjacent communities or neighborhoods. Community power in the United States has been mainly the power of provincial groups over their own members and derives more from their capacity to isolate residents from broader collectivities than to affect the policies and practices of national, state, and municipal administrations—in a word, provincialism.

The absence of sponsored community development is especially evident in the way in which administrative districts remain unconsolidated and fail to recognize any form of community boundaries. Some idea of how nearly these administrative districts are fragmented into a mosaic of uncoordinated units can be gained by looking at a map of Chicago. As can be seen from maps 1 through 5, those areas officially designated as community areas seldom coincide with administrative districts, and the net effect must be to diffuse the demands of residential groups to the point where they can mobilize to address themselves to one administrative hierarchy at a time for some special issue. The lack of consolidation in Chicago seems almost incredible, yet compared to other cities, Chicago is probably less fragmented than most. Detroit, for example, has totally done away with her local wards. One can only surmise that local groups must take everything to the city hall irrespective of how minor their grievances or how busy the mayor.

This lack of sponsored community development and the infrequent use of such communities to designate administrative districts can probably be traced to our doctrine of the separation of powers and the arguments in favor of this concept. The concept is founded on a basic distrust of government and assumes that any kind of procedural and administrative relationship between differ-

68

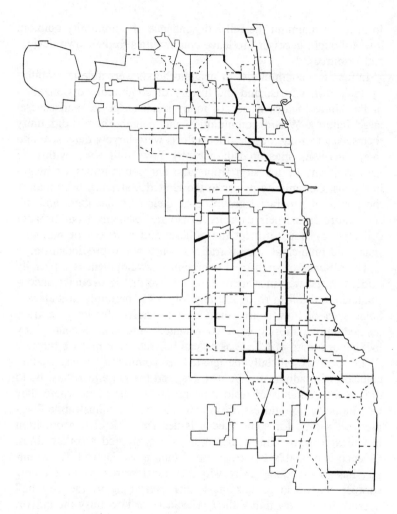

Map 1. Chicago: Ward Boundaries and Community Areas

———— Ward boundaries (1970)
– – – – Community areas (from Kitagawa and Tauber, 1960)
▬▬▬ Where boundaries coincide

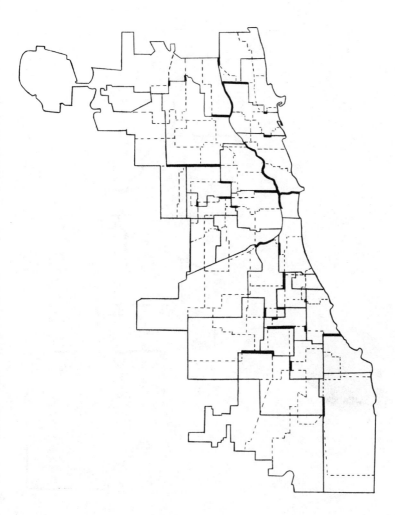

*Map 2. Chicago: School Districts
and Ward Boundaries, 1970*

———— School districts
– – – – Ward boundaries
▬▬▬▬ Where boundaries coincide

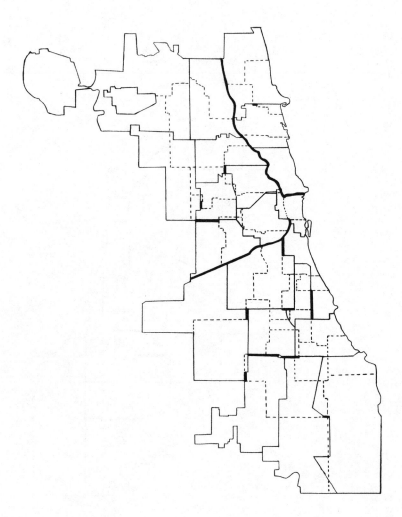

Map 3. Chicago: Police Districts
and School Districts, 1970

——————— Police districts

– – – – School districts

▬▬▬▬ Where boundaries coincide

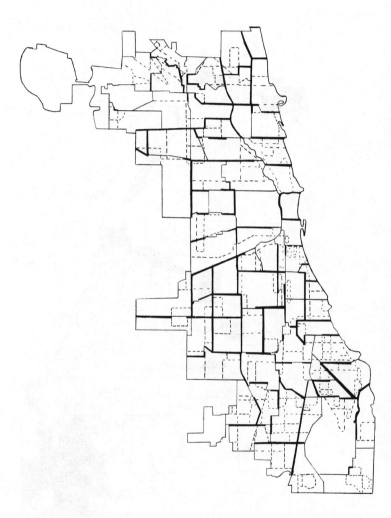

Map 4. Chicago: Community Areas

———— Community areas (from
　　　Kitagawa and Tauber, 1960)
– – – – Community areas (from Hunter, 1968)
▬▬▬ Where boundaries coincide

72

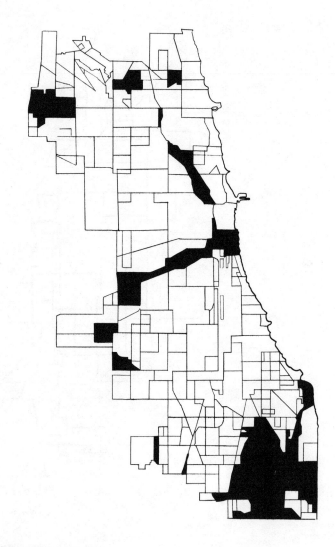

Map 5. Chicago: Community Areas

——————— Community areas as determined
by Hunter, 1968

Not included in any community area

ent centers of power is apt to result in a monolithic power structure in which the federal government dominates all other partners to the disadvantage of individual civil rights or individualism. Thus, private businesses, the different bodies of government, and separate communities have been allowed, even urged, to go their separate ways.

The argument in favor of a separation of powers was forged during a revolutionary period when the oppressiveness of a colonial government seems to have been equated with all forms of government. The confusion of this argument fits nicely into the view that all forms of government are inimical to individual rights and that the "least government is the best government." Countervailing powers, then, seemed a way of reducing the powers of government while increasing the rights of the citizen and thus a "good thing." The concept of a separation of powers and the arguments underlying it remained a sort of sacred cow to be trotted out whenever anyone suggested an administrative rather than a political solution to the problem of relating popular feeling to governmental policy. The citizens were to vote and the administrators were to govern, apparently without talking to one another between elections.

Judged in terms of its consequences, the concept of a separation of powers seems to have had almost the opposite result of that anticipated. The state governments were to defend individual rights against inroads by the federal government, but those who now cry out for states rights are certainly the most likely to curtail individual or civil rights. The lower and locally dominated courts are not more sympathetic to the rights of local residents but most subject to special influences. Local elections do not draw out a broad spectrum of participation and opinion but mainly those aroused by special interests. Since the Civil War, it is the federal government which has taken the most consistent stand on individual rights, whereas the states, municipalities, and counties have been most susceptible to narrow and self-interested groups.[28] The

28. C. Van Woodward, *The Strange Career of Jim Crow* (New York: Oxford University Press, 1955).

concept of a separation of powers succeeded consistently in one respect: it limited the power of the federal government in sponsoring individual civil rights and left localized government in the hands of special interest groups.

A cynical way of reviewing the separation of powers argument would be to dismiss it as simply a way in which various special-interest groups managed to weaken the federal government to the point that privilege could be bought cheaply from local governments rather than negotiated with a strong central government responsible to a broad spectrum of interests. Such an argument is persuasive since it relies on a utilitarian and mercenary imagery which is appealing to commentators on American society. In the relations between local communities and government much can be said in favor of such an argument. For example, the practice of gerrymandering tends to fragment natural communities and make it especially difficult for these communities to express their demands to politicians and administrators. Somewhat the same result may be achieved by the redistricting of areas where strong localized opposition emerges in reaction to a particular police, educational, or public aid administration. The general trajectory is one which tends to divide and conquer, leaving both government and popular groupings weak relative to the continuous influence of special interests.

Such an argument, however, does not ring true when brought into a wider confrontation with the facts. First, it is especially in machine politics—politics assumed most susceptible to special influence—where political parties have been most willing to form a structure of precinct politics which allows for some regularized expression of community opinion. Second, at-large elections and the general removal of informal procedures for consulting local groups have been sponsored by reformers rather than by the corrupted representatives of special interests. Corrupt or susceptible politicians seem to cater to every interest, including local community groups. It was reformers, seeking to eliminate special interests from politics, who sought to return to the image of an independent electorate whose contact with politicians was restricted to the voting booth. Apparently it is something more than the

politicians and their debts to special interests which militate against
a more regularized and procedural consultation between government and community groups.

The most obvious obstacle to bringing communities into regularized consultation with government was a model of community
development which implied the uselessness of such efforts. Since
de Tocqueville, such a model has been available in the form of the
local voluntary association, which was self-governing and self-
initiated.[29] Seen against the general view which judged all government intervention as bad, the grass roots voluntary association
seemed not only a positive good in itself, but an alternative to
something which was downright evil. The poor record of local
voluntary associations did not deter anyone; in any case it was
assumed that government could not contrive communities any
more than it could regulate love affairs. Communities emerged

29. In all fairness to de Tocqueville, it should be added that he was not
optimistic about the success of grass roots voluntary associations outside of
small towns and in the large metropolises of the United States (Alexis de
Tocqueville, *Democracy in America* [New York: Random House, 1945],
pp. 299–300n). "The United States has no metropolis, but it already contains several very large cities. Philadelphia reckoned 161,000 inhabitants,
and New York 202,000 in the year 1830. The lower ranks which inhabit
these cities constitute a rabble even more formidable than the populace of
European towns. They consist of freed blacks, in the first place, who are
condemned by the laws and by public opinion to a hereditary state of misery
and degradation. They also contain a multitude of Europeans who have
been driven to the shores of the New World by their misfortunes or their
misconduct; and they bring to the United States all our greatest vices,
without any of those interests which counteract their baneful influence. As
inhabitants of a country where they have no civil rights, they are ready to
turn all the passions which agitate the community to their own advantage;
thus, within the last few months, serious riots have broken out in Philadelphia and New York. Disturbances of this kind are unknown in the rest
of the country, which is not alarmed by them, because the population of
the cities has hitherto exercised neither power nor influence over the rural
districts.

"Nevertheless, I look upon the size of American cities, and especially
on the nature of their population, as a real danger which threatens the
future security of the democratic republics of the New World; and I venture to predict that they will perish from this circumstance, unless the
government succeeds in creating an armed force which, while it remains
under the control of the majority of the nation, will be independent of
the town population and able to repress its excesses."

from primordial sentiments, and by definition these sentiments could not be legislated into existence overnight.

Sociologists entered the picture in the 1920s and, while documenting the existence of urban communities, continued the tradition which stressed their natural development and the efficacy of the invisible hand. With rare exceptions people simply remained unaware of the way external forces helped define both the boundaries and identity of urban communities. A time-worn model, and now one commended to observers by "scientific facts," seems simply to have preempted other conceptual alternatives to the point that only the local grass roots community, self-governing and self-initiated, deserved to be called a community. Everything else was an artifact and, lacking the magic touch of the invisible hand, considered unreal or inauthentic. The model of such "natural" communities may have been a myth more often than not, but as a social reality it certainly excluded consideration of alternative possibilities.

At least one notable and interesting exception occurs in the writings of Lincoln Steffens, who, along with the Boston 1915 planners, "concocted a plan for a committee *to sit in a ward,* to be composed of a physician to give medical help, an attorney to give legal counsel, a businessman not only to give business advice but to find jobs for men in business as well as in politics, a clergyman to offer spiritual comfort, and one other, preferably someone who had done wrong enough himself to understand guilt."[30] Steffens does not elaborate on why he chose the political ward as a working unit nor does he spell out why he felt it was necessary for such a group of outsiders to take the initiative. In any case, the Boston 1915 planners failed because of their own pessimism about human nature and the fear that the plan would only increase the power of politicians.[31]

30. *The Autobiography of Lincoln Steffens* (New York: Harcourt, Brace and Co., 1931), p. 381. Emphasis added.
31. Ibid., pp. 384–90. Steffens was not the only one with such a plan. Ernest Burgess also attempted to get Chicago to consolidate its aldermanic and community areas (unpublished report found in Burgess's personal papers, called "A Ward Redistricting Plan," 1931), and Helen I. Clarke did a study proposing the consolidation of welfare agencies' districts:

The Boston 1915 plan has a modern ring to it and could have served as a model for some recent efforts along similar lines. In many respects, however, Steffens's plans and those of a more modern cast seem only to pile on top of existing community service agencies a volunteer or ad hoc organization to duplicate services already formally the right of residents. It is doubtful if people who are already paying taxes for these services can easily justify either the effort or expense required by additional but unevenly distributed programs. The interests of such local taxpayers probably lies in the formal recognition of community groups large enough to correspond to the governmental agencies which claim them as constituencies, along with the consolidation of a multiplicity of federal, state, and municipal districts, so that residential groups can effectively deal with a limited number of bureaucracies. Rationality would also seem to dictate a formal and procedural relationship between such residential groups and the public agencies meant to serve them. Yet it is exactly the local community group which seems most thoroughly trapped in the antebellum model of the grass roots community, autonomous, self-initiated, and uniquely able to determine its fate unilaterally.

Restorationism versus the Sponsored Community

The model of the grass roots community is especially appealing to residential groups. Its imagery makes them the original and final architect of their existence and they are beholden to no one. Such an imagery appeals to anyone reared in a society in which self-help, individual initiative, and personal responsibility are like the epitaphs that one puts on people's tombstones. It is within this broad cultural context that one must review recent social movements toward community control.

On the face of it, much of what is said by proponents of community control sounds like a patent example of restorationism.

"Uniform Areas for Chicago Citywide Social Agencies" (M.A. thesis, School of Social Service Administration, University of Chicago, 1926). Burgess's recommendations were ignored, and Clarke's dissertation led to only slight changes in some welfare agency districts.

There is a great nostalgia for an earlier and presumed golden age
of local determination. Spokesmen for the movement call upon
radical and militant tactics, but ideologically they would be most
at home with William Jennings Bryan. The precious autonomy
of the local community, its assumed ability to achieve justice and
equity through unregulated or unspecified interaction, and the
maligning of big government and big business are ideas which
have a durable history in the laissez faire state. It is entirely consistent then that supporters of community control call upon such
time-honored slogans as democracy, participation, the people, and
self-determination. And it is equally reasonable for them to accuse
big business and big government of being in conspiracy, of being
an establishment, and of forming an elite sensitive to only its own
wants. Guided by a model which emphasizes the justice and
efficiency of a system of totally unregulated competition between
small centers of power and authority, the spokesmen for community control need only to mouth worn phrases to embarrass their
opponents.

Such a movement draws on traditions already received, and
historically fits most closely into the populist camp. Like populism
in general, the community control movement arouses ambivalent
responses. It attracts wide sympathy, and people can scarcely resist being sympathetic since the movement can lay claim to most
of the slogans memorialized in high school civics texts. Despite
their sympathy, many people still draw back, saying either that
total community control is impractical or that the advances in
scale in government and business make it a lost cause. As with
other populist movements, this one seems to arouse sympathy, but
because of its lack of any new ideological vision, falls victim to
equally durable objections.

From the point of view of some observers, of course, local community control is simply a cynical or misguided way of returning
to river-ward politics and of abandoning any hope of meeting
national standards of education, welfare, and civil rights. Indeed,
the concept of local control seems to appeal equally to southern
racists and black separatists. Both are suspect in their ulterior
reasons, and one can readily imagine the favoritism and inequities

which would result from, say, community control of the police force. The alternative to inefficient, rigid, and arbitrary state, federal, and municipal programs seems to be a capitulation to even more arbitrary and less accountable local elites. Few people may be willing to make such an exchange.

As Lowie has pointed out, however, proponents or opponents of local community control seem less divided on national standards of community welfare than on the lack of uniform enforcement of these standards and the consequent poor delivery of services.[32] The implication, as he points out, is not for less centralization but for a more consistent and legislatively defined enforcement of national standards.[33] The present practice of piecemeal consultation with local groups and the pattern of episodic negotiation without explicit guidelines makes the delivery of governmental services very uneven and robs government itself of legitimacy. Meeting many of the objections of local community groups and subscribing to national standards would mean more rather than less government and, in many respects, it would be a more bureaucratic or legislatively guided government than it is now.

Whatever the broader implications of Lowie's work, it puts the controversy over community control on an entirely different footing by providing a new option, and for purposes of political mobilization, a new vision. The existence of national standards, big government, and big business need not be seen as antithetical or destructive to the local community so long as there is a thoroughly well-defined administrative framework within which consultation with local communities can be regularized and follow due process. The local community would not stand outside federal, state, and municipal bureaucracies but be officially recognized and included into their counsels. Both parties would be constrained by procedural and substantive guidelines and be accountable to higher review. But there is no inherent contradiction between centralized legislation and an administrative framework which is highly decentralized. The alternative which Lowie is proposing is an expansion

32. Theodore J. Lowie, *The End of Liberalism* (New York: W. W. Norton and Co., 1969).
33. Ibid.

of the explicit and accountable participation of groups within those bureaucracies which devise and deliver community services. This calls for a growth in administrative structure rather than a simple retreat into provincialism.

Those proponents of community control who look far enough will find precedent for such an administrative solution to the inclusion of residential groups into the orderly procedures of government. The expansion of regularized government consultation with lobbies, the armaments industry, labor unions, and other interest groups is already so extensive that it belies any simple laissez faire description of the relationship between the private and public spheres. As Lowie points out, this consultation between government and private interests has not developed from guiding principles but crept up on us in the form of ad hoc negotiations without much in the way of legislative guidelines.[34] For the residential community the most apparent model is the Department of Agriculture's farm extension program with its use of the county and country agent as a basis for relating farmers to policies of the federal government. No doubt such a program has the usual failings of other federal attempts to relate to the public outside the voting booth. But the existence of such a program at all provides a principle—or at least a departure from laissez faire principles—which by extension could include urban residential groups as well as rural ones. More extensive and refined models can be drawn from Scandinavia and Japan. The obstacles to such a solution are not a shortage of intellectual possibilities but those preconceptions growing out of vested interests and a sentimental attachment to the myth of the grass roots community.

Doubtless, the obstacles to such an administrative solution are very great, and a current assessment of them suggests that they may be so impressive as to constitute a self-defeating myth. The identification and definition of community boundaries would have to be initiated by government itself since most communities seem to lack sufficient consensus on any boundaries which go past the

34. Ibid., see particularly pp. 79–97, 125–56.

defended neighborhood.[35] With our characteristic distrust of government intervention, this is apt to arouse more apprehension than it quiets. The consolidation of an incredible number of federal, state, and municipal districts could be carried out only over the violent objections of higher administrators anxious to define whom they will serve. The nomination or appointment of community representatives and their monetary subsidization is sure to arouse the suspicion that they will be no more than mouthpieces for governmental agencies. The problem of developing concrete and clear legislative guidelines is not only onerous but subject to the current influence of special and sectional interests. These obstacles alone are probably sufficient to argue down without trial any attempt to include the local community as an administrative partner in the allocation of community services.

But the proponents of local community control are themselves likely to be one of the main obstacles to their success. Drawing on a model of community development which gave them sole credit for its existence they will be loath to admit the role of external forces in the origin of past communities or the necessity of such sponsors in the future. The image of the grass roots community beholden to no one and thoroughly in the grasp of its local elites has a symbolic attraction to many people and a mercenary utility to some of them. The images of the past will die hard, since local communities found in them a favorable if inaccurate resemblance of themselves.

35. In this instance, the case of Oceanhill-Brownsville is especially interesting because the proponents of community control often point to it as their signal success. Yet, as the hyphenated name suggests, Oceanhill-Brownsville was not an intact community with great solidarity before its separate constitutiences were thrown together by governmental decree rather than community action. (Mayer and Wade, *Chicago.*)

4. The Contrived Community

When Park, Burgess, and Wirth attempted to describe and analyze the Chicago of the 1920s and 1930s, they were essentially dealing with a city which had been built from scratch. Chicago was among the new cities of the New World, built on virgin land without the obstruction of prior installations. Today, however, the city of Chicago is no longer a new city. It has been condemned by time, neglect, and authoritative opinion. Of course, it is not that the physical plant of the city has just worn out. In some sense the city is wealthier, more efficient, and, believe it or not, handsomer than ever.[1] Certainly there are ghettos, children get bitten by rats, and many buildings are about to fall down of their own weight. But judging from reliable accounts, the city has always had its share of these troubles, only they were worse in previous eras. What has changed is mainly our own standards of what the accommodations of a city should be like. Not a little of this change is due to the competitive position of jurisdictionally distinct suburbs. It is no longer true that people must compete *within* the city for its land and benefits. Instead, the city must now compete for people, and to do so effectively it must be reconstructed to match the benefits and attractions of adjacent municipalities.

The reconstruction of Chicago provides an opportunity for re-thinking and redoing what Park, Burgess, and Wirth inaugurated. In a very true sense of the word, such a restudy represents a "replication," in which not only do the contours of geographic reality remain the same but it is at least within the realm of possibilities that the slate of existing construction could be erased and created again from scratch. As I shall point out, however, the past does not seem quite so easily removed.

1. For a visual demonstration see Harold M. Mayer and Richard C. Wade, *Chicago: Growth of a Metropolis* (Chicago: University of Chicago Press, 1969).

Douglas Park Community Area

The Douglas Park Community Area is only one of the seventy-five
to which Burgess gave names and can illustrate only a fraction of
the general pattern of urban development he described. Lying on
the Near South Side, just south of the Loop, the area was originally
developed by Stephen Douglas, who owned most of the area and
whose tomb lies in a small park at its southeastern corner. His
development became the Gold Coast of the day, and many of the
streets were lined with great mansions until Potter Palmer re-
located his own home on the city's Near North Side and started
an exodus from the area. Afterward the area underwent a period
of succession and became the northernmost portion of the Black
Belt by 1920. Since then the community area has become widely
known through the studies of St. Clair Drake and Horace Caton.[2]
As one of the primary areas of black settlement, the section gave
rise to the first black political machine and earned the nickname,
the "Mother Ward." The subject of several sociological accounts
and popular articles, the community area occupies a significant
place in Chicago's history.[3] Until recently, however, the area was
never known as the Douglas Park Community but referred to
variously as 31st Street, the Mother Ward, or the Black Belt.
Despite its richness, this history has been broken with such abrupt-
ness that even old residents who continue to live in the area no
longer think of it as the community in which so many famous
whites and blacks lived.

Shortly after the Second World War, clearance of the area was
started and later encouraged by two local but powerful institutions,
a hospital and university.[4] At first the cleared land was used for

2. St. Clair Drake and Horace Caton, *Black Metropolis* (London: J.
Cape, 1946).
3. James Q. Wilson, *Negro Politics* (Glencoe, Ill.: Free Press, 1960);
Harold F. Gosnell, *Negro Politicians* (Chicago: University of Chicago
Press, 1935); and Allen H. Spear, *Black Chicago* (Chicago: University of
Chicago Press, 1967).
4. Evelyn M. Kitagawa and Karl E. Taeuber, eds., *Local Community
Fact Book, Chicago Metropolitan Area* (Chicago: Chicago Community
Inventory, 1963), p. 84. Both types of institutions seem unable to adapt to

low income public housing, and two large developments were
located in the community area along with some others at its periphery (see map 6). This new form of housing for low income
blacks did nothing to reduce the high level of public danger in the
area and other threats to the local hospital and university. In the
early fifties both institutions joined their efforts with that of the
wider community and encouraged the development of middle class
housing to make the area safe for themselves and for their emblems
of a shared moral order. The first result was a high-rise development for middle income tenants, mixed according to race, ethnicity,
and all other characteristics. Subsequent rebuilding in the area
followed this course; in all, nine different developments have taken
shape either as totally new construction or as new residential
developments. Only a small portion of the old slum is left, and
approximately one-third of it has been cleared over the years.
Significantly, it is referred to as the "Gap"; a lapse in the encroaching wall of high-rise buildings.

Each of these developments is somewhat different from the
others, although they are primarily variations on a single theme
grown familiar to us by the widespread construction of inner city
developments. Although each development is interesting in its own
right, the most impressive aspect of the community area is the
sheer extent of redevelopment. By now, over twenty-two thousand
residents have been settled in the new housing, not including the
spillover of additional developments going up in adjacent community areas. Probably nowhere in the country and certainly not
in Chicago, can one find such a scale of inner city urban residential
redevelopment. Accordingly, what is interesting about the community area is not an intricate description of its internal structure, but
an analysis of those broad features which are apt to be general to
other areas once they also undergo redevelopment. The Douglas
Park Community Area is certainly not typical of other big city
neighborhoods, but something like it will probably be typical in

---

invasion by moving because their physical plant is so specialized that it
cannot profitably be passed on to other users.

85

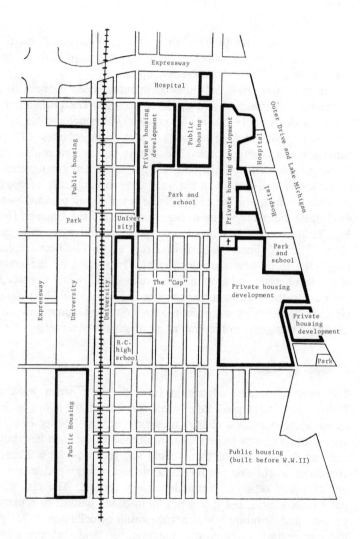

Map 6. Douglas Park Community Area

the future. The attempt here, then, has been to single out those processes and features which seem to be integral to both the scale and character of such urban redevelopment.

For these purposes, only limited attention need be paid to the population composition and the local ecology. The population remains predominantly black (76 percent), although whites are an increasing proportion. The lower and working classes (48 percent) are now a minority and a declining one as new middle class housing is constructed. Income groups are sharply separated by rental levels, and almost all the poor and working class people live in public housing or the Gap. Of the seven developments, two of the largest are managed by a single realtor, and the Chicago Housing Authority manages two more; the others have separate managers. The old linear pattern of street shops has been replaced largely by three new shopping centers. Impressed by the amount of glass, concrete, and monumental architecture, one of my students referred to the area as a "moonscape." That is one's first impression. I developed the concept of a contrived community after living for two years in the area as a participant observer.

Changes of Scale

The most noticeable alteration from the time when Park and Burgess first attempted to give an account of the Douglas Park Community Area is a change of scale. Until as late as 1945, the area could be seen largely as a multitude of independent buyers and developers. Wirth, then, could see the area as well as the entire city as the end product of a process of aggregation growing out of many separate and independent choices. The city had a pattern, of course, but it was not an intended pattern or a planned pattern, and certainly it was not the result of collusion. What gave the city pattern stability was the price of land and the relative economic position of many firms and individuals in the open market. No single individual or firm was so powerful or so well financed that it could reverse such general trends.

In the rebuilding of the Douglas Park Community Area, however, developers are not simply faced with the problem of making the most economical usage of cleared land. To a large extent their decision must be based on what they expect to happen to adjacent property. It made little sense, for example, to build a string of thirty or forty town houses if the adjacent land remained a deteriorated ghetto or was taken over by a series of new warehouses. The tendency of developers, and especially private developers, was to hang back until they could control a block of land large enough that the context of their development was less problematic.

Necessarily this meant that large blocks of land had to be cleared, procured, and managed in some thoughtful way. The land blocks which were amenable to this sort of management ranged anywhere from a city block to forty or fifty acres. Such purchases inevitably eliminated most of the small developers, small financiers, small realtors, small construction firms, and local politicians. Redevelopment was carried out by large operators, and even in a city the size of Chicago there are only a few developers, realtors, financiers, and politicians who can enter into so large an undertaking.

Accordingly, development in the Douglas Park Community Area has been undertaken by a very limited number of large organizations capable of mounting such large-scale projects. The Chicago Housing Authority, three very large private developers, the Illinois Institute of Technology, and Mercy Hospital are responsible for over 35 percent of the new construction in the area and continue to be the major agents controlling housing in the area. In all these housing developments, government money has been important, either directly in the financing of construction or in the clearance and sale of land to private developers. Government has also played a role in establishing standards for bidders on the cleared land since the proposed developments have had to be judged on the basis of quality as well as the size of the bids presented by prospective builders. Indeed, the burden of inducing builders to consider construction in the area has often fallen on local government since private firms are reluctant to risk investments in an area whose future is so problematic. Thus, many of the private developers regard their investment into the area as a sort of public service in which they are not aiming to lose money but in which they are balancing the gains for social welfare against relative losses from alternative investments.

One fairly obvious consequence is that the decisions made among so small a group of developers are no longer independent of one another. I do not mean to say that the parties involved are in collusion. As near as I can tell, developers and realtors are more competitive than ever because the sums of money at stake are so great. But as each large development goes in, it very much affects what other developers can do with adjacent land. If one developer earmarks a large plot of land for high income housing, then other developers of adjacent plots of land may follow suit, because the sale or rental value of housing depends heavily on its being placed in homogeneous batches.

As a result, developers keep a close eye on one another, and the first to enter a particular area may start a trend quite apart from the fact that it may not subscribe to the most advantageous economic usage of land. A fairly obvious example of this sort in Chicago and in the Douglas Park Community Area is the rather heavy concentration of public housing during the early stages of redevelopment. Lacking commercial bidders on land adjacent to inner city ghettos, government proceeded to use its own money to develop public housing, and once started, the placement of public housing made it very difficult for city planners or private developers to consider the adjacent land for any other purpose than additional public housing. This process went so far in some areas of Chicago that it encroached on the lake front itself, which normally would have been reserved for more expensive housing. Where there have been no institutional guardians to appreciate this "noneconomic" use of land, the expansion of low income housing and the ghetto has continued. In the Douglas Park Community such guardians were present in the form of two hospitals and a university which were able to encourage the use of government controls to obtain private development for higher income housing. The continuation of such government controls and favored rates of property exchange, however, is crucial to the future development of the area, since it is the main assurance that developers have for the prospective value of their properties.

Examples of this sort seem to be one among many reasons for
an increased insistence on planning and coordination among the
various parties affected by redevelopment. This insistence on planning grows directly from the scale at which redevelopment takes
place. Time was when a few new homes, business places, or a
subdivision were accepted for the uncertainties they posed, either
because they were not very important in their impact or because
they were undertaken by so many different individuals that the
burden of planning could not be assigned. Now, with only a few
developers and realtors engaging in reconstruction, the finger of
blame is easier to point. Moreover, the scale of development is so
great that the changes in demand placed on the schools, parks,
shopping areas, churches, and other public facilities is nearly
intolerable. During the period of clearance, for example, a school
district may find a good portion of its students removed, and then,
by the time the district has adjusted to these new population levels,
it may be swamped by a sudden influx of pupils coming from a
new development.[5]

One finds in the Douglas Park Community Area, then, a loud
outcry for planning and coordination which, however, is seldom
met. School officials complain that they are not forewarned about
the number of students they can expect to enroll from each new
development. Builders complain that the schools are not adjusting
their building and academic programs to meet the demand from
prospective renters. The situation of other publicly run organizations in the area is not very different from that of the schools, and
naturally there is a good deal of pressure on developers to make
known their plans and to coordinate their efforts so that they do
not press too heavily on existing facilities or leave those who run
public facilities totally unprepared. Such planning and coordination of the parties involved in urban redevelopment poses not only
practical but moral dilemmas. The developer, for instance, cannot
prognosticate his intentions very far ahead because they depend

5. This general absence of coordination among builders was highlighted in the early 1960s when a newly completed public school was torn
down before it opened to make room for a freeway under construction at
the same time.

so much on other contingencies, such as the national economy, the discount rate, plans for adjacent property, and alternative investment opportunities. In turn, to coordinate the plans of different developers violates the rules of free enterprise and lays each developer open to the charges of conspiracy and collusion. Even more suspect is coordination between politicians, developers, realtors, the federal government, and financial institutions. Seemingly, collaboration among these organizations is without legitimate precedent in American society, and their cooperation causes untold suspicion.

Cast of Characters

These problems of coordination and planning point up yet another difference between the Chicago that Park and Burgess watched grow from scratch and the one we are seeing reconstructed. In degree and kind, the cast of characters engaged in rebuilding the Douglas Park Community Area seems to be far more variable than in the 1920s and 1930s. Initially it is up to political bodies to come forth with plans and to bear the brunt of criticism for clearance and the dislocations that ensue. In turn, civil rights groups, residential aggregates, community organizations, local politicians, churchmen, and professional planners become aroused and enter the controversy over subsequent land usage. The developer who enters such a hornet's nest must not only assuage an indignant citizenry but engage both governmental and private financiers while also juggling his relations with realtors, chain stores, local institutions, and an occasional researcher.

No doubt this cast of characters was present at the time of Park and Burgess. Nonetheless, there remains a difference, particularly in the visibility of public and private agencies which are developing the area. The number of developers in the area is so small and each is so prominent that the local residents can identify and remember them. The role of federal and city financing for purposes of clearance and construction is openly publicized and widely known. This heightened visibility of the area's developers and their close connection to public institutions has raised a num-

ber of the residents' expectations about how the development of
their community can be coordinated and guided to meet local
desires. There is a tendency to attribute a considerable degree of
coordination to both public and private agencies and to assume
that they can be held jointly responsible for the development of
the area. Another expectation is that the coordination among
public and private organizations is or should be sufficient to raise
proposals for the betterment of the collective welfare of groups
of residents rather than centering only on individualized benefits.

The first expectation often takes the form of a local community
group's attempting to develop a grievance structure to redress
wrongs which are now thought correctable because control is so
nearly centralized in the hands of a few actors. Tenants' groups,
PTA's, Concerned Parents, and a number of other groups have
developed along this line and have acted on behalf of specific
individuals who complained about police harassment, the unfair
treatment of children at school, eviction notices, and so on. Sometimes these groups are unsuccessful, but they tend uniformly to
assume that the organizations they confront are able to make the
corrections they desire and should be held responsible. Their atti-
tude on these matters is one of considerable self-confidence, and
often they threaten to demonstrate publicly, although their threats
have usually been louder than their bites.

The efforts of these groups are paralleled by that of a few others
which have attempted to represent an entire development or, in
one case, the entire Douglas Park Community Area. All these
groups tend independently to foresee a great potentiality for coordination among the developers and public agencies. Thus, they
not only attempt to redress the grievances of specific individuals
but also attempt to get builders and public agencies to meet their
desires for public facilities which are to be shared by parts of the
community's population. Their objectives here have especially
centered on school programs, the safety of parks, traffic patterns,
and a host of issues which touch on their collective welfare. Obviously these concerns are not special to this area, but their tendency
to assume that almost any developer or public agency can initiate
the desired change is a qualitative change from our experience

with past community groups. This tendency to see public and private agencies as a single, consolidated establishment is especially irksome to some developers who feel that they are being asked to run the public agencies as well as their own businesses.

From my own observations, the coordination among these large public and private organizations is still minimal. Schools and parks are not built at the same pace as are new residential units. Commercial facilities lag behind the construction of housing and, once built, may not be occupied for some time. Additional police are not always keeping pace with the increase in population, and the same is sometimes true of the schools, parks, sanitation force, and so on. During the last election there was even an inability to increase the number of polling places. Inevitably, a large number of grievances arise, and they center on the politicians, realtors, builders, and planners who play such a large role in the area. Corresponding to this readiness to lay blame on the small number of people who take a role in the area's development is the assumption that any one of them can act in almost any area.

For example, police brutality has recently become an issue in the area, and some of the local developers and realtors, much to their bewilderment, have been asked to take part in restoring due process to police action. Similar requests have been made of some developers to provide a better school system. The continued presence of all-black populations in the two public housing projects has aroused interest in their managed desegregation, and one builder has responded by offering to take over the management of one of the public housing developments and desegregate it. Politicians are approached to force builders to include additional commercial properties in their developments, and developers are approached to force politicians to change traffic rulings or increase the number of crossing guards. The local builders ask city agencies, such as the Park District, to provide new recreation for the new renters, and the city agencies sometimes ask community organizations or builders to provide volunteer help or new resources. Many of these attempts at lateral coordination are clandestine and pursued as a kind of favor, but they show how obscure are the boundaries between private and public realms of responsibility. The assumption seems to be that the number of actors who manage local life are so small that any one member is in immediate consultation with the rest.

To a remarkable degree, the local developers and realtors have themselves moved in the direction of responding to those demands which go beyond their narrow role as private businessmen. As mentioned above, one of the builders has offered to help integrate one of the public housing developments. All of the developers have installed some public facilities, especially recreational space. One builder has constructed a school building in his development and subsequently leased it to the public schools. This has involved him and some of his personnel in the management of the school. Two of the developers have built community centers and have since been required to take some role in designing the activities these centers provide. The residents, then, are not simply demanding coordination of public and private organizations without justification; to a considerable extent, the developers and public agencies have moved toward a combined role.

Nonetheless, there still exists a general absence of any formal relationship between private and public organizations. More often than not, developers want to avoid responsibility for public facilities, and public officials insist on their inability to "force" the developers to follow their plans. For many of the residents, these disclaimers are merely examples of evasiveness and only further evidence that the developers and public officials are in collusion to the disadvantage of the residents. This view that there is a conspiracy behind the area's redevelopment has widespread credence although it is ill-formed. One extreme is the belief of a few people that the entire area was designed by some highly placed financiers at the close of the Second World War and that everything which has happened in the community since then is the unfolding of this plan. A few other people believe that the area was explicitly created on a strictly quid pro quo basis in bargaining with black politicians for the development of all-white North Side communities. Most of the residents do not believe any of these conspiracy theories specifically; rather, they listen to all of them seriously and weigh one against the other. Most people feel vaguely uncomfortable and feel that "something is going on" but are unable to pinpoint it.

This outlook leaves the residents poised to see conspiracy and to react forcefully when given the opportunity to confront what they regard as the establishment. For example, at a recent PTA meeting I attended in one of the racially integrated developments, several parents were up in arms over the failure of most of the white parents to send their children to the local elementary school. The mayor and other dignitaries were present and were told by numerous speakers that "if only they wanted to" the "power structure" and the realtors could "make" the recalcitrant whites send their children to the local elementary school. To press their point, the local dissidents went so far as not to allow the mayor to speak at all. It was as if the dissidents expected that by some verbal alchemy the mayor could convert all the whites to the call of racial integration or he would not be allowed to speak. The mayor, however, was not to be denied, and grasping the microphone despite the emcee, he told those present that the city and the realtors had gone as far as they could in providing for residential integration. Further integration, he suggested, particularly that in the school system, depended on the residents themselves. In their subsequent discussion, however, the residents were reluctant to take this responsibility because: "Unless the city makes its policy clear, we can't do anything."

In addition to this anticipation of conspiracy, there is a local school of thought which seeks to increase the extent of coordination among private and public agencies through the use of human relations experts. These people are seen as acting as jobbers who will meet with everyone concerned with a particular community service and help them reach consensus on what is to be done. Their role is to enter into the sort of collaborations which are already going on and insure that the community's interests are protected. So far there are only limited moves in this direction. One local school has an advisory board including members of the attendance district. One of the two community centers has hired a professional to coordinate its activities and to speak on behalf

of the residents to the local management of housing.[6] Residents
in one of the developments are forming proposals for federal
financing of a community coordinator who will meet with various
groups and the developers and the administrators of public agencies. There is widespread discussion of community boards who
will take a hand jointly in the management of housing, the schools,
parks, the police force, sanitation, and so forth. No clear formula
has been found for carrying through this type of community participation, and it is more symptomatic of the general malaise
present in the area than of an emerging structural pattern.

What does seem most clear from the Douglas Park Community
Area is its divergence from a traditional pattern of residential
development in which public and private organizations have been
seen as acting independently without much opportunity for large-
scale coordination or collusion. Instead, many of the residents
assume that any of the leading figures in the area's redevelopment
can speak with authority to the others. For their own part, the
area's developers and public administrators are reluctant even to
see each other lest they give further credence to the widespread
allegation of conspiracy. As a result, the degree of coordination
among them is very limited and likely to occur only in crises situations where a community group has threatened to demonstrate
or where a school or park finds its facilities totally overloaded.
The result is a pattern of grievances which add fuel to the fires
that keep conspiracy theories boiling. In a way, then, the Douglas
Community Area is neither fish nor fowl. It is neither a strictly
private development governed by the principles of laissez faire
nor a publicly and centrally developed community where broad
goals of public welfare take priority. Consequently, much of what
goes on in the community seems of questionable legitimacy to
the residents. Either there is collusion which is hidden from
their eyes or there is an opportunity to coordinate the activities
of both public and private organizations to obtain better community services.

6. The other is temporarily closed because of an inability to be self-
supporting.

The residents pursue both possibilities, sometimes simultaneously. If their attempts at coordination are rebuffed, they lean
toward one of the community's conspiracy theories. If builders,
public officials, or residential groups respond to their suggestions,
it is because the potentiality of coordination is there. Both the
residents and those who are taking a leading role in the area's
development seem to lack either an administrative or an ideological model which can explain their predicament or guide them
in it. Thus, one finds residents decrying centralization in the area's
planning and at the same time demanding more coordination
among builders, realtors, and public officials. Public and private
organizational heads still appeal to the independence of their
roles, but on occasion deviate from a faithful conformity to that
ideal. The result is a huge backlog of "irregularities" as gauged
from a model in which private and public organizations act independently. These irregularities are quick to be seized on and re-
interpreted by other community groups which share in a heritage
of distrust and pessimism.

Heritage of Distrust and Pessimism

Coincident with these time lags in construction, unscheduled public and private development, grievances, and allegations of conspiracy, there are a number of movements from the sidelines
which may prove to be of considerable significance for the community. As clearance in the area progresses, it does not simply
remove everyone but leaves sizeable portions of the indigenous
population in their previous position. In the Douglas Park Community Area, these are people who have often been wronged by
the politicians, the urban planners, developers, financiers, researchers, and institutions which now seek their cooperation.
These people have multiple grievances, and they share a legacy
of distrust for highly placed officials and entrepreneurs. All of this
occurs within a contemporaneous national context in which political and business elites suffer from a widespread credibility gap
and the suspicion of an establishment inimical to public welfare.
    All of these currents of thought find an objective in the Douglas

Park Community Area in the persons of its developers and public
officials. On the one hand, this means that many of the local
community groups make strong demands to have their questions
answered about the plans of public and private organizations
developing the area. On the other hand, continual threats of violence have lurked in the background, especially by vaguely defined
black militant groups living or working around the fringes of the
new middle class residential units. Both public and private officials have tended to put off the questions of the residents, generally saying that the way the area is developed in the future depends
on other builders, public decisions, and the availability of funds,
or on City Hall. The main reaction to the threats of violence is
a considerable investment in formal methods of social control.
Thus, the roles of policemen, doormen, security guards, and
watchdogs have been sharply increased, especially in the middle
class housing developments. Wire fences have been placed at
some strategic points to discourage cross pedestrian traffic. Tele-
vision monitors have been installed in some of the high-rise buildings so that residents can see who is buzzing their apartment before
they open the door. Peepholes are regular equipment on all apartment doors in the new middle income housing. Custodians and
doormen have been instructed to fill their formal role and provide
informal surveillance as well. It is reported that in one period after
the riots in Watts and Detroit, a machine gun was placed on one of
the high-rise buildings. In the main these threats emerge as vague
rumors, but it is obvious that no one is taking any chances.

Alongside this legacy of distrust goes a heritage of pessimism.
Some of the residual population left after the clearance of the area
are badly aggrieved because they were dispossessed of homes and
community institutions which they cannot replace. The new and
more affluent population moving into the area tend to understand
and sympathize with these suspicions and grievances. They are a
self-selected population with attitudes favorable toward the integration of social and economic groups. Thus, the most outspoken
among the new and affluent residents tend to sponsor the grievances of their less well off neighbors. These new residents also
take the view that the people who have been hurt by the area's

clearance have a right to be suspicious and even violent. This leaves the new residents in a peculiar position: they sometimes seem to be siding with other segments of the population but at the same time are willing to accept the alienation and avoidance which persist between the older and poorer residents and themselves.

The result is a tendency for some of the more outspoken middle income residents to sponsor the outrage of the older residents and to intensify some of the allegations of conspiracy. Correspondingly, there is great difficulty in supporting general community programs, because the more affluent and more recent residents have a tendency to accede to the older and poorer residents' claims that all new developments, programs, and buildings in the area are for the benefit of the middle income residents. Especially crucial in this context are the local schools. Practically all the local community groups publicly favor integrated education and a number of vaguely defined enrichment programs for the local schools. The poorer blacks tend, however, to support basic education, whereas some of the middle income parents want more foreign language and special programs in the schools. The middle income residents tend to support the poorer blacks' demands from the schools and then to withdraw their children because the schools are still unsatisfactory. A somewhat more subtle dilemma is created when the lower income blacks insist on a wholly voluntary plan of incorporating the incoming white children into the schools in which they would become an extreme minority if equally distributed across all schools and classrooms. The whites and middle class blacks seem totally unable to promote openly a quota system that would achieve a balance in the distribution of racial and income groups to some, but not all, of the schools. Indeed, some of the whites and middle income blacks go so far as to support the lower income blacks' demand for a general incorporation of all children into the school of their attendance area irrespective of considerations on racial or socioeconomic balance. Middle income residents who do not go this far are still inclined to admit to the moral correctness of the lower income blacks' demands, pointing out that lower income blacks have to send their children to schools that are practically all white. In actual practice, a large

number of the middle income residents have elected to send their
children to private schools partly because they are so small a
minority in the local schools but also because the schools concentrate so exclusively on basic training in reading and writing. The
lower income blacks take this as just another example of hypocrisy on the part of the higher income members of the community,
and it widens the gulf between them. This gulf of mistrust seems
self-perpetuating. The higher income residents bend over back-
wards to indicate their good intentions by acceding to the lower
income residents' demands and then, rather guiltily, do not follow
through by participating in the schools.

The schools, of course, occupy a crucial position in the redevelopment of the area, and practically everyone agrees that a
high quality, integrated program of education is essential to attracting people back into inner city neighborhoods. The schools
remain, however, among the most segregated institutions in the
community, and almost all of them are attended by lower income
blacks. Mixed classrooms are present in only three of ten schools
and are restricted to the first three grades in those schools. All of
the new developments have had trouble attracting middle income
families with children beyond this age level. Thus, many of the
high income blacks and whites are childless or have young children
below school age—a fact which makes it easy for them to support
the moral claims of the lower income blacks without having to
put their children in schools where they would be in an extreme
minority.

New Metes and Bounds

By now upwards of twenty-two thousand people are living in seven
new developments in the area, and within the next few years this
number may reach thirty thousand. It is estimated that eighty
thousand people will eventually be housed in the area, although it
is allowed that much deteriorated housing will persist until the area
is completely redeveloped. Although urban redevelopment is uneven and advances at unforeseen intervals, one can detect from it
at least some general patterns.

The first of these paterns is a considerable change in what Wirth called the "metes and bounds" imposed by the physical structure of the city. The original grid pattern of the city, for example, is being preserved only in its boldest outlines. Although some major thoroughfares of the grid pattern persist, they enclose islands within which the streets dead-end or wander around so that they are useful mainly to local traffic. Moreover, the main thoroughfares that remain are seldom the shopping areas they once were but simply traffic arteries used by the residents when they drive out of the area or by other persons from all over the city. Shopping areas are usually located in the interiors of each development-island, and the general trend is toward local autonomy through a complete complement of the facilities necessary for weekday life.

The overall pattern can be described as centripetal to distinguish it from at least some centrifugal elements of an earlier pattern common to inner city Chicago. The central location of shopping areas within each development tends to keep people within their own developments. The surrounding main streets are not colorful attractions but, for children and more so for their mothers, a place where life and limb are in danger. Sometimes these thoroughfares separate developments which are so dramatically different in racial composition and income that there is scarcely any basis for initiating a relationship. As a result, people tend to draw back into their own developments.

When people draw back into their respective developments, they find there a rather complete social world in many respects. First, they find an intact residential identity provided by the builder, and people are almost uniformly identified by the developments they come from. This fragmentation of the area has made it difficult for community groups to identify themselves in such a way that they can bargain for the entire area. Most generally, community groups emerge within a particular development and then find it difficult to enter into broader confederations because their interests are so narrowly associated with their own living quarters. To date there have been at least three attempts to start a community organization to represent the entire area, but all of them have floundered after a while because of the presumed predominance of sectional representation from one of the developments.

Second, the developments tend to be sharply differentiated by their racial and income composition. This seems to have heightened the residents' awareness of class status and, unlike other areas of Chicago which have been studied, the vocabulary of social classes is commonly used in everyday discussions among the groups and residents. In turn, the conflicts of interest which divide blacks and whites or high income and low income people are uppermost in the residents' minds, making them doubtful of the existence of any broad areas of consensus among themselves. Thus, where consensus may exist it is often precluded by the ecological legibility of income and racial differences and the general presumption that their differences outweigh their similarities. To a large extent this is an unexamined presumption, because there are not extensive and intense primary relationships throughout the area. The residents depend on collective representations of one another, and the discrete and distinctive composition of each development tends to set it aside as a special-interest group solely responsive to blacks or whites, high income or low income residents. This stereotypic view of the way community groups operate is not entirely due to the economic and racial distinctiveness of each development, but it is a large part of the visual contrasts in the community which give credence to such a point of view and help structure the community organizations which have emerged in the area.

Community Organization

Community organizations in the Douglas Park Community Area are distinctive to the extent that they are self-conscious in their pursuit of specified goals and lack a primordial or sentimental basis for cohesion. A large number of local groups have emerged over the last five years, and none of them has emphasized its ethnic background, prior associational experiences, or incidental reasons for common association. Frequently their first meetings have brought together people unknown to one another for the explicit purpose of community betterment, and the broad assumption is that people have come together for an instrumental purpose rather than because they have some prior associational background. Such groups are especially close to the form that Wirth thought characteristic of urban life.[7] They are secondary organizations with a shared set of goals rather than an ascriptive background which gives them a common set of goals.

The most frequent form of community organization is the community group which recruits from a single development and tries to represent the demands, desires, and hopes of the residents to what is locally referred to as management. Six of the seven developments have spawned such organizations, and some of these developments have given rise to such groups more than once, whereas others have more than one group trying to represent them. In addition, there are a number of special-purpose groups. There are groups aimed at improving schooling for youngsters and providing recreation for all the residents and advisory groups concerned with more narrow issues such as the education of pupils at a particular school or police practices in the local district. At this writing there are 22 intact organizations in the community area. They are preceded by many others, and doubtless some of them will be replaced with others. Community organizations in the Douglas Park Community Area emerge and decline with some instances of continuity. What is stable about them is their instrumentality and self-consciousness of community.

The most stable organizations are those which are based on the participation of residents in a single development and which attempt to act on behalf of the residents in that development. The most persistent of these community organizations is one that attempts to represent all public housing residents to the Chicago Housing Authority. It spans two public housing developments, but sometimes it separates into its two parts when negotiating with CHA. This seems to be the largest organization in the area simply because it attempts to speak for more than one development. Most

7. Louis Wirth, "Urbanism as a Way of Life," *American Journal of Sociology* 44 (July 1938): 8–20.

of the remaining organizations seem to originate as ways of dealing with a single landlord and are confined to the developments in
which they start; essentially they act as tenant unions, although
they are often more ambitious in their goals.

Another type of organization is the group brought together
around a social institution such as the schools or parks. In the
main these groups have been formed at the behest of public institutions which attempt to enlist those they serve into their management. The schools have their PTA's and in one instance an advisory board. The local parks have enlisted a temporary "working
group" into the role of helping to design the play activities of
youngsters and petitioning the city for additional funds. The local
library, charitable organizations, and a settlement house have
enlisted volunteer groups to help them perform routine functions
and obtain funds. Occasionally they are the source of difficulty for
their host organization because they bring together disparate elements of the community who raise issues which originate from
the heritage of mistrust and pessimism present in the community.

Another form of community organization present in the area is
the "special-interest group" preoccupied with entertainment and
personal enjoyment. These are groups which meet rather regularly
to pursue sports, cards, dances, parties, and whatever pleases them.
There are a number of such organizations, but they tend to stand
aside as other community issues rise to the surface, and they have
not yet thrust themselves into the controversial issues which other
groups have attempted to address.

One form of community organization which has been tried in
the area without much success is the Douglas Park Organization,
which attempts to represent all or most of the interests in the community and federate all the residents into a single combine which
can negotiate their interests with the public and private organizations which are developing the area. There have been at least three
attempts to start such an organization, the first of which lacked
any definition of the area and seized on the name Douglas Park
Community Organization because its supporters learned from the
Community Fact Book that this was the community in which they
lived. The group declined at first because one of its central figures

was alleged (falsely) to be an employee of CHA. It was resur-
rected twice but failed each time because the meetings were heavily
attended by middle income whites, and blacks and others feared
that they would take over. The ministers in the local area attempted
to form an equally overarching organization on several occasions
but were unsuccessful apparently because they could not get a
satisfactory representation from the black and poorer residents in
the community. The attempt to form a broad community organization will probably continue, and the residents seem to be fully
committed to the definition of their area as the Douglas Park
Community Area, because they have no other way of drawing a
boundary around themselves.

One form of community organization favored by some residents
of the area and especially by the builders and managers of the
developments is the professional community organizer or expert
who is responsible for community services and the negotiation
among residents. The schools have anticipated this demand by
providing school-community representatives whose responsibility
is to mediate between the schools and individual parents. One
community group is now attempting to raise funds to hire a community relations expert to whom they can hire out their problems
of dealing with fellow residents and adjacent developments. A
paid task force to humanize police enforcement is being proposed
by one community group, and they are seeking public funds to
support this venture. One developer has hired a specialist to organize recreation in his buildings and to act as a spokesman for the
local residents. In general, then, there is a tendency to turn community relations into a specialized task of human relations experts.

Within this proliferation of variant types of community relationships, the traditional political machine of the Mother Ward persists
in a limited way. Precinct workers in the area complain a great
deal about the unavailability of the residents and how they "can't
do anything for people anymore." Both complaints tend to have
credibility once one has looked into the matter. First, most of the
local precinct workers are black but are ineligible to live in public
housing where the blacks are most heavily concentrated. As high
income blacks with a "city job," they prefer to live in Chatham or

some other black middle class area which has higher status among
blacks than the Douglas Park Community Area. Naturally, they
are at a disadvantage when trying to approach residents of the
area when they are not also neighbors.

Second, the precinct workers are at a loss when most of the
residents ask for a favor from the local school system, police department, Chicago Housing Authority, or a local private developer.
Decisions in these organizations have been pushed upward over
recent years so that by now discretion is concentrated toward the
top of each organization. Most precinct workers have little access
to these higher levels of managerial discretion and, in any case,
the middling status of most precinct workers makes them hesitant
to approach people so highly situated. Thus, even the most important precinct captain in the area feels that he is powerless to
carry the residents' desires to the administrators who can make
final decisions.

Third, many of the benefits which precinct workers could dis-
pose of have now been incorporated into federal and municipal
bureaucracies which are accessible to the general public without
the jobber function of the political worker. Welfare payments,
medical care, unemployment benefits, and the like are often available on application or through one of the local community organizations. After a long delay, the Roosevelt New Deal has come to
this section of Chicago, and residents have the alternative of going
to a bureaucracy rather than to their precinct worker.

A final constraint on the precinct worker is the sheer size and
entry conditions of each new multi-family dwelling unit. The prevalence of high-rise buildings means that precinct workers must
gain admission without any chance to introduce themselves except
that offered over an intercom between the building's foyer and
the resident's apartment. Many people refuse them entrance
as they might a traveling salesman. Precinct workers also find
the large scale of the buildings forbidding and fear that they
will meet enemies as well as friends in so large a residential unit.
Some admit that they must bolster their confidence by a couple of
drinks before trying to face their "betters" in private housing or
make the round in a public housing development. In either case,

precinct workers are likely to admit that they can give the local residents little which they cannot obtain from the regular channels available through direct appeal to bureaucratic procedures.

The result has been a drastic shift in voting behavior as the ward voted out the established candidate for the first time since DePriest and Dawson established the black machine in the Mother Ward. During the elections in 1968, a candidate without the backing of either political party won the election as alderman. Some people fear that the newly elected alderman will be left out in the cold and unable to negotiate on behalf of the community. Since this same alderman has made overtures to the Chicago Machine, he is suspected of currying favor from installed powers. Either way he turns he is sure to gain enemies, and he has little patronage with which to make persistent followers. The area seems to be opening up to a new style of politics in which the attractiveness of the candidate, his special claims at election time, and the residents' ideology may have more effect than in the past.

Conclusion

Although its distinctiveness should not be overdrawn, the Douglas Park Community Area does incorporate a number of characteristics which move it away from the ideal model of the natural community. It is in many ways a contrived community, constructed by a small number of builders and public officials with a limited set of objectives in mind. Yet it is not a fully planned community, and neither the residents nor the developers and public officials seem to have a model by which a number of private builders, financiers, public service agencies, and local residents can jointly coordinate their aims, resources, and activities. At least part of the difficulty in originating such a model are some basic beliefs about the dangers of too close and formal a relationship among different private entrepreneurs or businessmen and public officials. The residents fear and sometimes allege a conspiracy or oligopoly of public and private officials who are running the area. It is doubtful, however, if anything less than such an oligopoly (perhaps one that

includes the residents as well) would be able to coordinate redevelopment of the area.

The result is often an ad hoc pattern of negotiations among
private and public officials and the local residents. Such ad hoc
negotiations tend to lack clear legitimacy and to raise questions
about the propriety of influence among organizations. This absence
of a model for urban redevelopment, however, has not discouraged
the existence of community in the sense that it provides a residential identity and a set of common aims. The area may lack many
of the ingredients of our traditional portrait of the neighborhood:
its sheer modern architecture, its lack of a primordial basis for
cohesion, and the prevalence of secondary relations among the
residents. Yet the exclusion of these features seems to have only
heightened a general awareness of community and made it a more
explicit organizational framework within which coresidents must
single out their special goals and try to achieve them.

Part 3

Territoriality and Human Behavior

5. The Ideological Overburden in the Study of Territoriality

In recent years the topic of human territoriality has attracted popular interest among both laymen and scholars.[1] Indeed the subject is part of a controversy to which there are several sides. One strand of this controversy is the question of how much space is a minimal necessity for agreeable human life.[2] A closely related issue is whether or not man's "territorial instinct" is always accompanied by aggressiveness and conflict.[3] A third issue pivots on

1. Works by Robert Ardrey (*The Territorial Imperative* [New York: Atheneum, 1966]), Konrad Lorenz (*On Aggression* [New York: Harcourt, Brace and World, 1966]), and Desmond Morris (*The Naked Ape* [New York: McGraw-Hill, 1967]) are probably the most popular in their appeal and the chief subject of this essay. More technical and restrained considerations of the same problem can be found in William Etkin, *Social Behavior from Fish to Man* (Chicago: University of Chicago Press, 1967); John Paul Scott, *Animal Behavior* (Chicago: University of Chicago Press, 1958); and V. C. Wynne-Edwards, *Animal Dispersion in Relation to Social Behavior* (New York: Hafner, 1962). The last three works tend to deal largely with nonhumans, with only implicit or occasional comparisons with humans. More straightforward attempts to compare territoriality among animals and humans can be found in H. Hediger, "The Evolution of Territorial Behavior," in S. L. Washburn, ed., *Social Life of Early Man* (New York: Viking Fund, 1961) and Edward Hall, *The Hidden Dimension* (Garden City, N. Y.: Doubleday and Co., 1966). For a thorough and technical examination of the first two of these books see M. F. Ashley Montagu, ed., *Man and Aggression* (London: Oxford University Press, 1968). There have been very few direct attempts to study territoriality among humans without reference to other animals, but in this line one should mention the work of Hall, *Hidden Dimension*; David Lowenthal, ed., *Environmental Perception and Behavior* (Chicago: University of Chicago, Department of Geography Research Paper no. 109, 1967); Kevin Lynch, *The Image of the City* (Cambridge, Mass.: The M.I.T. Press, 1960); and Alvin L. Schorr, *Slums and Social Insecurity* (Washington, D.C.: Social Security Administration, 1963).

2. See particularly Hall, *Hidden Dimension*; Schorr, *Slums*; and John B. Calhoun, "Population Density and Social Pathology," *Scientific American* 206 (February 1962): 139–46.

3. This is most evident in Ardrey, *Territorial Imperative*; and Lorenz, *Aggression*.

the continuity between the biological determinants of territoriality among human communities and those of other animals.[4]

Each side to this controversy bears ideological overtones which make it difficult to judge their merits as only explanatory analyses. Discussions of just how much space a man needs to carry on his normal functions quickly turn to public issues on urban planning, public housing, private ownership, and birth control. The assumption that man has a territorial instinct can readily mount into an argument for the inevitability of wars and any other types of human aggression. Finding parallels between human and other animal communities easily leads to the view that man's nature is fixed by biological universals and little affected by laws, institutions, or training.[5]

The foremost among those who have popularized the concept of territoriality are Ardrey, Lorenz, and Morris. Certainly there are other accounts which dwell equally on the topic of territoriality, but they are more fragmentary and specific.[6] The works of Ardrey, Lorenz, and Morris offer a holistic account of man, territoriality, animals, and aggression. Any interpretation of territoriality less general than these must be colored by their overriding conceptualization of what is otherwise a mass of discrete findings. The works of all three men, however, have fallen victim to a mass of criticism, much of it brought together in a book (*Man and Aggression*) edited by Ashley Montagu.[7] Most, if not all, of this criticism seems well placed and persuasive. Yet despite the telling quality of this criticism, we are left with a perplexing question. If these works are as full of flaws as the critics suggest, why have they become so popular, and why is there such a convergence among their points of view? No doubt, any one edition of these three books will out-

4. See John Paul Scott's review of Lorenz's book, *Science* 154 (November 1966): 636, for further comments on this issue.

5. C. Vann Woodward (*The Strange Career of Jim Crow* [New York: Oxford University Press, 1955]) points out how explanations of racism in terms of instinct or inflexible mores left certain segregation practices unchallenged.

6. See, for example, Daniel G. Freedman, "A Biological View of Man's Social Behavior," in Etkin, *Social Behavior*, 152–88.

7. London: Oxford University Press, 1968.

sell all the editions of Montagu and his associates' compiled criticisms. All three books have been widely quoted in the mass media and have found supporters as well as critics. Surely there must be a wider sense in which the works of Ardrey, Lorenz, and Morris touch on a vital issue on which the different sides are reluctant to wait for a more detached and equivocal point of view. The strength of these three works seems to lie in their immediate responsiveness to a fundamental ideological debate over the fixity of man's nature and, by extension, the flexibility of social structure.[8] Ardrey, Lorenz, and Morris provide a point of view which claims the futility of human contrivance in attempting to build a society other than what we have. By reducing human behavior to animal behavior and by reducing the latter to instincts, we are taken along a chain of reasoning which forecloses planned social change and promotes parochial conservatism. This point of view has its attractions, and it is my contention that it accounts both for the popularity of these three works as well as for some of their more obvious departures from evidence and reasoning.

Ideological Debate

The sudden confluence of these three works on territoriality—all three volumes were published in a two-year period—is probably no accident. In their broad perspectives these books counterbalance some equally ideological sociological postures. In this sense, Ardrey's, Lorenz's, and Morris's books are timely because they help arm a poorly armed and overly besieged group of people. Much present-day sociological writing, particularly that called

8. Kenneth E. Boulding hints at this responsiveness to ideological issues in his "Am I a Mouse or a Man—or Both?" in Montagu, *Man and Aggression*, pp. 83–90. Unfortunately Boulding simply criticizes Ardrey and Lorenz for being ideological at all, rather than recognizing the authenticity and sociological character of the ideological issues to which Ardrey and Lorenz are responding. For a general review of this tendency simply to debunk ideological perspectives as untrue without further analyzing the genesis of ideological questions see Clifford Geertz, "Ideology as a Cultural System," in D. E. Apter, ed., *Ideology and Discontent* (New York: The Free Press of Glencoe, 1964), pp. 47–76.

symbolic interaction or labeling theory has treated social structure as if it were only a game of "let's pretend" without serious foundation or causal necessity.[9] In some sociological versions, this view extends to the point that society is portrayed as only a series of allegations or labels which the powerful and affluent impose willy-nilly on the defenseless and poor. Thus, mental illness is said to exist only in the minds of those who claim to be sane.[10] Crime is something invented by meddlesome and narrow-minded law-makers.[11] Manners, civility, deference, and occupational prestige are regarded as whimsical conventions as arbitrary and inconsequential as the rules of checkers.

Taken to its extreme form, this sociological point of view suggests that society exists only in the minds of individuals and that those who by accident or circumstance happen to be the more powerful will force their views down the throats of those less forceful.[12] Social distinctions such as those represented in the division of labor or the primordial ties of race, kinship, ethnicity, and residence become mere conventions, either as atavistic survivals or as deceits practiced by self-interested and powerful groups. War-

9. This is at least one way of reading the works of Thomas J. Scheff, *Being Mentally Ill* (Chicago: Aldine Press, 1966); Erving Goffman, *The Presentation of Self in Everyday Life* (Garden City, N.Y.: Doubleday and Co. Anchor Books, 1959); Thomas S. Szasz, *The Myth of Mental Illness* (New York: Hoeber-Hoeber, 1961); and Howard S. Becker, *Outsiders* (New York: The Free Press of Glencoe, 1963). No doubt these writers see societies as causally related phenomena, but this will not be immediately apparent to the reader who thinks that cultural rules and organizational forms are purely arbitrary. Sometimes the above point of view has been called the "hollow man" theory, and it has been criticized by Dennis H. Wrong, "The Oversocialized Conception of Man," *American Sociological Review* 26 (April 1961): 183–93.

10. Scheff, *Being Mentally Ill*; and Szasz, *Mental Illness*.

11. A conclusion which, with some difficulty, can be read into Becker's *Outsiders* and Joseph R. Gusfield's *Symbolic Crusade* (Urbana: University of Illinois Press, 1963). Jack Gibbs has provided a criticism of the former ("Conceptions of Deviant Behavior," *Pacific Sociological Review* 9 [Spring, 1966]: 9–14) but the ideological and technical problems remain undifferentiated in his account.

12. Which is certainly one way of interpreting C. Wright Mills, *The Power Elite* (New York: Oxford University Press, 1956) and Thomas J. Scheff's "The Societal Reaction to Deviance," *Social Problems* 11 (Spring, 1964): 401–13.

fare, conflict, invidious distinctions, sacrifice, and abstinence, in turn, can be seen as mere rituals that are either holdovers from the past or token acts to be performed in the present.

This sociological ideology bespeaks its own utopia. If man truly makes himself, then he might as well make himself well as ill. As only a convention, society can be constructed according to any plan whatsover. Nations, states, and the wars between them can be discharged with as much ease as the rules of checkers. Race, income, sex, occupation, and age can be ignored as easily as they are now observed. Instead, equality, peace, and imminent gratification can be sought out as easily as the tough and uneven paths of competition, sacrifice, and aggression. All that is required are the right names and labels for people and situations. If society is only a game of "let's pretend," we might as well be in Alice's Wonderland as on Crusoe's grudging island.[13]

It is this fanciful world of words and social fictions that Ardrey, Lorenz, and Morris are challenging.[14] The message they bear is essentially a call for a return to a more simple biological determinism. It is a message which reemphasizes the harshness of competition and aggression, the sacrifices of group life, and the endur-

13. Which is not to say that Alice's Wonderland is preferable to Crusoe's faithful island. Alice's Wonderland is a nightmare precisely because it draws a full correspondence between reality, dream, and social fictions. It is worth noting that it is the Mad Hatter who makes the world correspond to his labels. By contrast, Crusoe's stolid island seems orderly even if ungenerous and stratified. At least it is the latter which has worked its way into our popular models of society by way of "Crusoe economics."

14. One should not get the impression that Ardrey, Lorenz, and Morris are challenging very directly these sociological works. Instead, they seem to be reacting generally to the widespread view that ideas or conventions may play some independent role in human behavior. Thus, they do not footnote their adversaries, although obviously there is an enemy which they are attacking. Undoubtedly this is one of the problems in their work; they have received their sociological news through second-hand and diffuse sources. At least their references lead one to this conclusion: Ardrey makes reference to a dozen or so social scientists; Lorenz refers only to Freud and Washburn; and Morris draws from eight sources which might be at least marginally in the social sciences. All or almost all of these references draw on the more archaic fundamentalists of the social sciences, themselves hard pressed to defend the extensive terrain of the social sciences.

ing biogenetic bases of social differentiation. The stories that Ardrey, Lorenz, and Morris tell are uncomfortable tales because they record the intransigent rather than the manipulable features of social life. First, they view conflict and competition as inevitable because man and other animals like him are 'built that way." It is the nature of man to be antagonistic whether as an individual or a member of a group. The floor plan for this type of behavior is blueprinted in his genetic code and for that reason not easily altered. The conflict between nations, states, races, ethnic groups, delinquent gangs, and social classes is inevitable, then, because they are as stubborn to change as one's chromosomal coils.

Second, Ardrey, Lorenz, and Morris make it clear that the limits of human choice are narrow whether these limits dictate peace or war. Most of man's choices are mere fancy or ideas which are transmitted through one's cranium without alteration between the viscera and muscles. Certainly people think, but thought serves mainly to cover one's tracks or salve one's conscience. Social ideas exist chiefly as just enough noise to obscure the nasty and evil designs which a people's testicles and viscera desire.[15] Social ideas, then, may alter from time to time, but man's history is a boring constant which consists of little more than competition, conflict, warfare, chauvinism, and selfishness. Thus, sociology is the study of half threadbare veils which conceal a little but shape nothing.

Third, Ardrey, Lorenz, and Morris find in the distinctions which mark any society—those of status, primordial ties, and wealth—a monotonous repetition of pervasive, genetic impulses. The fatefulness of these distinctions lends stability to societies because they inalterably separate people according to differences already extant. Social movements and new utopias, then, are only fool's gold, false tokens which allay but do not halt the impending advance of raw, visceral interests.

15. Why a social conscience should exist in the first place to be salved by social justifications in the second place is a problem that exists in all simplistic accounts of man which depict him as a narrow and utilitarian animal.

The upshot of this critique of recent sociological outlooks is that man is a victim rather than master of his visceral and muscular urges. Each author, of course, pays tribute to man's ideas as his loftiest accomplishment. But it is by being high, ethereal, or heavenly that man's ideas are disqualified from any direct role in the dirty work of ordinary life. The baser or major portions of human life cannot be seen as the result of what at least Ardrey, Lorenz, and Morris see as our "noble" ideas and culture. Thus, man's narrow and parochial interests must derive from basic and uncontrived biogenetic conditions. In exonerating our ideas and culture from causal guilt, however, Ardrey, Lorenz, and Morris also removed these same ideas and cultural guidelines from critical review: there is not much point in trying to change epiphenomena. In turn, even a reluctant acceptance of this type of biological determinism leaves little room for an active social policy other than a policy of eugenics.[16]

Yet Ardrey, Lorenz, and Morris are attempting to provide a counterbalance to an equally unbalanced view of human life, and one can sympathize with their intent if not with their claims. At least some sociologists have given the partial impression that society is little more than a contrived playhouse and as easily manipulated. What we may have here, then, is less a controversy over how to explain social behavior than a head-on collision between ideological views which are themselves determinative of social behavior. As I will argue later, the dividing line between nature and nurture has long provided a way of setting aside some features of social organization, such as sex, aggression, and territoriality, so that they are immune from even the suggestion of managed alteration. In turn, those who continue to see the social world in terms of this dividing line will read into the accounts of social scientists an unrepresentative concern with only the arti-

16. Oddly, these three authors do not suggest eugenics as a social policy, although it seems implicit in their respective works, unless we assume that there is so little genetic variability among men that selection would have no consequences. Their common assumption that man's nature will "catch up" if we hold off social change seems, however, to deny this outlook.

ficial dimensions or frills of society. What might be able to resolve
the controversy is a larger vision of what social relations and
functions are essential to society and one which juxtaposes these
relations against a new version of what is more optional in society.
Such a new ideology would be in rather than out of phase with the
social sciences. The topic of territoriality, however, is only a
specific case which belongs to this generic problem. It is the generic
problem which concerns us here, and at times we shall have to
forage widely beyond the issue of territoriality itself.

Analogy between Human and Animal Communities

The concept of territoriality can be broadly conceived to include
the total relationship between organism and space.[17] For human
communities it has been used to comprehend such disparate phenomena as distancing between individuals in visual contact; the
arrangement of rooms within a house; the play of gestures within
space; the esthetic and sentimental attachments associated with
things which occupy space; and the distinction between turfs,
neighborhoods, communities, cities, states, and nations. The sheer
range to which the concept is extended is enough to near bewilder
one. As a traditional field of inquiry it comes closest to fitting into
what is called human ecology. Ardrey, Lorenz, and Morris, however, are bent on a much more reductionist statement which goes
beyond mere environmentalism to the more indestructible elements
of man's biogenetic past. Their views, then, go well past the usual
claims of environmentalism implicit in some forms of human
ecology to place man's abiding characteristics in a universal

17. This is a broader usage than I would prefer since it lumps together
such things as private property with exclusive land holdings. But the above
statement is probably correct in the usual breadth given the concept, and
certainly it is common for Ardrey, Lorenz, and Morris to take all proprietorial claims as an instance of territoriality. Hall (*Hidden Dimension*)
occasionally makes an equally broad usage of the term, as do Stanford M.
Lyman and Marvin B. Scott, "Territoriality: A Neglected Sociological
Dimension," *Social Problems* 15 (Fall, 1967): 236–49.

framework which he shares with all other animals irrespective of
his environment, much less his culture.[18]

Each commentary on territoriality draws almost wholly from a
series of careful studies on nonhuman organisms and a few fragmentary observations on human societies. It is the studies on the
nonhuman organism, then, which must bear the overwhelming
burden of proof, whereas human communities enter in chiefly as
cases to be explained. There is always a danger in such abrupt
projections: substantiation for one's theories and hunches are
drawn from one source, and the theories and hunches are applied
elsewhere. This amounts to a kind of gross extrapolation in which
nonhuman organisms are substituted for humans with very little
conceptual or empirical justification. These extrapolations or projections may be exciting or instructive, but they remain gratuitous
extensions of a narrow body of generalizations.

In the case of Ardrey, Lorenz, and Morris, the gratuity of these
parallels between human and nonhuman organisms is peculiarly
important because of the nature of their argument. A central aim
of their work is to establish that man is "just another animal"
whose culture and social organization only gloss over the primitive
impulses and instincts which guide "all animal behavior." They
may be right, and certainly it is true that man is an animal. But
each author has tried to demonstrate his argument only by showing how generalizations drawn from studies of nonhuman organisms can be selectively applied to some incidents among humans.
Such incidental parallels between man and animal do not prove
their general comparability but assume such comparability.

Indeed this concatenation of empiricism and wholesale generali-
zation produces a paradox in the works of Lorenz and Morris.
Both are careful to marshal an overwhelming body of evidence to
establish territoriality and its consequence among nonhuman

18. In all three works there is only one reference to a major human
ecologist. What this points up is the general way in which the social
sciences seem to have invaded public consciousness and to have defined a
position which can be known without identifying its particular spokesmen.

organisms. They are equally willing to draw on the most clandestine anecdotes among human communities to substantiate their armchair assertions. Lorenz, for example, can say:

> Let us imagine that an absolutely unbiased investigator on another planet, perhaps on Mars, is examining human behavior on Earth. . . . He would never gain the impression that human behavior was dictated by intelligence, still less by responsible morality.[19]

Vague references to Alexander and Napoleon corroborate this observation and lead to the conclusion that man's emotions are so evil and animalistic that they must be countermanded by a mindless subservience to an irrational culture.

Morris is surer of his facts and far more entertaining when he says:

> There are one hundred and ninety-three living species of monkeys and apes. One hundred and ninety-two of them are covered with hair. The exception is a naked ape self-named *Homo sapiens*. This unusual and highly successful species spends a great deal of time examining his higher motives and an equal amount of time studiously ignoring his fundamental ones. He is proud that he has the biggest brain of all the primates, but attempts to conceal the fact that he also has the biggest penis, preferring to accord this honour falsely to the mighty gorilla.[20]

There is no disputing Morris's observations, but they carry overtones and implications as broad as those stated directly by Lorenz. The difficulty in either type of statement is that is substitutes verbal associations and stereotypes for empirical evidence and some form of rational argument. It is doubtful if either writer would tolerate similar connotative projections in their own specialized fields.

Certainly we cannot claim that there is no connection between human and nonhuman behavior. Arising out of a common process of evolution, all animals must have very broad areas of similarity

19. *Aggression*, pp. 228–29.
20. *Naked Ape*, p. 9.

among them, both in the adjustments they have made and the physiological mechanisms underlying these adjustments. Indeed it may be well worthwhile trying to take some of the extensive generalizations based on animal behavior and extend them in a straightforward way to human behavior. This is not, however, quite what Ardrey, Lorenz, and Morris do. Their course is much more indirect, and in the end they make man a very different beast from others.

This transition is most evident in the way each writer shifts ground when examining adaptive mechanisms among human and animal communities. On the whole, Ardrey, Lorenz, and Morris accept aggression, territoriality, and instincts as adaptive mechanisms within animal communities: they are part of the clockwork necessary to an orderly relationship among themselves and with their environment. For humans, however, aggression, territoriality, and instincts are cast into a destructive role, sometimes to man's relationship to man, sometimes to his relationship with the physical environment. For Lorenz, this turn of events follows the classical pattern of natural man's downfall because of a corrupting culture.

All the great dangers threatening humanity with extinction are direct consequences of conceptual thought and verbal speech. They drove man out of the paradise in which he could follow his instincts with impunity and do or not do whatever he pleased. . . . Knowledge springing from conceptual thought robbed man of the security provided by his well-adapted instincts long, long before it was sufficient to provide him with an equally safe adaptation. . . .

Conceptual thought and speech changed all man's evolution by achieving something which is equivalent to the inheritance of acquired characters. . . . Thus, within two generations a process of ecological adaptation can be achieved which, in normal phylogeny and without the interference of conceptual thought, would have taken a time of an altogether different, much greater magnitude. Small wonder, indeed, if the evolution of social instincts and, what is even more important, social inhibitions could not keep pace with the rapid development forced on human society by the growth of traditional culture, particularly material culture.[21]

Thus we have in rather clear and self-conscious form a restatement of the aged doctrine of original sin.

Ardrey, on the other hand, seems to take the view that man is simply perverse by nature.

I can discover no argument of objective worth which can effectively counter the claim that the psychological relationship of a lungfish to a piece of muddy water differs in any degree from the psychological relationship of the San Franciscan to the hills and the bay that he loves so well. Several hundred million years of biological evolution have altered not at all the psychological tie between proprietor and property. Neither have those unimaginable epochs of evolutionary time altered the psychological stimulation which enhances the physiological energies of the challenged proprietor. Nor have we reason to believe that the sense of security spreading ease through a troop of black lemurs in their heartland has changed a least whit throughout all of primate history in its effect on the sailor, home from the sea, or the businessman, home from the office.

War may be the most permanent, the most changeless, the most prevalent, and thus the most successful of our cultural innovations, but the reasons differ not at all from the prevalent success of territory. Both satisfy all three basic needs (identity, stimulation and security).[22]

Ardrey's outlook is a species of visceral materialism unrelieved by any historical dialectic. He recognizes the existence of culture and the world of ideas only in order to dismiss them.

While granting that the varying cultural achievements of human populations set man apart from other animals, still we must know that such cultures, however complex, simply serve to fill out behavioral patterns, some as ancient as recorded life.[23]

21. *Aggression*, p. 230.
22. *Territorial Imperative*, p. 337.
23. Ibid., p. 350.

Morris is more synthetic and at least attempts to restore some balance toward the end of his book.

As I have stressed throughout this book, we are, despite all our great technological advances, still very much a simple biological phenomenon. Despite our grandiose ideas and our lofty self-conceits, we are still humble animals, subject to all the basic laws of animal behavior. Long before our populations reach the levels envisaged above we shall have broken so many of the rules that govern our biological nature that we shall have collapsed as a dominant species. We tend to suffer from a strange complacency that this can never happen, that there is something special about us, that we are somehow above biological control. But we are not. Many exciting species have become extinct in the past and we are no exception. Sooner or later we shall go, and make way for something else. If it is to be later rather than sooner, then we must take a long, hard look at ourselves as biological specimens and gain some understanding of our limitations. This is why I have written this book, and why I have deliberately insulted us by referring to us as naked apes, rather than by the more usual name we use for ourselves. It helps to keep a sense of proportion and to force us to consider what is going on just below the surface of our lives. . . . Unfortunately, because we are so powerful and so successful when compared with other animals, we find the contemplation of our humble origins somehow offensive, so that I do not expect to be thanked for what I have done. . . .

Optimism is expressed by some who feel that since we have evolved a high level of intelligence and a strong inventive urge, we shall be able to twist any situation to our advantage; that we are so flexible that we can re-mould our way of life to fit any of the new demands made by our rapidly rising species-status; that when the time comes, we shall manage to cope with the over-crowding; the stress, the loss of our privacy and independence of action; that we shall re-model our behavior patterns and live like giant ants; that we shall control our aggressive and territorial feelings, our sexual impulses and our parental tendencies; that if we have to become battery chicken-apes, we can do it; that our intelligence can dominate all our basic biological urges. I submit that this is rubbish. Our raw animal nature will never permit it. Of course, we are flexible. Of course, we are behavioral opportunists, but there are severe limits to the form our opportunism can take. By stressing our biological features in this book, I have tried to show the nature of these restrictions. By recognizing them clearly and submitting to them, we shall stand a much better chance of survival.[24]

Statements of this sort lead not to a comparison of man and other animals but only to an alleged equivalence of the two. This error, occurring in each book, is rather obvious, and one could add to it several others. But their arguments are relevant and answer to pressing ideological questions: In the absence of full information and because of the necessity to make fateful decisions, how are people to devise a social order which seems both durable and morally correct? By insisting on their detached perspective, social scientists ignore their part in this controversy and thereby leave unclear the limits of their knowledge. In order to devise a society which seems to have firm foundations, the causal connections between aggression and social structure must be known—or at least assumed. In drawing this connection the social sciences are not just dallying with another hypothetical relation—a bit of hypothesis testing—but suggesting a prescription for society to follow. Ardrey, Lorenz, and Morris have made their formulations available through the commonplace metaphors and allusions which constitute our native ideology and its special problem of deciding one or another way in the face of a controversy. Thus, their works are popularly received because they boil things down to a single alternative. The simplistic way in which they have made their arguments is appealing because the practical decisions which face us are equally simple and come down to the primary response of "yes" or "no."

24. *Naked Ape*, pp. 196–97.

Parochial Conservatism

The works by Ardrey, Lorenz, and Morris, respectively, partake of a certain weltschmerz, reminding man of his limitations, of his commonalities with other animals, of the permanency of territoriality and aggression in human social structure, and of the continued presence of evil in the modern world. Each of them aims to correct our banal optimism and show us the difficult road ahead. All three authors are preoccupied by the bomb and man's self-produced capacity for self-destruction. Gathering from the recent findings of ethology, each of them has tried to shed some light on human behavior in order to show us the way.

Judged in these general terms each book is quite commendable. In their efforts to champion the rights of underdogs and to instate the values of an "open society," social scientists have helped create a prospective utopia free of aggression and primordial cleavages. Yet beyond their implied criticism of social scientists, these three studies are rather disappointing. They attempt a great deal but fall short of their own ambitions. What is new and exciting about the works of Ardrey, Lorenz, and Morris is their review of the findings of ethology and the idea that animal and human behavior bear many similarities. Each book starts with a rather thorough review of these findings on animal behavior and reserves only its later portions for describing some correspondences with human behavior. Ardrey devotes roughly six chapters to describing animal behavior and three more to saying that humans are no different. Lorenz does the same thing with eleven of fourteen chapters.

In part, this unbalanced ratio of attention to human and non-human communities is due to the availability of information; animals have been more thoroughly studied than man. There is, however, an additional stricture on their balance of attention and this is self-imposed. By examining first and most extensively animal behavior, they seem to be saying that we must understand animal behavior first, and we will then automatically understand human behavior. There is ideological precedent for this order of presentation.[25] In human communities, considerable importance is often attached to the primordial ties of residence, kinship, sex, age, blood, ethnicity, language, and race. These social distinctions make up what social scientists call ascriptive social criteria or those divisions of society which are not subject to current human management. By elevating these primordial ties to exclusive primacy, we may also downgrade the potential effects of such human contrivances as laws, legislation, and governmental programs aimed at resocialization. This outlook on human societies automatically advances the view that there is not much point in trying to change man, because his essential characteristics have been laid down by prior and immemorial principles of organization.

This outlook fits neatly into the views of parochial conservatives who at every turn counsel against legislation and the futility of trying to reorder societal relations. The basic structure of society has already been given, and there is not much point in tampering with it.[26] The poor will always be poor, and public assistance programs are only a way of countermanding sound selective prin-

25. In this regard, Ardrey, Lorenz, and Morris are not very different from most social scientists who also start with man's "human nature," and proceed to examine relatively small social units (e.g., the family) in such a manner that one is led to think that society is simply the additive product of such "basic" units. Two people who have argued quite a different approach to this problem are Earl W. Count, "The Biological Basis of Human Sociality," *American Anthropologist* 60 (December 1958): 1049–85; and Edward Chace Tolman, "Physiology, Psychology and Sociology," *Psychological Review* 45 (May 1938): 228–41. Indeed, what Count says about the family as a subunit of society might be said about almost any subunit of society: "In a final survey of the family, we may note [that] societies do not take form by a confederation of families, since family is a stable group recognized as such by the society . . . [and] from its earliest emergence in the vertebrate classes, it has always represented a mood of society, a phase in the biogram of the society . . . (p. 1080).

26. For an account of how Sumner's concept of inflexible mores were used to support the Jim Crow laws in the South see Vann Woodward, *Strange Career*. One oddity in the history of the Jim Crow laws not explored by Vann Woodward, but nonetheless characteristic of parochial conservatives, is their tendency to discount the utility of legislation which goes against ingrained mores or primordial differences while trying to obtain legislation to reinforce such ingrained mores. If such mores or natural tendencies are so intransigent and compelling, it seems scarcely necessary to pass laws against what people cannot do.

ciples. The move toward integration of the races and ethnic
groups is a utopian dream which violates the biological instinct
to love only one's own kind. Thus, joining the propertied and un-
propertied classes of society has no more future than combining
the geese of two flocks.

So long as primordial ties are regarded as the fundamental and
productive ties among mankind, there can be little argument for
change. Man will do what he has been selected to do and that is
that. Such an outlook forecloses the question of social change
while we wait for genetic change to "catch up"—and hopefully to
take the lead. Ardrey, Lorenz, and Morris make an easy addition
to this ideological package by selectively drawing a correspondence
between man's animal past and his "lower" rather than his
"higher" motives. Lorenz simply equates the terms *emotion, irra-
tionality*, and *instinct*, although, admittedly, he does not see our
culture as particularly rational or moral.

> For Kant it is self-evident that one reasonable being cannot
> possibly want to hurt another. This unconscious acceptance of
> what he considered evident, in other words common sense,
> represents the chink in the great philosopher's shining armor of
> pure rationality, through which emotion, which always means
> an instinctive urge, creeps into his considerations and makes
> them more acceptable to the biologically minded than they
> would otherwise be. It is hard to believe that a man will refrain
> from a certain action which natural inclination urges him to
> perform only because he has realized that it involves a logical
> contradiction. To assume this, one would have to be an even
> more unworldly German professor and an even more ardent
> admirer of reason than Immanuel Kant was.[27]

Ardrey describes our fundamental motives as perverse and successful champions over judgment and "dainty" moralism. In his
chapter headings, Morris restricts himself to such topics as eating,
sleeping, fornicating, and fighting. It is apparent in all three of

27. *Aggression*, p. 239. To speak of a culture as immoral seems somewhat contradictory since morality is a part of culture. But Lorenz, nonetheless, follows this course.

these accounts that all of our lower instincts have been gathered
from beasts of the field, whereas our higher motives are of our
own making.

To arrive at this conclusion all three authors make use of a
conventional imagery which draws more from biblical and poetic
tracts than scientific ones. Lorenz finds among rats the best analogy for what organizational principles he thinks most fundamental
to men.[28] Ardrey likens the voting habits of Italians to the
Planaria's unwillingness to respond only to offers of food. Morris
equates the size of man's penis to the size of his roguishness. These
are familiar and timeworn metaphors which grow out of our tradition of literature and poetry. They may be right, but mentioning
them again does not make them so.

Such timeworn images are persuasive even when they are only
literary similes. They take what is small, mean, and simple about
man and impute them to his most durable heritage from his fore-
bears. The most limited and destructive portions of man, then, are
rooted in circumstances which cannot be changed. Man's loftier
and moral portions, in turn, are seen as supremely human but
ineffective constructions. Thus, on the one hand, our moral and
learned institutions, such as the church and the university, are
exonerated from causal guilt. On the other hand, narrow primordial ties are retained as the basic building blocks out of which
societies can be constructed. To put it in the words of a practical
politician, "Reformers only mornin' Glories."[29]

A persistent theme of all three books, then, starts with the connection between territoriality and aggression and proceeds from
there to explain all aggression as a consequence of territoriality.

28. As Scott ["That Old Time Aggression" *The Nation* (Jan 9, 1967),
pp. 53–4] points out, this analogy between rats and men seems to derive
more from literary similes than sound evidence. Kenneth E. Boulding
appreciates the simile in the title of his review, "Am I a Man or a Mouse
—or Both?" Understandably, neither Scott nor Boulding is concerned primarily with why the tested routines of our language are more available to
Ardrey and Lorenz than other points of view. That, however, is a primary
concern of this essay.
29. George Washington Plunkitt's ungracious evaluation of morally
charged attempts to guide social policy, in William L. Riordon, *Plunkitt of
Tammany Hall* (New York: E. P. Dutton, 1963), pp. 17–20.

Racial, economic, and ethnic distinctions tend to be ignored as distinct sources of aggression probably because they have already been so thoroughly reviewed and left in an equivocal state. The notion of territoriality is a relatively new primordial distinction growing out of the large volume of recent work by ethologists. Yet the notion of territoriality is extremely adaptable since there is scarcely any human organism or organization which does not have some territorial bases. Wives can be seen as defending their kitchens from their marauding husbands. A man's home is his castle, and all of his proprietorial interests may need the defense of walls and moats. Nations are clearly territorial groups and often engage in the most serious and terminal forms of aggression. It is through these archaic images that Ardrey, Lorenz, and Morris manage to connect the ubiquitous territorial bases of all social organizations with whatever forms of aggression they happen to discern.

This rhetoric is one of the most durable features of Western Christian civilization. It has also had the function of preserving primordial social relations from criticism and doubt. It is evident that Ardrey, Lorenz, and Morris have not intended to take their own argument to this conclusion. All three authors make a further recommendation for additional scientific knowledge of man as both an animal and cultural creature. This seems a blunt contradiction with their general thesis that conceptual thought and verbal speech have progressively perverted and thwarted man's natural impulses. This contradiction, however, seems proper to the first stages of ideological debate. At the outset of ideological debate, it is as essential to discredit one's opponents as to systematize and extract the latent conclusions in one's own counter ideology. This seems to have been what Ardrey, Lorenz, and Morris have done. They are quick to recognize the absurdity of a popular sociology which seems to say that social life is a rootless and arbitrary contrivance. In making their own recommendations for social policy, however, they become more or less run-of-the-mill liberals who think highly of sports, birth control, and basic (but not applied) scientific advances. These proposals do not follow from their argument but seem tagged on only after they have spent their wrath on the opposing point of view.

What Ardrey, Lorenz, and Morris seem to have done in opposing an unduly naïve popular sociology is to fall back on the same
distinctions used in this popular sociology. The distinction between
nature and nurture is an old one, and although popular sociology
has done much to discredit the causal importance of the former,
Ardrey, Lorenz, and Morris fall back on it. This is the sort of
seesaw battle one expects of ideological debates, for, as I have
emphasized earlier, ideology is a practical theory of society and
must bring its doctrines to the point where decisions can be seen
in terms of binary or practical alternatives. The distinction between nature and nurture has functioned this way in the past, and
parochial conservatives have emphasized especially the importance of the former in decision making. In this respect parochial
conservatives as well as Ardrey, Lorenz, and Morris are guided
by a very durable and vigorous Judeo-Christian tradition.

The Rhetoric of Nature and Nurture

A peculiarity of the Judeo-Christian tradition is its tendency to
impute what this same tradition regards as small, mean, and selfish
about man to his natural condition. The doctrine of original sin
is the sacred charter for this outlook, but it is also ingrained in
our literary metaphors and those linguistic shortcuts which we can
quickly understand. To say that a man is animal is a quick way
of saying that he has few virtues and numerous vices: indulgence
in sex, food, drink, or sloth, for example. "Flowery ideas" is an
almost incontestable judgment, whereas "flowery guts" seems only
a contradiction in terms. Platonic love—love without vice—seems
possible only among philosophers. Morality is high or lofty,
whereas avarice and greed are low instincts, and generosity and
charity are noble gestures. Most or all of a child's vices—mastur-
bation, greed, selfishness, and gluttony, for example—are usually
described as inborn, whereas his virtues are achieved through
insistent and disciplined labor. Our entire vocabulary of motives
is so cast in this form that it works an insuperable bias against any
view of human nature which allows man's recommended virtues
an easy and direct line of expression.

It seems odd that a culture would define its most cherished values as the least available and the most fragile. But there is no paradox here, for Judeo-Christian societies have relied, in the main, on these natural vices both to distinguish among the statuses of people and to induce them into the routine activities which these societies have required. Primordial distinctions such as those based on sex, age, residence, or nationality have been a common feature of Judeo-Christian societies as well as most others.[30] It would be extremely destructive to these societies, then, not to attribute to these natural distinctions the most abiding and indestructible human impulses. If men are to govern women and children, then it should be that men have a natural urge to do so, however deplorable this situation may be. Similarly, if men are going to have to defend any territory whatsoever, it is best that they do so thinking themselves natural, if not virtuous. For in the Judeo-Christian tradition, to be without virtue is preferable to being "unnatural."

Thus, people sharing in the Judeo-Christian tradition have gone about their work not altogether because it was good but because anything else was deemed "unnatural." It is only in recent history that emphasis has shifted from this primordial or "natural" division of labor to one based more nearly on evidential ability. This is most obvious in work places where careful records of performance are kept, but it may encroach even into the home where men and women increasingly exchange tasks according to their proven abilities rather than on the twin cults of mother love and masculinity. This shift in allocating responsibilities seems to require altogether different justificatory principles than those contained in the archaic distinction between nature and nurture.

---

30. Indeed, this emphasis on primordial differences may be more pervasive in cultures which do not share in the Judeo-Christian tradition. What may be most distinctive—though not most characteristic—of the Judeo-Christian tradition is its allowance for some degree of redemption from one's natural condition through good deeds or achievement. Many other cultural traditions seem to foreclose most of the possibilities of achievement which gain at least a grudging admission to the Judeo-Christian tradition. (Max Weber, *The Protestant Ethic and the Spirit of Capitalism*, trans. Talcott Parsons [New York: Charles Scribner's Sons, 1958].)

Ardrey, Lorenz, and Morris, then, seem to be resurrecting an ideology based on so primitive a set of social distinctions that it is neither explanatory nor prophetic when applied to contemporary or modern societies. Yet these are the twin responsibilities of ideology, and shortcomings in these respects are fatal. On the one hand, ideology must provide a vision of society which is capable of concerting the efforts of the members of that society. On the other hand, ideology must explain—perhaps by simplification and overdrawn dichotomies—the present as an instrumentality to that vision. As Geertz might put it, ideology must furnish a vision of society capable of explaining and honoring the current sacrifices people must endure.[31] The works of Ardrey, Lorenz, and Morris fail to do any of this for people already caught up in an achievement society.

Essentially their direction is reformist or nativistic. They hark back to a period when primordial categories were the main assortive principles for distributing people in a division of labor and accounting for the prevalent forms of conflict and sacrifices to be endured. The connection between territoriality and aggression fits rather well into this line of argument because territoriality has only recently received wide recognition as a principle of social organization through the research of ethologists. Without criticism or qualification, then, Ardrey, Lorenz, and Morris take an imperfect correlation between primordial territorial consignment and aggression—a correlation documented only in the case of nonhumans—and extend it to conclude or imply that there is a wholesale and perfect relationship between all primordial categories and all human vices and virtues. Had they attempted to make the same and equally complete connection between aggression and race or sex, the available research would have required greater caution.

Descent Categories and Cultural Innovation

A more serious difficulty with these three studies is that they

31. Geertz, "Ideology as a Cultural System."

really shed very little light on the variable elements of social structure. Men eat, sleep, fight, fornicate, look out for themselves first, their children second, their friends third, and their fellow nationals fourth. There is not much sociological news in this. Moreover, there is a subtle tendency to suppress human variability and what may be one of the main lines of continuity between our cultural and biological heritages. As Ardrey, Lorenz, and Morris point out, man is a very mixed beast who is not highly specialized for his present ecological niche. Following Morris, it is clear that the large cats are far more specialized and better fitted to their environment.[32] But the large cats are a dwindling species and seem utterly to lack enough genetic variability to move effectively into the new regions which are encroaching on their traditional lairs. Man, on the other hand, is quite variable with regard to both his cultural and biological heritages. This probably creates an awesome amount of difficulty within human populations because of their enormous differences in biological and cultural endowment as well as the tendency for these two lines of adaptation to diverge from one another.

Such wide cultural and biological variability may be troublesome, but it also holds open for *Homo sapiens* many options of adaptive radiation. There is great danger in a very close correspondence between biological equipment and present environmental requirements. As the large cats and shoe repairmen are just now learning, one's environment is at best a temporary condition, and a range of skills is often more adaptive than high levels of specialization. Heritable specialization would seem especially maladaptive in periods as brief as those between changes in human environments. It is to be expected, then, that humans are not only very generalized and malleable animals but highly variable in their inventory of biological proclivities and capacities.

This brings up an issue which Ardrey, Lorenz, and Morris ignore but which is critical to any similar analysis. Genetic transmission, including that which may help govern territoriality, is inevitably a stochastic process in which there is only a probabilistic

32. *Naked Apes*, pp. 22–23.

relationship between the characteristics of parent and descendent generations. In actual practice this means that there is no singular and complete relationship between descent groups and their alleged genetic characteristics except, possibly, in the case of some species like the large cats which may be almost invariant in their genetic makeup. In individual cases, then, it will be impossible to make firm projections about those descent groups—racial, native, national, ethnic, regional, and the like—which constitute a large part of our primordial categorical system. Thus, so long as subsequent evidence of these alleged characteristics is tested for rather than simply assumed, there will always be an overlap between these primordial descent groups. What modern societies do by testing for these characteristics (for example, aggressiveness, territoriality, intelligence, familialism) is to disclose this overlap and bring into question the legitimacy of any classification system which marches people into a division of labor in lockstep.

It follows then that even where genetic transmission is the prime basis for determining individual characteristics, classification according to descent group is not an adequate basis for projecting individual characteristics. Some form of social testing and periods of trial are essential if people are to be placed defensibly according to their talents, vices, or virtues. Such a trial-and-error approach to the determination of the characteristics of people changes wholly our outlook on how the social order is to be constituted and how people are to be fitted into its various niches.

Most especially this means that a moratorium on our cultural and technological innovations will not give heritable characteristics a "chance to catch up." Social selection for roles, membership, and ability represent a selective pressure which is one of the main sources for adjustment to contemporaneous circumstances. Thus, a moratorium on social change and technological innovation would probably only lower the selective pressures that are operating on genetic transmission and forcing us to catch up with contemporary circumstances. Genetic structures do not change of their own accord except in very small populations and on the occasion of rare mutations; cultural and social structure, then, are not a passive cart drawn by genetic alteration but they are the horse of selective pressures which direct our variable genetic heritage. Without such selective pressures man would not catch up but just remain the same.

Summary and Conclusion: The Burden of Ideology

In large part the ideological overburden in the works of Ardrey, Lorenz, and Morris can be seen as a reaction to a contrary ideological overburden in some recent sociological works. The view that the social order is a mere contrivance of arbitrarily selected rules is at least implicit in some recent and popular sociological writings if read without considering their broader theoretical underpinnings. For the layman this sociological outlook may suggest a dubious utopia where wish and reality are one. Certainly this is an unbalanced point of view and contrary to the general experience that it is extremely frustrating to make even minor changes in the social order. Ardrey, Lorenz, and Morris have tried to correct for this exaggerated voluntarism by their own overemphasis. Taken in this way, their accounts are part of the usual clockwork of public controversy where the pendulum swings back and forth to touch base with opposing positions in popular opinion.

Like many social scientists, Ardrey, Lorenz, and Morris have phrased their arguments in terms of the exclusive alternative between heritable and acquired characteristics. In responding to pressing and meaningful ideological issues, they could scarcely avoid some kind of categoric approach, since one of the services of ideology seems to be its simplification of social decisions to the point where they can be brought to so decisive a state. Instead, the problem seems to reside in the continued wrangling over the nature-nurture dichotomy rather than some other.

Something more than the mere truth or falsity in the application of these terms is at issue here. The basic lineaments of most past societies have been grounded in the belief that primordial relations are essential (that is, "natural"), whereas all others are artificial, transient, or externally imposed. This makes good sense in a society where the main divisions and affiliations are formed on the basis of age, race, nativity, sex, residence, and the like. In modern industrial societies, however, social divisions and affiliations are enlarged to include more contractual, civil, and voluntaristic forms. The emergence of these additional principles of social organization[33] creates a mix of essential social institutions which range from the most primordial (for example, families) to the most voluntaristic (for example, political elections). A sharp dividing line between "natural" and thus permanent categories as against "artificial" and thus transient categories leaves many essential institutions ideologically defenseless.

Barring a continued and crippling disaccreditation of voluntaristic relationships, what seems likely in the more technologically advanced countries is a larger view of social relationships which gives moral worth to both primordial and voluntaristic categories. It is hazardous to make predictions at this point, but the most obvious resolution may be some variant of the dichotomy between spontaneous and coerced forms of social affiliation and division. The former term automatically includes primordial groupings and divisions since being natural implies also the spontaneous expression of native impulses. But the term *spontaneous* is broader and also includes extremely voluntaristic relationships and social divisions such as those found in occupational or political groupings. Alternatively, this categoric distinction still discredits authoritarian and unpopular modes of organization which, in any case, may not be very essential to modern societies. Negotiated and multilateral relationships have widespread support in modern societies.[34] In turn, social divisions and affiliations which are externally enforced are rare or relatively unpopular. Disaccreditation of the latter, then, may not materially impair the central institutions of modern society.

This dichotomy between spontaneous and coerced social affiliations is continuous with our established rhetoric for making

33. What Parsons calls "achievement criteria" in T. Parsons and E. Shils, eds., *Towards a General Theory of Action* (Cambridge, Mass.: Harvard University Press, 1954), pp. 76–88, but in some ways more nearly what Marshall Sahlins calls "socio-centric" (Elman Service, *Primitive Social Organization* [New York: Random House, 1962], pp. 185–92).
34. Which is one way of viewing David Reisman's *The Lonely Crowd* (New Haven: Yale University Press, 1950).

categoric and practical evaluations. There already exists widespread conviction that "free," "voluntary," and "heartfelt" distinctions and affiliations are proper and durable ways of ordering society. In fact, long-standing strains in this direction can be found in much of the social science literature attempting to compare democratic and authoritarian modes of organization.[35] Similar trends can be seen in social movements in which self-determination or local control have become terms of approval. Emphasis on being oneself, on social moratoriums, and on persuasion point in the same direction. The dichotomy spontaneous-coerced, then, does not represent a sharp break with the dichotomy between nature and nurture; it seems only to broaden the scope of approved affiliations and divisions. If such a new dichotomy successfully works its way into our ideology, it will not be because of its eternal verity but because this dichotomy draws a line, however gross, between the durable and more transient structural forms in modern societies.

Of course, the terms *spontaneous* and *coerced* may not be the exact nomenclature for this basic division. There are a number of terms in the works of social commentators and political activists which may prove more compelling. *Freedom, self-determination* or *democratic* are terms which may substitute for *spontaneous*. In turn, *passive, co-opted,* or *machinelike* are plausible alternatives to *coerced*. In fact, both families of terms, as well as many close relatives, are likely to be incorporated into the same ideology. The dichotomy spontaneous-coerced includes many possible contradictions so long as there are no further distinctions to identify gray areas and special cases.[36] The full elaboration of such an

35. See, for example, Ralph White and Ronald Lippitt, "Leader Behavior and Member Reaction in Three 'Social Climates,'" in Cartwright and Zander, eds., *Group Dynamics* (White Plains, N.Y.: Row, Peterson, 1953), pp. 585–611; and Theodor Adorno, et al., *The Authoritarian Personality* (New York: Harper, 1950).

36. For example, the student movement has assigned great value to both the possibilities of local, neighborhood control and the right of separate ethnic or racial groups to reside wherever they like. Clearly this poses a real contradiction unless further distinctions are developed to single out those persons who "spontaneously" want to live in desegregated neighborhoods.

ideology would have to be carried out in conjunction with a detailed projection of the major decisions likely to face modern societies. What I have tried to present here are only the basic dividing lines which would make such decision making defensible and clear to those involved.

From these remarks one can draw some tentative observations on the meaning of reductionism, on the one hand, and the role of ideology, on the other hand. Positivistic reductionism has a long and troubled history in the social sciences, and the works of Ardrey, Lorenz, and Morris are relatively new additions to the controversy. In singling out territoriality and aggression as native or inborn characteristics of man, they are following a set trajectory which emphasizes the permanent and nonmanipulable character of social relations. So long as there is much variation in the genetic background of different ethnic, regional, or racial groups, there is not much veracity in this reductionism as a portrait of societies. As an ideological model of society, however, this emphasis on nonmanipulable and inborn traits has defended the basic divisions and organizational principles of those societies based primarily on descent groups: race, nativity, ethnicity, regional grour. linguistic group, and the like. An unconditional preference for reductionism, then, has clear ideological meaning because it removes from consideration any marked departure from the present operating relations between descent groups.

The ideological role of reductionism points up the substantial and effective part ideology in general plays in total societies. Dogmatic reductionism drew a forbidding line between the durable and transient forms of preindustrial society. It developed a model of society which brought decisions down to the simplified alternatives between nature and nurture and made binary decision making possible and defensible. This same type of reductionism also provided a vision of society which promised the full or unavoidable expression of natural inclinations. At the same time, this vision of society made endurable the intermediate sacrifices thought worthy in light of the long-term gains to be obtained. These seem to be the basic hallmarks against which the adequacy of any ideology must be judged.

These chores of ideology become important when we consider what happens when there is either a clear or partial absence of ideological guidelines to direct the decision making of people included in a total society where direct communication and negotiation are no longer possible. Ideology, then, becomes increasingly important as we approach the condition of a mass society where people must depend more and more on a conceptual model of their society rather than on direct accounts from their primary or secondary relations. Similarly, the absence or partial absence of a coherent ideology in large-scale modern societies leaves people without any broadly defined vision within which they can set defensible priorities. Instead, they become "disenchanted," "hedonistic," or "jaded." Without a larger vision of society, current inequities seem irremediably unfair and unjust. Ideology, then, gives us a practical model of society which is able to provide vision and justify sacrifice. And unless people are willing to work for the future and tolerate the present, social life in modern societies is probably impossible.

6. Territoriality and Aggression

The central theme which is shared by many studies of territoriality is its connection with aggression.[1] Humans along with many other animals kill, maul, and pillage individuals from outside their own territory. At the same time, there are many self-sacrificing loyalties and nonutilitarian exchanges among members of the same territorial group. This inverse treatment of in-group and out-group members seems to be a widespread and problematic feature of many different kinds of social structures.[2] Recent studies on territoriality among nonhumans may help to clarify and generalize the competitive structure which draws so sharp a distinction between in-group and out-group members.

What seems most distinctive about this association between territoriality and aggression is the way territoriality can become part of a competitive structure in which one group's gains are automatically another's losses. In the classical case of mutually exclusive territorial groups, the resources that groups compete for are coextensive with their territories, and one group seems able to gain only at another's loss. Such a competitive structure seems calculated to encourage aggression and a narrow range of loyalties. But this type of territoriality is scarcely the only type we can find in the literature, and in a different kind of competitive structure territoriality may not automatically signal aggression.

1. Konrad Lorenz, *On Aggression* (New York: Harcourt, Brace and World, 1966); and John B. Calhoun, "A 'Behavioral Sink,'" in Eugene L. Bliss, ed., *Roots of Behavior* (New York: Harper, 1962), chap. 22, are examples to which one could add numerous others. For a general review see C. R. Carpenter, "Territoriality," in A. Roe and G. G. Simpson, eds., *Behavior and Evolution* (New Haven: Yale University Press, 1958).

2. The general formulation owes much to William Graham Sumner's *Folkways* (Boston: Ginn and Co., 1940) although the tradition of inquiry he established has not been drawn on much in recent studies of territoriality.

Functional Interpretations of Territoriality among Nonhumans

Most of what we know about territoriality has been drawn from studies on nonhumans. From these studies a number of interpretations have been formulated and expanded. Foremost among these approaches is Wynne-Edwards's view that territoriality is a way of dispersing the individuals of a species so that their numbers remain roughly commensurate with the available long-term food supply.

> We have already the strongest reasons for concluding, however, that population-density must at all costs be prevented from rising to the level where food shortage begins to take a toll of the numbers—an effect that would not be felt until long after the optimum density had been exceeded. It would be bound to result in chronic over-exploitation and a spiral of diminishing returns. Food may be the *ultimate* factor, but it cannot be invoked as the *proximate* agent in chopping the numbers, without disastrous consequences. . . . we should therefore look to see it there is not . . . some kind of density-dependent convention . . . based on the quantity of food available but "artificially" preventing the intensity of exploitation from rising above the optimum level. Such a convention, if it existed, would have not only to be closely linked with the food situation, and highly . . . density-dependent in its operation, but, thirdly also capable of eliminating the direct contest in hunting which has proven so destructive and extravagant in human experience.
>
> It does not take more than a moment to see that such a convention could operate extremely effectively through the well-known territorial system. . . .
>
> The substitution of a parcel of ground as the object of competition in place of the actual food it contains, so that each individual or family unit has a separate holding of the resource to exploit, is the simplest and most direct kind of limiting convention it is possible to have. It is the commonest form of tenure in human agriculture. It provides an effective proximate buffer to limit the population-density at a safe level . . . ; and

it results in spreading the population evenly over the habitat, without clumping them in groups as we find in many alternative types of dispersion.[3]

A second approach has been to emphasize the biogenetic basis of territoriality. This outlook has highlighted aggression as the key biological mechanism for maintaining territorial groupings. In this case, territoriality and aggression are part of a genetic "package deal" in which the defended territory and territoriality are the same thing. The relationship between territoriality and aggression are definitional matters, then, and empirically unproblematic.

> Animals fight amongst themselves for one of two very good reasons: either to establish their dominance in a social hierarchy, or to establish their territorial rights over a particular piece of ground.[4] . . . From that day to this, biology as a whole asks but one question of a territory: is it defended? Defense defines it. Variability became the final description.[5]

A third approach has stressed the way in which territoriality tends to moderate, although not eliminate, aggression and subsequent injury or loss of life.[6] The relative peace among territorial groupings is here compared to the alternative of internecine conflict among isolated individuals. This same point of view emphasizes the ritual character of most acts of territorial defense and the general absence of conflict which results in serious injury.

None of these approaches really excludes the others. Animal dispersion may operate through a biogenetic "package deal" join-

---

3. V. C. Wynne-Edwards, *Animal Dispersion in Relation to Social Behavior* (New York: Hafner, 1962), pp. 11–12.

4. Desmond Morris, *The Naked Ape* (New York: McGraw-Hill, 1967), p. 120.

5. Robert Ardrey, *The Territorial Imperative* (New York: Atheneum, 1966), p. 210.

6. F. M. Chapman, "The Courtship of Gould's Manakin (Manacus vitellinus vitellinus) on Barro Colorado Island, Canal Zone," *Bulletin of the American Museum of Natural History* 68 (1935): 471–526; W. C. Allee, "Animal Sociology," *Encyclopedia Britannica*, 1954, pp. 971–72; C. R. Carpenter, "Sexual Behavior in Free Ranging Rhesus Monkeys," *Journal of Comparative Psychology* 33 (1942): 113–62.

ing territoriality with aggression; for surely aggression is one way of getting animals to disperse. In turn, any cooperative community, however parochial, may represent an advance over individualistic and continuous conflict. Yet, although these approaches do not obviously contradict one another, no attempt has been made to comprehend them in a single theoretical outlook. Lacking such a general argument, it is difficult to see the limits to each approach as applied either to various nonhuman groups or to humans themselves.

Initially it should be recognized that all three approaches are hemmed in by numerous empirical qualifications. Not all animals achieve dispersion through territoriality and aggressive attacks on approaching strangers.[7] There are also compact and localized animal groupings in which aggression is not the mechanism for marking off their particular area of exploitation.[8] Even the acts of aggression which take place between adjacent territorial groupings are usually minor and tend to take the form of threats rather than terminal or injurious combat.[9] And, finally, most of the interpreters of territoriality have already exempted humans from the same governing principles either as genetic or adaptive forms. The works of Ardrey, Lorenz, and Morris are exceptional in insisting that man is a simple and territorial beast.[10] Wynne-Edwards openly suggests that only primitive societies conform to the laws of dispersion which regulate population density in other animals; modern industrial societies are considered to have achieved independence of these laws, and this is one reason they are approaching a crisis in regulating their numbers.[11]

These restrictions on the connection between territoriality and aggression have been introduced in a retrospective and ad hoc manner. Theoretically, no general reason has been suggested why

7. Wynne-Edwards, *Animal Dispersion*, pp. 98–101.
8. Ibid., pp. 90–113.
9. K. R. L. Hall and Irven Devore, "Baboon Social Behavior," in Devore, ed., *Primate Behavior* (New York: Holt, Rinehart and Winston, 1965), pp. 53–110.
10. Ardrey, *Territorial Imperative*; Lorenz, *Aggression*; and Morris, *Naked Ape*.
11. Wynne-Edwards, *Animal Dispersion*, pp. 187–91.

the same regulatory principles which govern dispersion in non-humans should not apply to humans. Nor is there any good reason to believe that some animals can or cannot maintain compact and localized groupings without engaging in aggression. Also the degrees of aggression, ranging from mere threat to terminal conflict, are too wide in variation simply to be aggregated. The aim of this essay is to take some steps toward a broad formulation which can find those points at which territoriality among humans and nonhumans may be expected to be accompanied by aggression.

Elements of Territoriality

Territoriality, even among nonhumans, often does not appear to be a unitary sequence of responses as are some forms of grooming or sexual behavior. Wynne-Edwards speaks of the "territorial system," which means a series of behavioral forms that can be combined or abridged in various ways so long as they operate together to disperse animals and keep their numbers roughly commensurate with long-term food supplies. The elements of this territorial system are extremely numerous and include several types of aggressive displays, a series of dominance relations, seasonal fluctuations, precedent, spatial movements, and a range of other communicative devices which include everything from electrical signals to olfactory scents.[12] All of these various elements never seem to occur together in the territorial system of single species, colony, or community. Instead, a selective few of them are often strung together in some type of orderly sequence. Sometimes this order is rigidly followed and closely corresponds to Tinbergen's "releasors."[13] In other cases, it seems a loose concatenation of acts which may or may not be carried out in full.

What gives the concept territoriality broad application, then, is not a uniformity in its elements and their causal connections, but the uniformity of their consequences. First, territoriality involves some restriction on totally unselective movement. But this may be

12. Ibid., pp. 23–126.
13. Niko Tinbergen, *The Study of Instinct* (New York: Oxford University Press, 1951).

achieved by aggressive displays, by urine markings, or by conventionalized precedents.[14]

Second, at least some of the elements of territoriality draw a line between members and nonmembers. Members, of course, may include only one individual, but the mutual exclusiveness of the distinction is the important point. As with the restriction on unselective movement, the distinction between members and nonmembers is often confined to particular seasons, breeding periods, or portions of the life cycle.[15] In fact, territorial groupings, on balance, may represent a very limited and atypical formation in the total biogram of some animal groups. Still, the effects of territoriality are to create what sociologists call segmentary groups, although additional lines of affiliation can easily mar such a discrete system of boundaries.[16]

Third, territoriality assumes some form of group or individual recognition. Again this may be achieved by several different methods relying on scents, facial recognition, spatial markers, and the like. What seems most important here is the historical continuity of occupancy and the connection between the specific members who make up a single functioning group: a pair, family, colony, or community.

At least these three conditions seem to be the parameters by which territoriality is judged to have some commonality. These conditions, however, are achieved by a welter of separate elements drawn together in somewhat different causal relations. Both rats and skunks, for instance, have objectional scents. Skunks use their scent to ward off strangers, whereas rats use their scent to identify territorial members. In both animals, scent is an element in distinguishing territorial groups, although it serves in contrasting ways.

Competitive Orders and Aggression

Why should the conditions identifying territoriality—restrictive

14. Wynne-Edwards, *Animal Dispersion*, pp. 23–126.
15. Ibid., pp. 145–92.
16. Emile Durkheim, *The Division of Labor* (Glencoe, Ill.: Free Press, 1960).

movement, mutually exclusive membership, and individual or group recognition—be associated with aggression? The most obvious reason is that groups with mutually exclusive memberships belong to a competitive order in which there are only winners and losers. Such a competitive structure is formally referred to sometimes as a "zero-sum game" or one where one group's gain equals another's loss. This type of competitive structure seems especially likely among territorial animals in the classical case of mutually exclusive territorial groups where the resources they compete for are coextensive with the territories they occupy. Their segmentation is complete, and the boundaries between them can be represented by aggressive displays.

Among nonhumans, such an argument is persuasive because the resources which animals compete for are often coextensive with the territories they defend. Where mutually exclusive human groups compete for resources which are equally coextensive with their territories, then, one ought to expect the same association between territoriality and aggression. Such a conclusion probably has wide application, judging from the available literature.[17] Yet for both humans and animals this line of argument has limits, first, because aggression has other sources and, second, because some types of exclusive territories do not seem to belong to such a competitive order. Since the situation is somewhat better charted for nonhumans, they probably best illustrate the general case.

In the literature on social groups among nonhumans, one may distinguish three distinct ways by which exclusive territorial usage is maintained. The first of these is the familiar fixed territory marked off by permanent and defended boundaries and continuously occupied by some animal group throughout their life, for a particular season, or during a part of their life cycle. Many birds develop such territories, although their occupancy often continues

17. Alexander M. Carr-Saunders, *The Population Problem* (Oxford: Clarendon Press, 1922); Wynne-Edwards, *Animal Dispersion*, pp. 187–91; Isaac Schapera, *Government and Politics in Tribal Society* (New York: Schocken Books, 1967) and *The Khosian Peoples of South Africa* (London: Routledge, 1930); and Elman Service, *Primitive Social Organization* (New York: Random House, 1962).

only during a season or portion of breeding cycle.[18] For a time at
least, however, such territories remain the exclusive province of
one group or individual within a species, and the boundaries of
these territories are fixed and defended.

Closely resembling these compact, fixed, and exclusive territories are leks and nesting sites. Leks consist of little more than
customary sites where males display their virility to attract females, who are subsequently enticed into breeding. Typically,
these leks are in limited supply since the same ones are occupied
year after year. Usually males compete for these breeding sites,
and some males fail to obtain a spot on which they can parade
their sensual capacities. These leks are reported to occur in close
proximity, and the neighboring males who achieve continuous
occupancy may develop a rough dominance hierarchy among
themselves. Thus leks are like exclusive territories where occupancy
is continuous, excludes other individuals of the same species, and
consists of a small plot of land, which is spatially fixed and defended.

Nesting sites are similar to leks in their small size, the customary nature of their occupancy, and the exclusiveness of the
occupancy. Many animals, particularly birds, return to the same
nest year after year. In turn, these same species do not establish
new nests on virgin land but either usurp the nest of a previous
tenant or remain excluded from the joys of connubial and domestic life. Thus, nesting sites are like leks or exclusive territories in
their spatial fixity, in their limited supply, and in their exclusive
tenancy. Exclusive territories, leks, and nesting sites, then, seem to
belong to a single class distinguished by certain shared features.
First, they are scarce goods in the sense that a limited number of
these territories are available and that they are not shared among
groups or individuals. Second, exclusive territories, leks, and nesting sites have fixed or settled boundaries which draw a sharp line
between individuals or groups and exist as a feature of their social
structure irrespective of group composition. Each of these structural features seems to juxtapose groups into an adversarial com-

18. Wynne-Edwards, *Animal Dispersion* pp. 145–64.

petitive structure where what one territorial group or individual gains is an equivalent loss to the other.

In contrast, home ranges constitute a very different and less competitive structure of territorial segregation. Home ranges consist of a sort of circuit of resource sites, each of which is essential but included in a sequential and proximal itinerary of some animal group. Gorillas, for example, seem to travel between a series of sites which include among themselves a full complement of the resources necessary to their livelihood: feeding places, sleeping sites, nesting areas, and breeding refuges. These home ranges are specialized somewhat in that separate sites are exploited in temporal order so as to meet a range of needs. Thus an animal group may move from site to site in order to find food, a safe place to sleep, or a breeding spot. Also, their short movements may be geared into the quick exhaustion of available food supplies and a selective appetite which applies high pressures to food sources which are easily pushed beyond their capacities for regeneration.[19]

Home ranges, then, consist of an intricate balance between several more or less specialized resource sites to be used in a temporal and spatial order. By their very proximity and interdependence these resource sites circumscribe the movement of an animal group. Movement beyond the customary circuit of resource sites may remove them from the next available resource site and is hazardous. Correspondingly, incursions into the home range of other groups is not a sure gain but likely to result in losses because of the distance between resource sites and the uncertain cropping potential of a new resource site. Thus, adjacent groups who occupy home ranges are not embraced in a zero-sum competitive structure, because what they might gain from one another is counterbalanced by possible losses.

A third, and even less competitive, structure of territorial segregation is evident among animals who shoal or school. Shoals or schools are constituted of animals who are remarkably similar in size or their stage in the life cycle. These shoals move about and do not continuously occupy any single territory. Yet animals

19. George B. Schaller, *The Mountain Gorilla* (Chicago: University of Chicago Press, 1963).

of the same size or stage in the life cycle remain in close and uniform proximity to one another, whereas distinct shoals avoid one
another even when they are similar in size or stage of life cycle.
Shoaling is especially common among fish, who occupy a relatively
undifferentiated medium without clear territorial markers or
spatially fixed resource sites. Each shoal may make use of the same
general area but at different times. Apparently, their segregation
or mutual avoidance is governed by a simple trophism which
guides fish toward others which are similar in size, of the same
species, and nearby. Aggression between shoals seems scarcely to
occur at all. Separate groups, usually different in size or stage of
development but also separated by historic precedent, simply avoid
one another, although they may use the same areas in consecutive
order.

Exclusive territories, home ranges, and shoals probably do not
exhaust the range of possible methods of territorial segregation,
but taken together they still cover enough variation to make plausible our general argument. Aggressive displays seem to be increasingly present where competitive relations are cast into a
zero-sum structure between animal groups.

Obviously humans do not possess exact replicas of the types of
territories common among animals. Yet looked at in terms of
their competitive structure, many human social groupings, territorial and otherwise, may bear strong similarities to those described for nonhumans. The rivalry and conflict of interests
between different American states or regions, for example, is
quite strong and well represented in the aggressive displays of
sports teams. Indeed sports teams in general seem to be representative of segmental groups—school districts, towns, counties,
states, regions, and the like.

Similarly, the conflict between political parties, between some
commercial firms, and between farmers sometimes verges toward
a zero-sum game. More often than not, however, the possibility
of coalitions and common interests makes aggressive displays inappropriate as a way of typifying the relations between such
groups. Thus, political parties tend to restrict aggressive attacks
on one another to election time; unions and management cooper-

ate for the most part while confining their conflicts to periods of
wage bargaining; and nations occasionally send out a "white fleet,"
but for the most part their transactions are restricted to a peaceful
maritime trade.

Even among human groups, however, which are drawn into a
zero-sum competitive structure, the consequences may not be quite
the same as among nonhumans. Typically, animals belong only to
one territorial group and their loyalties are undivided. Just the
reverse is probably most typical of humans; ordinarily they belong
to more than one group, only some of them territorial. Humans
are more than a "bundle of roles," but they are at least that. This
means that their loyalties are seldom undivided among groups, and
the prospects of aggression between groups with apparently exclusive interests is not necessarily agreeable to their individual members. Republicans and Democrats may both be good Rotarians.
The exclusiveness of group interests, then, is not necessarily
reflected in individual perspectives, and humans, unlike other
animals, often have a difficult time finding an unqualified enemy.

Dominance Hierarchies

This difference between group and individual competitive outlooks
among humans and other animals is paralleled in the comparison
between their dominance hierarchies. Among many nonhuman
social groups, there are clear dominance hierarchies expressed
partially by shows of aggression. Sometimes males cow the females. Older members of the group may chase off the younger
ones. An estrous female is often treated more deferentially than
one not in heat. An individual with an established position in a
dominance hierarchy is given signs of respect not accorded to
lower status individuals. Aggressive displays and signs of submission, then, generally follow a pattern which is part of an
existent and continuous hierarchial division of labor.

Some of these aggressive displays seem to be only constituent
elements of a hierarchial division of labor. Such a division of labor
must be recognized some way, and aggressive or submissive displays seem to be the signs that both researchers and the animals

they are observing manage to objectify status differences. These
shows of aggression are simply those inherent in the power differences of a hierarchial division of labor: a mother controlling the
movements of her young, a dominant male preempting sexual
rights from other males, and the like. These evidences of difference
in power are only a part of the individual's specialized role.

Other instances of aggressive display among nonhumans seem
less essential to the individual's role and more emblematic in
character. Thus, pecking orders among chickens are sometimes
represented in aggressive displays which seem gratuitous except
as reminders of status differences. Previous analysis of these
aggressive displays has approached them as essential because they
help maintain individual awareness and the stability of dominance
hierarchies.

Rough parallels for either type of aggressive display may be
found among humans. Foremen tell workmen what to do, initiate
conversations, and criticize performance. Similarly, in the regular
performance of her role, a mother may force her child to take her
hand upon crossing the street. These are examples of dominance
or aggression in the sense that those in the dominant position must
take the initiative while those under them show submission. They
are examples of aggression, however, which are integral to an
accepted hierarchial division of labor and seldom arouse much
curiosity.

In addition to these instances of aggression and submission
among humans, there are others of a more emblematic character.
Military parades, terms of address, or formal seating placements
may seem only gratuitous shows of strength or submission. As
among nonhumans, these representational forms may serve only
as reminders to keep in people's minds their place in a dominance
hierarchy and to deter them from further competition over dominance relations.

To this extent aggressive displays are probably comparable
among humans and nonhumans. Yet beyond that point, the two
seem to diverge rather sharply. Among nonhumans, aggressive
displays seem the common and appropriate way to represent
dominance relations because animals tend to occupy a single posi-

tion in a dominance hierarchy which is exclusive of all others. Individual animals are fully identified with their position and do not alternate between definite roles in more than one hierarchy. At any one time, then, individual animals tend to belong to a single dominance hierarchy and to have no conflict of interests. Appropriately, the emblematic representation of their status differences can take on the form of aggressive displays. Once again the zero-sum competitive structure is the important consideration.

By contrast, humans are seldom related to one another through a single dominance hierarchy. Individuals ranked by their occupations, for example, must also deal with one another as friends, pedestrians, motorists, customers, and so on, where their rights and privileges are ranked in different ways. An attempt to claim universal dominance then, would be extremely disruptive to practically any group other than the military. Accordingly, the competitive position among humans is seldom a simple zero-sum game. Correspondingly, aggressive displays are often inappropriate representational forms for typifying differences of social rank. This is probably especially so in modern societies where groups are less all-encompassing and multi-group membership is the rule rather than the exception. Under such circumstances, aggressive displays on the part of dominant individuals are probably disruptive because they do not accurately represent the multifaceted stratification systems which humans have constructed. Aggressive displays, then, are apt to arouse a sense of outrage because they suggest a more universal form of dominance than actually exists. More importantly, aggressive displays may provoke an attempt to retaliate when, as often happens, the tables are turned between individuals in another dominance hierarchy. As sales clerks, policemen, school teachers, and employers are apt to learn, their authority has sharp limits, and aggressive displays on their part are more likely to create retaliation than to restore dominance relations.

This, of course, does not mean that humans lack ways of representing their dominance relations or that aggressive displays are wholly lacking among them. Rather, conventionalized aggressive displays seem to be limited to those circumstances where relations are cast in a zero-sum game, as in sporting events or between complete strangers whose likelihood of meeting again is very low. What may be more common among humans are displays of submission without a corresponding show of aggression. Here the burden of representing dominance relations falls on the junior member who signals his relative status first without forcing the hand of senior people. Thus, terms of address, eye movements, and distancing tend to be the forms which provide status superiors with the rightful exercise of their position. In turn, the junior member of the pair can portray his compliance as a voluntary act and control the limits to which he concedes the dominance of superiors. In this case, respectful titles (Dr., Professor, Officer, and so on) are especially serviceable since they not only show respect but also delimit the capacity in which other people are regarded as superiors. Much the same kind of message can be constructed from eye movements, clothing, and distancing relations which are situation-specific (for example, in the classroom) and do not express universal submissiveness. Under these circumstances, submissive displays are substituted for aggressive ones, and social life can proceed without the continual threat of retaliation.

Certainly this does not mean that humans are unaggressive and that status superiors are unlikely to use aggression in dealing with their juniors. Instead it means that aggressive displays are far less a conventionalized emblem of dominance relations among humans than among animals. When humans use aggressive displays to represent dominance relations, they are likely to be going beyond the accepted forms, and it is precisely this which makes shows of aggression so much more serious and destructive in human societies. Attempts to symbolize status differences by aggressive displays seldom achieve unqualified submission but often end in an escalation of retaliatory acts in a vicious circle far more destructive than aggressive displays occurring among nonhumans. For this reason, aggressive displays among animals and humans are not often comparable.

Conclusion

Some of the literature on territoriality has been confusing because of an attempt to draw a direct causal relationship between it and aggression. Aggressive displays, however, seem most closely associated with a win-or-lose type of competitive structure, and only some forms of territoriality produce this competitive structure. By focusing on the competitive structure among animals or humans, somewhat different implications can be drawn for further comparative work.

First, the competitive structure among many human groups, especially those in complex societies, is not nearly so close to a zero-sum game as is true of many animal groups. Human groups often share members, group mobility is frequent, and the possibility of coalitions is very common. Thus, it is often inappropriate to use aggressive displays to represent the relationships between these groups.

Second, humans often belong to several dominance hierarchies and the relationship between any two individuals cannot be expressed uniformly in terms of superiors and inferiors. This is especially so in complex societies where people shift among a vast array of roles in which they are sometimes inferiors, sometimes superiors, and sometimes equals. Aggressive displays, then, become progressively improper as conventionalized representations of social rank, because people now have the occasion for retaliation. The limited authority which most people exercise in social hierarchies, in addition, is not authentically represented in aggressive displays which suggest the general dominance of one individual over another.

Third, the major alternative to aggressive displays as a way of representing differences of social rank are displays of submission. These displays of submission consist of token acts which recognize the limited dominance of superiors. Such displays of submission are often situation-specific and designed, as in titles of address, to identify a superior role rather than a superior individual. Above all, these displays of submission are initiated by the junior member and therefore seem like a voluntary act which is removed from any appearance of force or coercion. Conversely, it is the appearance of force in aggressive displays which makes them treacherous in societies where people have the opportunity to turn the tables on one another.

Fourth, the relative infrequency and inappropriateness of conventionalized aggressive displays is probably what makes shows of aggression so destructive and dangerous in modern or complex societies. Among nonhumans, aggressive displays are correct in the sense that one animal or group does thoroughly dominate another. Similarly, groups in simple segmentary societies may represent their relations as one of mutually exclusive interests. But the more organic a society, the more difficult it is for individuals or groups to separate their interests or to speak of generalized dominance relations. Shows of aggression, then, tend to overstate the division between groups or the power of one individual over another. Thus, when people or groups do resort to shows of aggression, they are likely to arouse a sense of outrage and subsequent retaliation. The possibility of escalation of shows of aggression into outright violence is very real among humans as compared to animals. It is a matter which is most likely to be understood by an examination of the continual struggle to find representational forms which accurately portray the changing relationships between groups and individuals. The difficulty of such a task is obviously great in complex, pluralistic societies where an increasing number of social distinctions are piled on top of one another. In the confusion, some people have been tempted to reach back and find an overly simple model which mechanically relates aggression to territoriality. This oversimplification is symptomatic of a wider tendency and one among many reasons people resort to shows of aggression ("putting people in their place") in the absence of more accurate representational forms. The results seem typically abortive; they achieve not quick submission or the segregation of groups but the escalation of shows of aggression into actual violence.

7. Territoriality and Distancing

As Wynne-Edwards points out, territoriality is less a distinct structural form than one result of several communicative devices for governing the spatial distribution of individuals and groups.[1] Thus, he speaks of a territorial system which includes a vast array of signaling devices which help control the density, distribution, and reproduction of animal groups. This same outlook may be profitably extended to humans, although the role performed by these spatial communicative devices may be only partially the same as that among nonhumans.

In no human community is totally unselective spatial movement permitted. There always seem to be sharp differences between individuals according to the territories to which they have rightful access. There is also a wider variety of spatial signals which indicate the gradations of interaction—distancing—between individuals at near or far levels of affiliation. As with both territorial and spatial displays among animals, these communicative devices seem to operate together as a single language for objectifying some common features of social differentiation.

The crucial reason for considering together all these types of spatial signaling is that they appear to have an unequivocal and unavoidable meaning among human communities. Spatial propinquity or mere copresence alone make people available to insult or injury. In part this follows directly from the normative character of social relations. Since society is constituted by norms and standards, compliance with these norms and standards is at least partially voluntaristic. The prospect of deviance, then, is always possible in human societies in a way in which it is not clearly present among, say, a colony of bees dancing after they have dis-

1. V. C. Wynne-Edwards, *Animal Dispersion in Relation to Social Behavior* (New York: Hafner, 1962), pp. 98–101, 162–64.

covered a new supply of nectar.[2] Humans can and do intentionally
or self-consciously violate social norms despite the most forbidding
sanctions. Since deviance is so possible among humans, copresence alone lays people or groups open to victimization, because
one man's deviance is generally a threat to at least one other's
welfare or assurance of social order.[3] Social proximity, even of
the most adventitious sort, then, is one of those occasions which
can arouse fears and requires regulation.

The conventional character of social standards also means that
failure is always possible in every social relationship. Humans
can always fail to meet each other's standards because they cannot
depend on their instincts to guide them mechanically through
every social relationship. Ignorance, incompetence, and variations
in expectations mean that social relations are perilous and have
judgmental consequences. It would seem essential that people
have some way of reading each other's likely responses so as to
estimate the risks they are taking. Copresence alone makes people
captive judges of each other's conduct and requires them to develop at least some communicative devices for anticipating and
interpreting each other's judgments. Like the child who drops his
ice cream cone on the street and then looks around to see if he
has been seen, we need conventionalized signals to weigh our
fortunes within the earshot and eyesight of others. Even where the
standard reaction is one of feigned ignorance, it is undertaken
with a mindfulness that it is harmful to the other individual to
stare.

Taken together, the prospects of failure and deviance mean
that spatial propinquity is more or less problematic and treacher-

2. K. von Frisch, *Bees: Their Vision, Chemical Senses and Language*
(Ithaca, N.Y.: Cornell University Press, 1950).

3. Edwin M. Schur (*Crimes without Victims* [Englewood Cliffs, N.J.:
Prentice-Hall, 1965]) has argued that deviance can exist without victimization, and he is right in saying that there are crimes or instances of deviance
which attack our cultural symbols rather than specific individuals. This
does not lessen the danger of such crimes or forms of deviance. The
legitimacy of cultural symbols and standards is as essential to life as is
food. Thus, one can agree with Schur that some cultural symbols and

ous.[4] People must feel their way into situations with varying degrees of apprehension over failure or victimization. It is vital, then, that people possess some type of "early warning system" which alerts them to the intentions and standards of other people. Thus, eye movements, arm gestures, stance, walk, and following the rules of the road, for instance, seem to be para-linguistic modes of communication which help us sort people according to our own concerns with safety and success.[5] In some instances this sorting process goes to the extreme of total segregation, and we may speak of territoriality in its classical form. Such regulation of the possibilities of copresence seems aimed simply at the elimination of social contacts and is most likely to occur where outright conflict is a clear possibility, as between racial groups in South Africa or to a lesser extent in many parts of the United States. In other instances these para-linguistic devices seem only to promote graduated levels of avoidance or interaction. In all cases, however, these communicative devices appear to dictate degrees of avoidance which are commensurate with the anticipated dangers of failure or harm.

---

standards no longer draw widespread support or respect without also agreeing that attacks against any of the standards of society are immaterial and unimportant. Otherwise his own critical account of our standards should be ignored as inconsequential or harmless.

4. Erving Goffman also frequently mentions this treacherous and problematic aspect of social relations (for example, see his *Interaction Ritual* [Garden City, N.Y.: Doubleday and Co., Anchor Books, 1967]). His assumption, like my own, is not an empirical observation but a preliminary starting point for making empirical observations. The treacherous and indeterminant character of normative relations is an underlying assumption which allows us to understand why special provisions exist to avoid treachery and indeterminancy. As with Hobbes's "war of all against all" there need be no empirical referent, but only a hypothetical alternative against which we can assess current social arrangements. Following Hobbes and Goffman, I assume that it is necessary to construe such idealized states in order to analyze actual social structures within the full range of conceptual possibilities.

5. See Erving Goffman, *Behavior in Public Places* (New York: The Free Press of Glencoe, 1963). I do not mean to indicate here that all spatial movements are discernible or that they are uniform in all cultures. I only aim to indicate that spatial movements and propinquity always make possible the difficulties of insult and injury.

The extent to which anticipated conflict figures into the segregation or distancing of groups and individuals is evident in some of the most obvious forms of either. Nations, for example, are the largest human groups which maintain an internal civil order through the efforts of a police force, constabulary, or military power. Within such a population there exists a third party to preserve order and restrain potential combatants. Without deemphasizing the conflicts occurring within many nations, they are still terminal societies, and relations which fall outside their acknowledged boundaries—for example, in frontier regions or no-man's-lands—are hedged in by comparatively gross apprehensions and a heavy emphasis on avoidance.[6] Moreover, when conflict between groups within a nation becomes so imminent, as in South Africa, the country may bifurcate into practically two nations, spatially distinct.

Similarly, cross-sex relations are overshadowed by the perpetual dangers of sexual violence and uncontinued exchanges. Thus, during their periods of sexual vitality, men and women tend to be segregated or subject to close surveillance. Territorial segregation is most apparent when individuals are clearly exposing their sexual organs: when they are defecating, dressing, or bathing. Even, however, where the imminent visibility of sexual organs is not so apparent, an elaborate range of avoidance practices is usually evident between the sexes. Women sit with their legs crossed or together, guarding the proverbial "gates of hell." Men open doors for women, place chairs for them, and rise when they enter the room, acknowledging both the weakness of women and the restraint of potential masculine forcefulness. No doubt there is great cultural variability here, but as I shall try to point out later, even very liberated dating partners in the United States adopt a series of spatial moves which help make them their own chaperons.

6. Encounters in international waters or air space seem to be characterized by extensive avoidance (e.g., the "rules of the road" observed by air and sea craft) or by elaborate rules of etiquette. Either type of behavior seems to betray the apprehensions of individuals caught in an area where they have no common referee.

Interracial, ethnic, and class boundaries are often equally volatile and likely to be hedged in by territorial segregation or elaborate signs for insuring avoidance relations. These same communicative devices, however, may be extended to regulate the relationship between persons who are unidentifiable except as individuals. Strangers, for example, are considered among the most dangerous of people simply because they are not easily identifiable and thus accountable. Indeed, within a whole range of social relations the structure of affiliations is problematic or voluntaristic. It is in these relations that the para-linguistic devices of spatial movement are especially helpful in developing an exploratory structure within which social relations can reach some stable pattern. Perhaps the most prominent examples are those of neighbors, friends, and casual gatherings. Within these groups we may expect a rich variety of communicative devices to regulate the spatial relations among individuals.

Many examples of segregation and distancing, of course, do not hinge so much on the dangers of physical harm as on the dangers of invidious comparison, insult, and the degradation of status differences. The private office, for instance, allows higher administrators to make mistakes and forego keeping up appearances without being seen by their inferiors. Generally this type of privacy becomes less treasured for people of lower status whose performances are not expected to be so exacting and for whom the judgmental consequences are not so grave. Similarly, the practice of having separate sleeping quarters for children and adults does not indicate the strong possibility of conflict, but allows connubial partners to drop certain parental pretenses while also maintaining a desexualized image for their children. The dangers here derive from the contradictory roles that people must play and the unfavorable judgmental consequences of having an audience who can make comparisons between these roles.

Some of these examples may suggest that the role of these communicative devices is only to duplicate structural differences (for example, race, sex, ethnicity) already present in most societies. Often this is true, but it does not detract much from the importance of such signaling devices. The social differences present in any society have to be indexed or conveyed in some manner, and signaling devices which use space are one way of doing this. The boundaries which surround an ethnic neighborhood, for example, are not simply there or an epiphenomenon of national extraction. Such boundaries must be constantly reconstituted by boundary displays (for example, threatened gang fights) which continually alert people to the meaning of these neighborhood boundaries. Spatial signaling devices, then, may not be the ultimate sources of social differentiation, but they are often the proximate sources of such differentiation.[7]

But the representational role of spatial signaling devices is not the only role they play. Even the most evident lines of social differentiation do not seem adequate to give a determinant form to all social affiliations. People may and commonly do associate primarily with others of the same social standing, as determined by religion, ethnic background, race, income group, and the like. In a community of any size, however, there exist choices even within such narrowly defined groupings, and moreover, relationships between these groups can be avoided only at grave costs. There are strong reasons, then, for finding some additional assortive process which will further refine the selection of eligible associates. Spatial signaling devices are a primary way of managing these choices for the same reason that many other lines of social differentiation narrow the range of eligible associates: they indicate with whom it is safe to associate.

Variations in the Function, Form, and Identity of Territorial Groups

Function

The great practical advantage of territorial groups is that they help designate the range of associations which an individual may consider trustworthy. To this extent, territoriality is like any other

7. See Wynne-Edwards for a similar comment regarding the role of territoriality among animals and its relationship with the ultimate determinant of food supply (*Animal Dispersion*, pp. 11–12).

selective principle such as those a parent might invoke to choose
his children's playmates. The practicality of territorial groupings,
however, is ramified by a number of further considerations. First,
spatial proximity simply cannot be avoided as it might be for some
other possible basis of grouping. People literally have to be somewhere, and although they might possibly ignore racial, ethnic, or
age groupings, spatial propinquity inevitably makes them vulnerable to one another.

Second, the structure of exclusive territorial groups helps to
impose the sorts of social control necessary to insure relatively
peaceable social relations. The opposition between territorial
groups aids continued membership by the exclusion of other alternatives if not through positive choice. The enduring character of
territorial membership and the lack of alternatives keeps groups
together willfully or unwillfully and makes short-run opportunism
a dangerous proposition, since the opportunist must continue to
live with his victims. Similarly, the involuntary confinement of
such a group allows its members to gain an intimate knowledge
of each other's personal character, abilities at joint and artful
tasks, and the highly specialized routines which any cooperative
group must develop on its own. Territoriality, then, builds accountability into a society without anyone's having to work at it.

This, of course, does not mean that territorial groups emerge
automatically whenever people are faced with the problem of
order or the execution of complicated and artful tasks. Rather, it
means that some territorial groups are able to survive because they
share a common fate and can be drawn together into a small-scale
but intricate division of labor which requires habitual cooperation. One of the difficulties faced by some other groupings, such
as social classes, intellectual circles, or interest groups, is that their
members can easily shift sides, avoid one another, or engage in
transient relations. Such groupings may not survive, because their
members can be fickle. As with some other primordial bases of
organization, (sex, age, language) the mutually exclusive character of territorial groups forces continued participation and thus
accountability.

Territorial groups go further by providing a sort of basic partitioning of society so that other selective principles of membership will be equally forceful in confining people to a single continuous grouping. For example, age grades are even more involuntary and prone to opposition between different age levels. To become effective, however, a group of individuals must be closely committed to one another and unable to seek anonymity. An initial partitioning of age groups according to territoriality imposes continuity on localized age grades small enough to insure face-to-face recognition and thus accountability. Much the same might be said of almost any categoric designation where the number of eligible numbers exceeds the possibilities of individual recognition. Territorial divisions, then, may be regarded as a first step toward the division of a population into units such that other principles of association will place people in groups which are small enough for them to be recognized and their members held accountable for their past actions.[8]

Despite all these advantages, territorial groups seem always to work in conjunction with other principles of affiliation. This is true even among very small scale societies such as the relatively autonomous and localized hunting band in which kin ties are the major internal bases of differentiation.[9] In large-scale societies, territorial groupings provide an even less complete model. One of the basic consequences of territorial divisions as well as many

8. And one may safely claim that practically all selective principles of affiliation operate within some framework of territorial boundaries. Sometimes these territorial partitions include enormous numbers of people, as in nationally based organizations. Even kin groups, which might conceivably consist of an unlocalized network of affiliations, seem to recognize mainly those kinsmen who remain within some locality. See Edward H. Winter, *Bwamba* (Cambridge: Heffer, 1956).

There are, of course, groups which attempt to define membership on an undifferentiated and worldwide basis. Such groups are bound to be unwieldy in their numbers and beset by defection through shifting claims of affiliation. Even the international communists develop localized cells which have mutually exclusive memberships.

9. Isaac Schapera, *The Khosian Peoples of South Africa* (London: Routledge, 1930) and *Government and Politics in Tribal Societies* (New York: Schocken Books, 1967).

other primordial distinctions is that they fragment populations into relatively discrete units in opposition to one another. Although these small units can be combined temporarily through a variety of alliances, the opposition between them is essential if they are to avoid defection and opportunism among their members. The mutual exclusiveness of their membership, then, makes it difficult to concert the action of people except through the unselective or mechanical aggregation of territorial groups. Large-scale industrial societies, however, often require intricate coordination between specialists in a widely distributed division of labor. Therefore, totally exclusive territorial divisions ought not be expected in an industrial society or, if found, must constrain the free operation of the marketplace in either the demand for labor or the distribution of products.

Territorial groups are further limited by their inability to provide a gradation in levels of affiliation or a series of stages along which individuals can move toward progressive affiliation. In their simplest form, territorial groups simply define individuals as in-group or out-group members in a relatively prescribed and enduring fashion. One of the most prominent requirements of large-scale industrial societies, however, is that people be able to change their affiliations and work their way gradually into new ones. Territorial groups of this kind provide essentially an all-or-none type of affiliative structure which does not easily permit this type of mobility between social relationships.

This does not mean that territorial groups disappear from modern societies but that their size tends to expand while other principles of affiliation become more important in their internal differentiation. The modern nation with its various subunits is probably the most obvious example of this expansion. The growth and internal differentiation of cities and regions seems to follow a similar course. Even the parochial inner city neighborhood often includes a large population when compared to residential groups in more simple societies.[10] Also, territorial groups can be trans-

---

10. Gerald D. Suttles, *The Social Order of the Slum* (Chicago: University of Chicago Press, 1968).

formed into alliance structures in which larger collectivities can
be formed by telescoping small locality groups into larger ones.
This simple principle of ordered segmentation seems to have been
shared by some of the most technologically primitive societies[11]
and advanced societies. The general trajectory in modern societies,
however, seems to aim toward a loose confederational form in
which small territorial groups not only give their members an identity that distinguishes them from the outside world but provide
identities which selectively align them into coalitions which facili-
tate cooperation. Among such societies, the small and self-suffi-
cient locality group may seem scarcely to exist, since it is so often
joined with collaborators in some larger enterprise. Yet the primary building blocks which occur in such advanced societies are
worthy of analysis even though they seldom occur in atomic form.
Here it is most important to point out how territorial groups and
their identities become progressively less exclusive as they are
incorporated into shifting and temporary alliances. In such circumstances territoriality becomes less a holistic design for life
than a social role, partial and incomplete in its demands on the
individual's loyalties and less than commanding in determining
his accountability.[12]

Forms

From the available literature it is possible to detect at least four
forms among those groups which are explicitly identified as territorial. First, there are exclusive territorial groups which are relatively autonomous and not further divided within themselves. This
seems a rather rare form among humans, very concentrated among
primitive peoples, and directly comparable to the defended and
exclusive territories found among some nonhumans.[13]

Second, we find populations in which territorial groups roughly
similar to the ones mentioned above can be drawn together in a

11. E. E. Evans-Pritchard, *The Nuer* (Oxford, Clarendon Press, 1940).
12. Suttles, *Social Order*, p. 105.
13. Wynne-Edwards, *Animal Dispersion*, pp. 109–10, 187–91, 219–20;
and Shapera, *Khosian Peoples*.

series of shifting alliances as each group selects sides in an oppositional structure. A third, and similar form, is one where alliances
between groups are pyramided into increasingly inclusive units in
some fixed order of combination while remaining in opposition
to equivalent territorial combinations.[14] The distinction here is
between a loose and optional affiliation among territorial groups
and a progressively inclusive order of combination following traditional lines and a fixed sense of common identity. Both combinations of smaller territorial groups preserve the opposition between roughly equivalent units. The first combination, however,
brings territorial groups together as allies, and the second brings
them together as a unified body with a persistent identity.

A fourth form is the administrative pyramid which draws a
series of subunits into increasingly inclusive units until they finally
combine in a single territorial unit. The administrative pyramid
bears a certain formal similarity to the pyramid made up of groups
which combine according to a traditional order. There are three
differences, however: the administrative pyramid remains continuously intact, it includes all subterritorial units into a single
pyramid, and the differences between levels of combination in the
administrative pyramid are paralleled by a dominance hierarchy
of officials whose authority is commensurate with the territorial
level with which they are associated.

The striking feature of the first three of these forms is the way
in which they are nested within a larger competitive structure
where territorial groups or combinations of them are joined in a
win-or-lose type of struggle. The exclusive and undivided territorial group stands alone in competition with others like itself.
Shifting alliances develop only as a way of seeking an overpower-
ing or equivalent advantage in a similar struggle between un-
compromising opponents. The ordered combination of territorial
groups into increasingly inclusive ones is only an escalation of
hostilities and competition between equivalent alliances. For at
least these forms of territoriality, one can say that human groups

14. Evans-Pritchard, *The Nuer.*

which explicitly identify themselves as territorial are comparable
to some of those found among nonhumans. They are embraced
in a zero-sum competitive struggle where membership is mutually
exclusive and territorially prescribed. Humans differ from animals
primarily in their ability to escalate these confrontations to include shifting alliances and the ordered combination of territorial
groups. This represents a considerable change in the scale of
opposition between territorial groups, but as these groups escalate in extent, they remain opposed in a win-or-lose game.

The administrative pyramid of territorial units is quite distinct
because it expands to include all potential opponents or competitors. Such a structure does not represent the clear division of
interests between equivalent territorial groups so much as the
creation of progressive levels of authority associated with increasingly inclusive territorial units. Thus, the administrative pyramid
is essentially a dominance hierarchy in which inclusive territorial
units unilaterally dominate less inclusive ones. Opposition and
competition, then, tend to be focused at the interface between
administrative levels. To this extent the administrative pyramid
shares with the other forms of territoriality a sort of win-or-lose
competitive order. Beyond this point, however, there are sharp
differences.

First, the basic units in the first three forms seem to develop
easily from the general tendency of people to withdraw into the
safe confines of their own membership in a relatively treacherous
world. These territorial groups, then, develop along traditional
lines with a minimum of self-conscious and planful guidance. For
the most part people see their membership as a natural event
which is not very susceptible to current human management. In
turn, shifting alliances or ordered combinations develop along
traditional lines or by short-term agreements for very specific purposes: often for war making or to obtain a brief competitive edge.
The administrative pyramid, on the other hand, is generally a
self-conscious attempt to create territorial groups, and it is frequently imposed by a ruling elite or external power. The entire
history of colonialism and the emergence of the established or

developing nations is marked by a self-conscious and purposive attempt to create subordinate territorial units.[15]

Second, the first three forms of territoriality tend to preserve a traditional division of labor, whereas the administrative pyramid is often revolutionary in its consequences. Shifting alliances and the ordered combination of territorial groups do not effectively disturb the basic working units which carry out routine and essential daily tasks. They gather their strength and develop wider perimeters of trust only for short durations: for a war against some other alliance, for brief smuggling ventures or similar economic operations, or for a festival or ceremony. Afterward, everyone goes back to his own parochial group without much or any change in the expanse of productive activities.

The administrative pyramid tends to create much-enlarged areas relatively free of internecine conflict and able to mount large-scale productive and distributive economic institutions which function on a continuous basis. The successful administrative pyramid must be accompanied by police powers which usurp the right to make local wars and a variety of courts, negotiating bodies, and referees to settle disputes without overt conflict. The *Pax Britannica* is only the most obvious example of this type. The result, whoever its sponsor, is a much-enlarged number of people who can safely engage in joint productive efforts and casual relations. There is no point here in developing the argument which can show the economic advantages of size or scale. The point is that these economies of scale can be realized only within an administrative pyramid which first monopolizes the rights to coercive power and second enlarges the population within which trust can be insured by an external referee.

Within such an administrative pyramid, conflict and competition can still occur in incipient forms, but they tend to be regulated and deescalated by the presence of an external referee. Out-

15. Which is not to say that only colonial regimes are prone to initiating such administrative pyramids. See Clifford Geertz, "Form and Variation in Balinese Village Structure," *American Anthropologist* 61 (December 1959): 991–1012; and Albert Beebe White, *Self-Government at the King's Command* (Minneapolis: University of Minnesota Press, 1933).

right conflict of a physical sort is likely to bring in a police force
or armed body, whereas differences get forced into the courts
or before some other arbitrating agent. Competition over goods,
services, and power is most often regulated through some type
of representational system, appointive or electoral. Certainly the
potential for conflict and competition is great, as evidenced by
the considerable number of people involved in forestalling conflicts and regulating competition. But, where they are successful,
these peace keepers help create an extensive area within which
trust can prevail as a precondition to larger organizational forms
that are not themselves territorial in their basic identity or structure. Thus, while the territorially defined administrative pyramid
is vital to modern societies, territoriality itself declines as a major
or exclusive principle of organization.

In this sense, the administrative pyramid is the most successful
form of territoriality because it can expand the limits of trust and
thus the complexity of a division of labor on both its productive
and distributive fronts. This does not mean that administrative
pyramids are especially liked. Indeed, colonial regimes have been
the most active in creating such administrative pyramids, and
they tend to be detested. Indigenous but ruling elites are probably
the next most active in creating such administrative pyramids,
and they are often only a little more popular. These reactions,
however, do not detract from the dominant role of administrative
pyramids or their important role in establishing the modern industrial nation. It is to be expected that they will be resisted,
because they go against the grain of traditional and small territorial units that consider themselves natural and are anxious to
preserve their privileges of offending their neighbors and making
small-scale wars. The external or elite origins of administrative
pyramids also arouse existing hostilities among the more powerless and provincial who find their prerogatives curtailed and di-
minished by comparison to the new scale of authority with which
they are confronted. A lack of sensitivity to local customs and
elite pride further offend the tiny groups which get thrown together into the same administrative unit. These sources of opposition are firmly rooted but unequal to the battle. Even where they

win, they are bound to be dominated by other populations which
have gone beyond the simple segmentary structure of small traditional groups bound together by face-to-face familiarity and the
inability to move elsewhere.

Identity

It goes without saying that every social activity must have some
locational base. It is not equally common, however, for the par-
ticipants in these activities to use their locational base to represent membership. Some churches, for example, have territorial
or parish boundaries, but others do not. Occasionally but not
always, kin groups are identified with some traditional home,
burial spot, or natal community. Governmental units are perhaps
the most uniformly territorial in their identity and membership.
Terminal societies seem almost always to be territorial in both
form and identity.[16]

Perhaps the most outstanding way to demonstrate the representational meaning of territorial identities is to portray clearly
their exclusive claim on members and the clear distinction between groups. The designation of a territory sharply divides those
within it from those outside it. Similarly, membership tends to be
presumed by those who remain within the territorial unit. Thus,
a Frenchman is known not only to be a citizen in France but to
lack citizenship in all other countries. Furthermore, even when
a person alters his residence and citizenship, his loyalties will be
presumed to shift even to the point that he becomes an opponent
to his country of origin. Territorial identities, then, tend to high-
light the division between groups and their unchallenged dominion over members.[17]

16. R. M. MacIver has argued otherwise (*The Web of Government*
[New York: Macmillan and Co., 1947], pp. 158), that territorial identification is especially undeveloped among tribal or primitive societies. Judging from Schapera's findings (*Government and Politics*), almost the reverse
seems to be true.
17. The British Dominion may be regarded as a single territorial unit
for purposes of this example. The free interchange of citizenship among
the dominions exists, however, more on paper than in fact. When faced
with large-scale immigration, of West Indians, East Africans, and Pakistani,
for example, the Dominion fragments into separate national territories.

As a result, groups with territorial identity tend to adopt a rhetoric of struggle which emphasizes the mutual exclusiveness of their interests and the omnipresence of force. The language used to describe international relations, for instance, is laced with such words as *power, struggle, domination,* and *cold* or *hot wars.* Similarly, turf-bound street-corner gangs espouse a sort of paramilitary vocabulary with their warlords, sergeants at arms, and war councils, all of which may be more myth than reality.[18] Even state university football teams, who would find it impossible to exist without one another, exercise to the utmost the sportswriter's ability to find terms that suggest terminal conquest. A striking and recent example in Chicago is the segregated black community's threat of a curfew for whites entering their neighborhoods. Obviously, neither nations, street-corner gangs, football teams, nor the Chicago Black Belt are autonomous territorial groups able to wall themselves off from one another without dire consequences. Indeed, such groups are probably as dependent on one another as on fellow members of the same territory. Yet, territorial identities tend to suggest such a rhetoric of struggle both because of a long history of struggle between autonomous territorial groups and because the mutual exclusiveness of territorial groupings, like those of age and sex, suggests an equal exclusiveness of interests.

These representational aspects of territorial identities make them problematic for two types of groups which are unable to achieve a full correspondence between form and identity. In the first type of group the leadership and ideology insist unsuccessfully on an exclusive claim to the loyalty of members and the unchallenged dominion of the group over its membership. In the second type of group the members are actually locked into a win-or-lose competitive structure with other territorial groups but are still unable to represent themselves in this form because a formidable elite embraces a counter ideology. The American Catholic church and certain immobile groups of workers are good examples of both types of group because they show the extremes of this predicament.

18. Suttles, *Social Order.*

In the United States, the Catholic church has preserved its parish structure despite a clear inability to turn everyone into Catholics. The parish structure is effective only in the sense that it can restrict membership to a local congregation and curtail the free selection of congregational membership despite residence. The monopolistic or universal claims of the church, however, have been subdued and deemphasized to the point that other faiths are tolerated or treated as relatively fair competitors.[19] In addition, nonlocalized ethnic churches have developed in the form of national churches.

Despite all these concessions, however, a parish structure has been retained at the insistence of the church's leadership. This is to be expected: the basic tenet of the Catholic church is its exclusive and preeminent claim to universal membership. This ideology is rooted in the church's identity and continued by an administrative elite which is drawn almost wholly from countries where the church retains a monopoly on congregational membership. These extraneous constraints seem to make it impossible for the church fully to abandon its exclusive and forceful claims to loyalty. This has left the Catholics open to accusations of Popism and the monopolistic management of religious life by most other American denominations which have long abandoned a parish structure in favor of a more laissez faire model of recruitment. The exceptions seem to include only such religious groups as the Mormons and Amish, who claim a second revelation that has made them the new and authoritative arbitrators of men's souls. And, like the Catholics, they continue to place a territorial claim on members through a parish or ward structure. Once again, their leadership is rooted in remote regions where the prescribed relationship between residence and religion can be enforced.

The reverse of this pattern can be found among some occupational groups in the United States which are territorially fixed but

19. Recently, the author was told by the local archdiocese that parish boundaries are no longer important for church attendance but only for school attendance. This represents a very recent change and apparently is further evidence that the church is relenting in its universalistic claims especially since Vatican II.

are not widely represented as territorial in character. Most typically these seem to be work groups whose fate is more determined
by the local firm than by multiple alternatives in the labor market.
The most obvious case is that of employees in a company town.[20]
Often these workers and their families are locals in the most fundamental sense; they can leave their places of livelihood only by
giving up any assurance of employment. The same is true of many
lower income occupational groups who have skills or "connections" which are nontransferable. Of course, this lack of transferable skills and connections is not unique to poorly skilled workers.
A common predicament faces the most prestigious of people
whenever their marketable talents appeal only to a localized clientele or employer: artists with local patrons, precinct captains with
a backlog of favors to be collected, or a restaurateur in the habit
of preparing dishes which will appeal in a local ethnic neighborhood. They are, in a sense, "company men."

The important point, however, is not the class or occupational
distribution of these localized commitments, but (1) the extent
to which such localized commitments place workers into a win-
or-lose competitive structure and (2) the general absence of an
identity for these locals which represents them as territorial
groups. Where the members of a work group are heavily dependent on a specific place of employment or local clientele, they may
rightfully see themselves as spatially bound. Their fortunes are
tied closely to that of their firm or their clientele. Either type of
dependency preempts their loyalties and gives them little or no
obvious interest in the fate of similar firms or different clienteles.
Social relations, then, can approach a zero-sum competitive structure in which employees follow their local employers or clients
to the exclusion of other collectivities. The situation, then, seems
ripe for the development of full-scale territorial identity.

The peculiarity in the predicament of these very localized
groupings is that their attempts to represent themselves as territorial groups does not find wide-scale and sympathetic acceptance.

20. John Kenneth Moreland, *The Millways of Kent* (New Haven:
College and University Press, 1965).

Sociologists, for example, do surveys in which questions about occupation are aimed exclusively at job titles, and probes have been designed to avoid obtaining only place of work. The tendency of sociologists to leave place of work uncoded seems to be typical of the way in which the territorial character of some work groups is ignored and therefore remains poorly represented as a part of their identity.

The territorial character of some work groups, then, is incompletely developed and seldom gains full recognition beyond their own ranks. A rudimentary step in this direction is evident in the union local, although these groups mar this local identity by assigning themselves a number rather than the name of their firm or shop. By contrast, the medieval guild system was much more overt and acceptable as a locality group.

An indirect way in which some work groups represent their fixed membership and opposition to other work groups is through team sports. The United States is saturated by athletic teams which range from industrial leagues to the spontaneous workshop group that forms its own bowling team. These teams must receive the widespread support of workers, management, and owners who are occupationally immobile and whose loyalties can be so clearly cast. The lack of publicity and attention directed to these leagues and teams, however, is indicative of their marginal acceptance as the proper representational form for occupational groups. Even more furtive forms of representing the localized character of work groups are evident in their company uniforms (worn only at work) and occasional insignias (such as decals which identify one's place of work). But all of these symbols are incomplete in their spatial references, and it is doubtful that many workers would explicitly describe themselves as company men.

The situation facing these immobile work groups seems to be the mirror image of that facing Catholics in the United States; the workers are confronted with indigenous laissez faire ideology which makes an ideal of everyone's full ability to bargain in the labor market. To openly recognize that many workers are in effect company men would at least question the ubiquity of the laissez faire model. The problem, however, seems to extend further to the point of intruding a vocabulary of motives which would not only be different from the laissez faire model of economic relations but disruptive of it. As I have emphasized at several points, the representational content of territorial identities tends to emphasize the sharp division between groups and the involuntary aspects of membership. Our image of the company man carries both of these connotations. Such a portrait of social relations suggests an order in which different work groups are belligerents, unable to trust one another and incapable of transferring their loyalties through verbal agreements, contracts, negotiations, persuasion, and similar forms of manipulation. The notion that people are susceptible to such manipulation, however, is vital to a modern economy which must constantly alter the composition of work groups irrespective of their current loyalties. Such an economy would seem to require an intact concept of economic man which has broad application simply because the extent to which work groups may have to be reconstituted is unpredictable. Even minor exceptions, then, cannot be given full expression lest they cast into doubt the unfractured and holistic character of economic man. Even more importantly, the notion that primordial loyalties, including those of territoriality, are terminal and unnegotiable promotes a vision of society which drives people back into small and hostile camps and arouses exactly those sorts of premonitions which help give rise to territorial groups. A modern industrial society cannot function if it is fragmented into territorial groups of such a small scale.

American Catholic parishes and immobile work groups represent two of the extremes in how ideological orders may retard the correspondence between territorial forms and group identities. There are numerous other examples of an intermediate character. College students, for instance, are closely identified with their place of learning and find it difficult to transfer their status elsewhere. Public school students generally find their movements closely circumscribed by curfew and censorship laws that regulate their patronage in commercial and public establishments. The founding fathers of many industrial firms are often local heroes and respond by becoming local philanthropists. Prominent politicians often have no attraction beyond a local ethnic group or community. None of these groups or individuals is wholly territorial in character or membership. Indeed no person or group is ever wholly territorial in this sense, but all of them share some features which are territorial in character. What needs pointing out is the way modern industrial economies cannot easily tolerate collective representations which seize solely on territorial identities because they emphasize only the exclusive, terminal, and oppositional posture of individuals and groups.

Distancing

Whereas mutually exclusive territorial groupings tend to emphasize the absence of choice, distancing seems to belong primarily to an opposing vocabulary of motives. Mutually exclusive territories help solve the problem of order essentially by segregating opponents. Distancing, however, consists of a wide range of spatial signs, some of which may be exploratory, some invitational, and others discouraging in a sequence of progressively more or progressively less intimate stages. Among animals, distancing seems to consist of a series of gestural signs or spatial markings which have conventionalized significance and help define gradations in status relations: grooming, bared teeth, urine markings, and the like. Essentially the same rough definition may be used for distancing among humans, with sufficient allowance for differences in form.

The distinctive feature of distancing, as against territoriality, seems to be that it does not simply divide individuals or groups into mutually exclusive affiliations but defines their associations at discrete points along a continuum. Distancing, then, does identify a range of alternatives from which individuals may advance or retreat with at least some liberty. This sense of liberty or freedom derives at once from the range of choices but also through the obvious necessity for mutual and personal agreement. Perhaps one of the most evident and complex examples of this type is dating or courtship relations in the United States. The United States is notable for the freedom unmarried couples are allowed, and some foreign observers have gone away with the impression that dating is only another word for clandestine sexual exploitation.[21] As most American males know, however, sexual relations, much less sexual exploitation of one's date, are possible only after a great deal of careful navigation. Much of this navigation consists of spatial moves which penetrate further and further into a couple's respective personal space. Since dating relationships in the United States start without any clear assurance of each companion's terminal interest in marriage, seduction, friendship, or entertainment, apprehensions must run high. These apprehensions ought be greatest with a pickup, somewhat less with a blind date, considerably less in a double date, and almost nil with a prostitute or between a couple who have known each other for most of their lives in a small town. The familiar dangers are twofold: making a miscue—failure—or being exploited—deviance. Each member of a couple, then, must read more or less closely the moves of his partner to define both his partner's intentions and his own reactions. These moves include a welter of separate steps which represent choices to be mutually endorsed, rather than a single and fateful sequence of stages: for example, the choice of how far apart to walk, of whether to hold hands, of whether to exclude other dancing partners, and so on. The general progression of these moves seems to hinge on two reasonably well understood patterns. First, there is a tendency to rely more and more exclusively on distancing or nonverbal forms as the nature of cross-sex relations becomes more clearly defined and fateful. This is most evident at the outset of petting and the irretrievable steps which can be taken from there on. What was once a quite voluntary and rather awkwardly formal relationship becomes progressively determinant and terminal.

Second, it seems that there is a general understanding that the human body itself makes up a sort of globe distinguished into center and periphery. The nearer partners advance to each other's equitorial and sexual regions the further one can expect to ad-

21. See Willard Waller, "The Dating and Rating Complex," *American Sociological Review* 2 (October 1937): 727–34) for an overall description of the developing obligations of dating relations.

vance and the more difficult becomes retreat. The general trajectory, then, is aimed toward an early and stabilized relationship.
At every point, however, and especially on the earlier and asexual
ones, there is occasion for calling the entire progression to a halt.
It is this element of mutuality in the dating cycle which preserves
it from indiscriminate sexuality while also retaining a sense of
choice or romanticism.

There have been attempts, of course, to define a singular order
for dating relationships and prescribe for them a unique and final
outcome.[22] But the very nature of such a relationship forbids such
a prescribed pathway, since it would make every dating relationship preliminary to marriage, deny the element of choice or risk
in romantic love, and make too explicit the dangers of rejection
and failure. What we must note instead is the way that dating
relations hone down to a form that is almost exclusively nonverbal
in form (for example, petting) and although at first voluntary,
become progressively fateful. The broader pattern, then, is one
in which dating relations vacillate from one peak of uncertainty
to another while following a secular trend toward routinization.
Such relations must be portrayed as a series of contingencies
which are essentially unknown at the outset but conclude in a variety of outcomes which make exploitation difficult rather than impossible. In the hands of a practiced couple, distancing, rather
than a chaperon, becomes their guide to security.

Parallel to the erotic and unsettled relationship of dating partners, one may detect somewhat the same pattern in the households
of American couples long married and settled in their domiciles.
Whereas the relationship between dating partners is less fixed,
that of husbands and wives is more nearly developed in the brick
and mortar of their dwelling units. Nonetheless the American
household preserves much of the voluntarism, asymmetry, and
staging already mentioned in connection with dating relations.
The living room circumscribes the family's collective character

---

22. For a diligent try, see the booklet by Ann Landers, *Love or Sex:
How to Tell the Difference* (Chicago: Field Enterprises, n.d.). See also
Willard Waller, "Dating and Rating Complex."

but, at the same time, opens the family to outsiders or visitors who can easily manage to get past the front door. The master bedroom is a partial sanctuary for the parents and by name and location is remote from the children's rooms; but on a Sunday morning or stormy night even the sanctity of the couple's connubium can be interrupted by childish pleas or curiosity. The children's rooms are generally smaller, more remote, and until puberty likely to be shared even if the children are of the opposite sex. The kitchen is a feminine world, decorated in that manner, and as nearly the exclusive province of the wife as the garage is that of the husband. The "rec room" is the most fluid of all, since it can be reserved by teenage children and their guests or used by any of the combinations which constitute a family.

At first sight, then, the family household appears to be a collection of territories, but on second thought, each of its portions seems only a membrane which sorts entrants rather than rejecting them altogether. The family is open to the wider community through its living room entrance, although a person who feels that he must remain there—or in the living room itself—will be only a peripheral associate of the family. The neighbor or kinsman who can enter and settle himself in the kitchen has a firmer and more central claim to extended affiliation. Entrance into bedrooms is more nearly restricted to children and marital partners within the same family, although once this barrier is crossed other barriers may become more permeable. Stage in the family cycle, sex, and age can all be associated with the portions of the family domicile to which a person has access. But none of the boundaries of the family household is totally impermeable, and as a matter of routine hospitality, parents, children, neighbors, kinsmen, strangers, peers, and guests are invited to trespass on one another's terrain. And as in dating relations, increased access is negotiated through preliminary exploratory movements and a range of responses.[23]

23. One might note here also that progressive access within the household is also accompanied by an increasing reliance on spatial signs as against verbal ones; e.g., lovemaking between marital partners, the fondling of children, the embracing of relatives, etc.

These examples seem to point up three features of distancing which are important to any society but especially important to modern industrial ones. First, distancing helps individuals preserve a sense of voluntarism or choice. From the point of view of an external observer with complete information, of course, such relations may be predictable and determinant. In large-scale societies which are highly mobile and have a changing role mix, however, the general situation is one of incomplete information among people at the outset of any new relationship. The steps in distancing are ways of disclosing this information and allowing people to make a refined choice of associates. At the same time, this sense of choice in one's associates gives both parties a personal commitment that might not be present in relationships imposed by authoritarian decree.[24] Such a personal commitment is of obvious value where affiliations are not otherwise supported by strong economic interests or extensive guarantees of prolonged reciprocity: for example, dating, the early periods of marriage, gang membership, neighboring in a transient residential area, and so on.

Second, distancing seems to help develop a stable affiliation along a gradient which reaches from complete strangers to extreme intimates. Individuals are not juxtaposed into neatly divided in-group or out-group members but stand at different levels of association. Aggressive displays, then, are appropriate only in a limited range of associations where people can be permanently thought of as strangers or friends. For most other relations, distancing signs must represent levels of positive association where the counter claims of individuals and companions are not mutually exclusive or independent. This, of course, does not mean that distancing never leads to outright conflict and aggression. Where individuals with different cultural backgrounds do not share the

24. Which should not be read to say that all prescribed or imposed affiliations will lack such a personal commitment. Primordial relationships seem to be viewed as "natural" since they are thought to derive from generic impulses which are both personal and social. The proper contrast to be drawn is between those externally imposed and those established through a graduated series of disclosures which have drawn positive responses (e.g., courtship).

same distancing vocabulary, sharp and violent encounters may result from one member's thinking he has been encouraged past a point which the other would deem proper.[25] These instances of aggression, however, generally overstep the bounds of aggressive displays and the normatively acceptable limits of distancing: unlike the aggressive displays which mark territorial boundaries, only one member to the relationship regards them as rightful or routine. Distancing, on the whole, seems calculated to avoid aggression or aggressive displays. Its preliminary stages are themselves ways of forecasting and avoiding aggression rather than of using it as a communicative device in its own right. Aggressive forms of distancing, then, may persist in human groups or institutions which have cast their members into a monolithic dominance hierarchy where one's status is singular and graduated along a scale of inferiors and superiors. This type of dominance hierarchy seems pervasive among social groups of nonhumans. Yet among humans, such a dominance hierarchy seems most restricted to groups where all of one's roles are contained within a single and terminal territorial grouping.[26]

Finally, distancing signals seem especially able to allow people to hint at and move between levels of intimacy without making themselves fatally culpable for their actions. This is evidenced both in the independence of action and reaction and the absence of an explicit verbal translation of nonverbal materials. For example, a peer who invites comradeship by backslapping need not be called to account for his action; without endangering the previous state of their affiliation, he can be dissuaded or encouraged by the direction his companion leans afterward. If necessary, he can plead that it was a joke or act as if he did not know it hap-

25. In fact, rape between couples who are previously acquainted with each other may derive from this sort of systematic difference in their views on what has been "promised." See Amir Menachem, "Patterns of Forceable Rape" in M. L. Clinard and R. Quinney, eds., *Criminal Behavior Systems* (New York: Holt, Rinehart and Winston, 1967), pp. 60–75.

26. Morris Janowitz, *The Military in the Political Development of New Nations* (Chicago: University of Chicago Press, 1964), pp. 31–74; and Erving Goffman, *Asylums: Essays on the Social Situation of Mental Patients and Other Inmates* (Garden City, N.Y.: Doubleday and Co., 1961).

pened. Because there is no authoritative dictionary for translat-
ing nonverbal into verbal behavior, actions of this sort can be
disattended or dismissed as ambiguous events still available for
interpretation.[27] Thus, distancing remains a way of developing
social relations rather than of foreclosing them through overt ad-
missions. Once again, this symbolic form seems to fit into the
requirements of a modern and industrial society where what is
most important is that people find some level at which they can
interact rather than quickly to define one another as total enemies
or unqualified friends.

Conclusions and Observations

In a mechanical overview, distancing and territoriality may seem
to have almost opposing functions and to operate at different
levels of social organization. Distancing seems most prevalent in
face-to-face relations, whereas territoriality seems to exclude such
face-to-face relations. Territoriality seems to separate groups into
opposing camps, whereas distancing provides for a gradation in
more or less positive associations which emphasize choice and
flexibility of affiliations. No doubt such an empirical association
might be found, but the larger context is one in which both territoriality and distancing are responses to common systemic problems: the apprehension of failure and harm. In this respect,
territoriality is only a more drastic solution than the many solutions of distancing. Territoriality seems to occur among individuals where the negative judgmental consequences and the
potential of conflict are greatest, and since unregulated conflict
without quarter is most likely to occur between distinct cultural
groups, territoriality is most likely to separate groups. At lesser
levels of conflict or when the judgmental consequences are not so
grave, distancing provides an avenue of approach between individuals busy at working out the extent of their own interpersonal
affiliations.

27. Which leads one to question the potential danger of a sociology
which would make clear the relationship between verbal and nonverbal
forms of communication.

One way of conceiving of the relationship between distancing and territoriality is to see them as a single dimension in which territoriality is an extreme form of segregation on a scale which extends through a series of relations in which distancing is less and less marked. Such a dimension, however, would not be very useful except to show that the more extreme forms of segregation are associated with the more extreme apprehensions of failure and physical harm. An alternative conception is a series of sieves in which territorial differentiation is the first in a telescoped series which sorts people so the possibility of affiliation minimizes the potential of physical harm and negative judgments. The latter metaphor seems the more appealing because it makes distancing and territoriality coexisting bases of social differentiation whose joint product is to sort people into groups which can get along with one another. It is appealing because all societies continue to use both territoriality and distancing as bases for social differentiation. It is also appealing because the ways in which territoriality and distancing operate are not independent but must be harnessed together to serve different but complementary functions.

The need for such a complex metaphor is especially evident in view of the different forms and functions of territorial groupings. In the simple structure of mutually exclusive territorial groups, spatial segregation occurs primarily between groups, whereas distancing is confined largely to intragroup relations. Beyond this level, however, the exclusiveness of territorial groups tends to be limited, and distancing becomes a more generalized vocabulary for developing social relations along more voluntaristic lines. The ordered combination of territorial groups, for instance, provides a pyramid of territorial identities which allows for cooperation, albeit a pyramid that persists in its opposition to equivalent units. Similarly, the administrative pyramid encompasses a range of territorial groups and makes them the building blocks in large-scale economic, political, and military enterprises.

As territorial groups become less exclusive and more nearly a part of a larger structure, people must rely more on distancing as a means of sorting among a much increased number of people eligible for association and affiliation. Such large populations force on people the necessity to make choices in their affiliations and the exploratory gestures of distancing produce the alternatives among which these choices can be made. Thus, with the decline of exclusiveness of territorial groups, territoriality and distancing become more complementary in their roles of social differentiation.

This, of course, does not mean that there is any simple or mechanical causal relationship between the expansion of territorial groups and the refinement of their distancing vocabulary. It is for functional reasons that the two are related, and this leaves ample room for each to lag behind the other. With the aggregation or enlargement of territorial groups in large cities, emerging nations, or composite populations, the difficulties of sorting among a wider range of associations must be apparent. The development of a shared vocabulary of distancing will not be automatic but takes time, effort, and insight.[28] Similarly, the consolidation of territorial groups into larger structures and the transformation of territorial identities into partial identities or roles, is often something that occurs at the insistence of centralized government or is the result of demographic growth, conquest, or cultural assimilation.

The expansion of territorial groups and distancing vocabularies brings with them a great advance in the number of people one can know, a greater sense of choice in social relations, and the opportunity to participate in large-scale enterprises. Societies able to increase their scale of economic and political organization without sharp strictures on the internal allocation of personnel tend to be dominant in current affairs and likely to be emulated. Yet, to the individual, the choice between atavistic and exclusive territories or the prospect of voluntarism are not unmixed blessings. Small-

28. And this effort is sometimes in the hands of specialists such as writers on etiquette. For example, American writers on etiquette at the turn of the century included ample warnings to young girls not to speak to strangers on the street, not to stand in hotel doorways, and the like. Current books on etiquette leave out such warnings, presumably on the assumption that these elements of distancing are already common knowledge. (Lyn Lofland, "In the Presence of Strangers," [M.A. dissertation, University of Michigan, 1968].)

scale territorial groups have a certain finality and security about them because they prescribe not only one's own membership and identity, but also the reciprocal obligations of others. In this small world, the individual finds security of continuity in his own identity and the near unimpeachable loyalty of a few other people. These attractions, however, are offset by the narrow and parochial extent of his associations, by the routinization of his opposition to other territorial groups, and by the small scale of human enterprises.

The prospect of voluntarism as expressed in distancing vocabularies is also counterweighted by a negotiated social world in which there is little that is constant or dependable and a persisting sense of danger of betrayal or defection. The singular feature of relations based on distancing is that one must make a first move without complete foreknowledge of someone's response, without a guarantee of his continued loyalty and, in fact, no strong means of making one's alters accountable for what they hint at rather than what they say. When distancing becomes the prime nonverbal way of identifying levels of intimacy, fraud, rather than violence, becomes the main item of concern.[29]

This expansion of distancing relations, along with the whole social order that accompanies them, brings forward a great apprehension of personal betrayal and deception which contrast sharply with the polite appearance of social relations. It is the quiet terror of the cocktail party rather than that of outright physical combat which troubles the sophisticated or advanced segments of such a complex society. This concern can be expected to take a number of different courses. One may be the increasing concern of social scientists with the intricacies and innuendos buried in the negotiations of face-to-face relations in everyday life.[30] A similar way

29. In a different context, Sorel remarks on how fraud replaces violence, in modern societies (*Reflections on Violence,* trans. T. E. Hulme [London: George Unwin, 1915]).

30. For examples, see Erving Goffman, "On Face Work," in Goffman, *Interaction Ritual,* pp. 5–45; Harold Garfinkle, *Studies in Ethnomethodology* (Englewood Cliffs, N.J.: Prentice-Hall, 1967); and Aaron Cicourel, *Method and Measurement in Sociology* (New York: The Free Press of Glencoe, 1964).

of grappling with these personal issues may be in a surge of novels which deal with the manipulative or conspiratorial aspects of face-to-face relations.[31] A further development along the same lines seems to be a loud outcry for community, sincerity, and credibility.

Understandably then, we must expect to find in complex societies a certain nostalgia for times past when territorial groups were sure and fateful in their associations. This nostalgia is present in the ideological overburden in the works of Ardrey, Lorenz, and Morris. Such a romantic backward look can survive in large part because it need not confront any concrete examples in modern societies. The idea of the small, tightly knit, ascribed community can remain an uncontested ideal, not much resembling any actual communities, but powerfully attractive to those heavily burdened by the continuous necessity to negotiate interpersonal relations.[32]

The general direction of large-scale and dominant modern societies, however, seems fixed. Ascribed territorial groups will be expanded to the point that they are very large, sometimes coinciding with the boundaries of the nation itself. The question which remains, then, is how small-scale territorial groups and their functions will survive in a modified form. Presumably the guarantees of reciprocity and security from victimization built into territorial groups are still essential or comforting conditions for the social order. This probably means a considerable reconceptualization of the territorial solidarities which span the distance between face-to-face groups and terminal societies. Somehow, these groups must be able to adjust to voluntaristic participation, to achieve recognition or legitimacy in the wider society and, above all, to develop new alliance structures so that various levels of social solidarity short of nationalism can be expressed. Jano-

31. Which may reach their peak in the fraudulent and deceptive characters included in Ian Fleming's thrillers. A self-conscious commentary on this literary type is carried out in Eric Ambler's *To Catch a Spy* (New York: Antheneum, 1965), pp. 12–13. Needless to say, Goffman has anticipated this potential of heroic treachery and has written a book on its strategies: *Strategic Interaction* (Philadelphia: University of Pennsylvania Press, 1969).

32. For a different approach to the same problem see Erik Fromm, *Escape from Freedom* (New York: Farrar and Rinehart, 1941).

witz's "community of limited liability" is a sort of floor-level reconstruction in this direction, although it is presently conceived
of as only appropriate to the most rudimentary levels of community organization.[33] The elements included in the community of
limited liability—its voluntarism, its responsiveness to the wider
community, and its degree of self-conscious purpose—are capable
of elaboration, and it is through the elaboration of these civil
ties that one may expect new territorial solidarities to develop.
This seems a far cry from the parochial conservatism which was
evident in the vocabulary used to describe natural areas and which
justified territorial groups as a primordial solidarity. The elaboration of these civil ties among territorial groups depends also on a
new vocabulary which is not only evocative but also more realistic
in terms of how it can persuade people to believe that their collective fates can be pursued by territorial constructs which are more
artificial or contrived than those which have received loyalty in
the past. This will require a new model of how territorial groups
can be fitted into modern societies like that of the United States.
It will probably also require a new model of human nature itself
in which the emphasis is shifted from the persistence of primordial
loyalties to an equal emphasis on man's capability to honor contractual agreements.

Nonetheless, there is nostalgia for a past in which interpersonal
relations and territorial solidarities were more fixed because they
were thought to be outside the realm of human choice. This
nostalgia has given rise to a resurgence of primordial groups and
at least a loud outcry on the part of new separatists. These developments are paralleled by an intellectual analysis of territorial
groups which reasserts the limits of human nature to expand
loyalties past local and parochial groups.[34] This nostalgia for the
past and for a more permanent sense of community and interpersonal loyalty is expectable where large numbers of people
throughout the world are being urged out of their local confines

33. Morris Janowitz, *The Community Press in an Urban Setting: The
Social Elements of Urbanism* (Chicago: University of Chicago Press,
1967).
34. For further discussion of this intellectual analysis, see chap. 5.

and for the first time included in mass society.[35] Social analysis of this nostalgia and the movements growing out of it, however, need not follow in its steps and reaffirm the inalterable character of small-scale localized collectives. The functions of territoriality and distancing in human societies are to preserve people from the prospects of insult and injury while introducing accountability into interpersonal negotiations. As the boundaries of social groups change or expand, new forms of territoriality and distancing are required to serve these functions. The general drift of modern societies seems to be toward a more voluntaristic and contractual relationship among territorial groups and a greater reliance on personal accountability in interpersonal relations which involve distancing. There are those who shrink from such an increase in personal responsibility, those who simply do not believe in the capacity of others to honor these responsibilities, and those who are ignorant of how to manage the negotiations in so flexible a social world. Their responses will be very important in determining how nearly territoriality and distancing lose their primordial trappings and come to be seen as a part of the civil order. To understand their impact, however, we cannot accept their own view that territoriality or distancing are outside the realm of human manipulation.

35. See Edward Shils, "The Theory of Mass Society," in *Selected Essays by Edward Shils*, Center for Social Organization Studies, Department of Sociology, University of Chicago, 1970, pp. 15–36.

8. Vigilante Peer Groups and the Defended Neighborhood

Inquirers of adolescent street-corner gangs have placed great importance on economic conditions,[1] cultural conflict,[2] social disorganization,[3] and especially, variants of the broken family.[4] One need not deny the utility of these lines of inquiry to see their limitations. The adolescent street-corner gang is found almost exclusively in the lower income slum communities of our large cities and scarcely occurs elsewhere in its classic form as a named group with a reputation for fighting and other types of predatory behavior.[5] Such a close association between type of community and this particular kind of adolescent peer group suggests that both the adolescent street-corner gang and its correlates belong to a larger pattern in which a number of institutions have under-

1. Robert K. Merton, "Social Structure and Anomie," *Social Theory and Social Structure* (Glencoe, Ill.: Free Press, 1957), pp. 131–60.

2. Clifford R. Shaw and Henry D. McKay, *Juvenile Delinquency and Urban Areas* (Chicago: University of Chicago Press, 1942); and Solomon Kobrin, "The Conflict of Values in Delinquency Areas," *American Sociological Review* 16 (1951): 653–61.

3. For a review of this literature see Daniel Glaser, "Social Disorganization and Delinquent Subcultures," in Herbert C. Quay ed., *Juvenile Delinquency: Research and Theory* (Princeton, N.J.: Van Nostrand, 1965).

4. W. B. Miller, "Lower Class Culture as a Generating Milieu of Gang Delinquency," *Journal of Social Issues* 14 (1958): 5–19; W. B. Miller and W. C. Kvarceus, *Delinquent Behavior: Culture and the Individual* (Washington, D.C.: National Education Association, 1959); U.S. Department of Labor, *The Negro Family*, prepared for the Office of Policy Planning and Research by Patrick Moynihan (Washington, D.C.: Government Printing Office, 1965); Hyman Rodman and Paul Grams, "Juvenile Delinquency and the Family: A Review and Discussion," *Task Force Report: Juvenile Delinquency and Youth Crime* (Washington, D.C.: Government Printing Office, 1967), pp. 188–221; and Abram Kardiner and Lionel Ovesey, *The Mark of Oppression: A Psychological Study of the American Negro* (New York: Norton, 1951).

5. Louis Wirth, *On Cities and Social Life: Selected Papers*, ed. Albert J. Reiss, Jr. (Chicago: University of Chicago Press, 1964); and Frederick Thrasher, *The Gang* (Chicago: University of Chicago Press, 1927).

gone adjustments to general conditions characteristic of inner city slums.

The purpose of this chapter is to point out some of the mutual adjustments which the adolescent peer group and associated institutions make in coming to grips with an inner city slum neighborhood. This is done primarily through my findings on adjacent black, Italian, Puerto Rican, and Mexican inner city neighborhoods in Chicago during the period 1962–65. Variants in streetcorner gangs, family type, voluntary associations, and cross-sex relations seem to make up a single complex which, in large part, could be traced to the inadequacy of formal bodies of social control under conditions of great suspicion and actual danger. In all four communities the protection of property and day-to-day security had become largely local community responsibilities. Like early settlers on the American frontier, residents in the four slum neighborhoods were forced to take on themselves some or all of the functions of the police, the courts, and civil adjudicators. As with frontiersmen, their behavior became that of vigilantes dispensing homemade justice and exercising grass roots police power.

In the four neighborhoods studied here, the inadequacy of formal bodies of social control tended to induce local males, especially adolescent males, into the role of an informal police power. In turn, this required a considerable adjustment in the structure of a number of families; it gave a definite character to cross-sex relations; and it modified the relative importance of local voluntary associations. Each ethnic neighborhood, however, made these adjustments somewhat differently, partly because of the size of each community, but also because each had had a longer or shorter time to complete these adjustments. Yet, in all cases somewhat the same generic process seemed to be taking place, and the residents themselves regarded their communities as something incomplete or short of what they would ideally prefer.

My own observations on these ethnic neighborhoods are drawn from a three-year period of field work, much of which has been reported elsewhere.[6] The aim of this chapter is to elaborate some

6. Gerald D. Suttles, *The Social Order of the Slum* (Chicago: University of Chicago Press, 1968).

of the findings of this earlier work and to dissuade any previous
readers from the view that the social order of the slum is an inevitable societal formation because of its ethnic or lower socioeconomic composition alone. In a very real sense, many of our
slum communities in large cities come to approximate warrior
societies because they must perform so much of their own policing
and other functions which are ostensibly the responsibility of
public institutions.[7] The failure of these public institutions has
left the adolescent peer group with a number of unauthorized
functions, primarily in the areas of social control and socialization.
No one, least of all slum residents, is very happy over the vigilante
solution which the street-corner gangs or their adult counterparts
provide. Nor are people, slum residents included, very satisfied
with a number of other characteristics of slum neighborhoods:
their high rates of marital dissolution, their emphasis on sex segregation, and their lack of self-improvement through voluntary
associations. Yet, as I shall argue, a different pattern seems impossible unless public institutions such as the schools and the
police can adequately perform the tasks which remain the unauthorized charge of the vigilante adolescent gang.

The Lawlessness of American Cities

The lawlessness of American cities is notorious, and for good reason. No nation so wealthy and so industrially advanced has such
high crime rates and such a regularity in the practice of fraud and
deception. In part, the lawlessness of the country derives from its
ethnic, regional, and economic pluralism. Americans share among
themselves all the distrust and suspicions which have driven

7. The term *warrior societies* is used purposefully here for there is some
comparative merit in the concept for analyzing communities which have
strong peer associations and a reduced family structure. The Nyar and the
kibbutz are the most celebrated cases in studies of the universality of the
family. Both communities lack very distinct nuclear families and both
make heavy military requirements of the young men. See Melford Spiro,
"Is the Family Universal: The Israeli Case"; and Kathleen Gough, "Is
the Family Universal: The Nyar Case," both republished in Norman W.
Bell and Ezra F. Vogel, eds., *A Modern Introduction to the Family* (Glencoe, Ill.: Free Press, 1960), pp. 64–92.

several European nations to war and to adopt far more restrictive immigration policies than would be acceptable to rabid isolationists in the United States. Americans who differ in ethnicity and wealth are literally so frightened of one another that they carry on a sort of slow-paced, internecine war with one another, triple bolting their doors, buying guns by the carload, and frantically searching for a safe neighborhood or suburb in which to live and bring up their children.

Americans come by this source of lawlessness honestly, for they have inherited much of it from the traditional antagonism and ethnocentrism which the European immigrants brought with them. The United States has added to its lawlessness by a series of heavily loaded stereotypes which presume that poverty and even a low income is such an intolerable condition that disadvantaged people will resort to any means to better their personal situation. The American Dream is largely a dream of pecuniary success without reputable alternatives for those who fail to reach a fairly ample level of economic security. For those of us who believe in the American Dream—or at least those of us who believe that others believe in it—there must exist the lurking suspicion that the poor are wholly dissatisfied and always just at the brink of becoming total opportunists. As in Merton's classical article, there is the assumption that greed, violence, and theft have simple and direct explanations: those who have nothing will simply take it however they can get it.[8]

The implications of such a belief must have frightening consequences for low income people in the United States, for they must live in close proximity to one another and deal with each other in additional realms of life as well. When these stereotypes of low income people are joined to ethnic differences and these to racial differences, the result is an extremely defensive posture on the part of both individuals and ethnic neighborhoods. People lock their doors, fear to walk on the streets, stockpile weapons, and are quick to assume that a good offense is the best defense. To a large extent this belief is self-fulfilling. It is fairly easy to steal

8. Merton, "Social Structure," pp. 131–60.

from or molest people in these neighborhoods simply because the residents frequently assume that their victims are not crowning examples of virtue themselves. Our economic, ethnic, and racial stereotypes give even the worst of us an easy conscience.

Such broad cultural definitions mean that there is a remarkably large potential for violence and property loss in the slums of our large cities. Balanced against this is the weakness and slow development of law-making and law-enforcement bodies in the United States. The general population of the United States has never favored a consolidation of its many police forces because of a widespread fear that the government would turn the country into a police state. This belief has probably been cultivated further by business elites who preferred to do business with very little police supervision.[9] These same elites have had a similar influence on the development of our courts and legislative bodies so that the law is often poorly defined or interpreted in courts which are so crowded they must hand out "mass justice" to the masses if not to the elites.[10]

The result has been a police force which is inadequately manned, which has low prestige, and which is so angry at the overcrowded courts that it frequently appoints itself judge and jury. This reaction has helped erode confidence in the police, but the practice of subordinating the police to serve special interests has all but undermined their role in some slum communities. Sometimes police practices are blatant, as when they stop low income Americans from entering neighborhoods other than their own, stop and frisk blacks on the presumption that they are "always up to something," or simply sweep low income neighborhoods to find every wrongdoer at large. Often the police protect property and life in the better-off sections of the city. In inner city slums they are more likely to look for people who are presumed a threat to property and life. This partiality in the policies of our police has left many low income residents in the large

9. David Bordua, ed., *The Police* (New York: John Wiley, 1967).
10. The President's Commission on Law Enforcement and Administration of Justice, Task Force Reports, *The Police and the Courts* (Washington, D.C.: Government Printing Office, 1967).

cities with little or no faith in police protection and with a tendency to take the law into their own hands.

Within this general situation, the public schools have done little to remedy the situation—either by developing a new set of cultural stereotypes or by socializing youngsters into a realistic assessment of life opportunities and the means for obtaining them. A vast number of Americans, especially low income ones, grow up in families and schools which share a public morality that has little descriptive or instrumental merit. In many families with an immigrant or rural background, traditional forms of total obedience to the family are taught along with a complete proscription of dating relations and discussions of sex. In turn, traditional heroes are spoken of reverently as if they were inhumanly moral, while contemporary politicians and public authorities are often assumed to be wholly corruptible.[11] Children in the entire society, and especially those in ethnic slums, have a difficult time getting some grasp of just what is proper moral conduct and how nearly people actually subscribe to it. The morality held up by precept in the schools and the family often seems like a quaint extract from one of Henry James's novels. The morality held up by example in the schools, in the family, or on the streets is exactly what drove James himself to live in England.

The result, at least in the slum communities I observed, was a sort of underground intelligence run by the adolescent peer groups themselves. In large part these groups were devoted to iconoclasm: the systematic destruction of images or morality and their replacement with "gutter knowledge." Although this gutter knowledge did not promote among them high aspirations for public service, it did free them from a naïve moralism and allow them to seek more realistic careers and develop a more differentiated concept of how people actually behave. Doubtless such a massive underground morality erodes commitment to broad collectivities and fosters cynicism and opportunism. It is another source of our lawlessness and general belief that the law and public morality are noble gestures to be honored but not obeyed.

11. Arnold Rose, *The Power Structure* (New York: Oxford University Press, 1967), pp. 456–82.

The schools do little to correct this either by providing a more realistic version of how people behave or by critically examining the social consequences of alternative courses of action. The morality most schools teach is "Dick and Jane" morality, and so long as this is taught we must expect children to search for a non-fictional account among themselves. The fact that they resort to situational ethics exacerbates the problems of a society noted for its lawlessness and, as I wish to argue here, gives the vigilante adolescent gang a new lease on life.

Variants in Local Gangs

The four ethnic neighborhoods which I studied lay adjacent to one another and were located on the Near West Side of Chicago. About twenty thousand people lived in the area, falling into four rather distinct ethnic groups: blacks, Puerto Ricans, Italians, and Mexicans. The residents shared a single collective representation for the entire area, but each ethnic group made up a distinct residential entity which was also acknowledged by the residents. A fuller report on the population is available elsewhere[12] and only the following will be essential to this analysis. The Puerto Ricans made up only a small proportion of the population, numbering about eleven hundred. The Italians were the largest group (eight thousand or 40 percent) and had lived there the longest of any of the ethnic groups. The Mexicans and the blacks made up respectively about 30 and 25 percent of the population. All the groups were relatively poor, although the Italians were somewhat better off than the others. The area was both officially and unofficially regarded as a slum, and this definition was the basis for the clearance of most of it in subsequent years. The area has had an enduring reputation for juvenile gangs and organized crime, including among its alumni Frank "the Enforcer" Nitti and the "Forty Gang."

In each of these ethnic neighborhoods the association of male peers was a frequent and prominent occurrence. Judging from

12. Suttles, *Social Order.*

my own calculations, roughly half of the male adolescents in the
total population eventually worked their way through a named
street-corner group which is accurately described as a gang. Many
more, of course, belonged to unnamed and unnoticed groups
which "hung" on the sidewalks but never achieved a reputation
and any publicly ackowledged identity.

Among the Italian male adolescents there were twelve gangs
which were quite stable in their organization, and some of them
possessed names which are reputed to have endured in the
neighborhood for over twenty years. Five of these groups were
arrayed in two hierarchies indicated by prefixes (Junior, Senior,
Midget) to their names. All of these groups claimed a reputation
for fighting, and stories of old battles were a frequent source of
conversational entertainment. Relations among the Italian gangs,
however, were relatively peaceful and could better be described as
rivalry than as conflict. Fights sometimes occurred among the
Italian boys, but they were not usually referred to as gang
fights, and ordinarily the two individuals involved were allowed
to settle it among themselves. Relations outside the local Italian
neighborhood were treated quite differently, for the slightest altercation was referred to as a gang fight. In fact, however, full-scale
gang fights were almost nonexistent. The frequent pattern was
one where one or a few Italian boys would get into difficulty with
some others from another neighborhood, sometimes the local
black, Mexican, or Puerto Rican boys but also boys from a large
number of surrounding neighborhoods of which a few were also
Italian. Afterward there would be a great deal of talk and threats
of a gang war. Sometimes this might grow to the point that groups
of two or three boys from different neighborhoods would jump
one another after some unforeseen encounter. It was these altercations which later formed the bases for most stories about gang
fights. Otherwise, there was much boasting about fighting ability
and a very careful avoidance of going into other neighborhoods
at times when these boasts might be tested.

The Mexican boys possessed a structure of adolescent gangs
which was remarkably similar to that of the Italians. The twelve
groups they manned were quite stable and equally intent on

building a reputation for fighting and toughness. Six of the twelve gangs were formally allied in three age-graded hierarchies, and some of the older groups boasted a predecessor with the same name. Relations among the Mexican gangs were those of rivals, and while there was an occasional fight, it did not mount into stories or rumors of a gang fight. As in the Italian gangs, difficulties with boys from adjacent neighborhoods were seen as qualitatively different, and almost any type of altercation would initiate a round of rumors about the impending gang fight. These fights seldom took place, but the pattern of jumping boys from adjacent neighborhoods was as common as among the Italian boys. Lest these altercations be interpreted as examples of interethnic hostility, it should be pointed out that both the Mexican and the Italian gangs seemed to have their greatest difficulty with nearby neighborhoods which were of the same ethnicity.

Among the black adolescent males much the same structure of peer groups prevailed. Seven named gangs were known throughout the neighborhood, and two of these were formally allied in an age hierarchy. Rivalry among these groups was strongly expressed but fell short of outright conflict in the form of gang fights and colorful recollections of past gang fights or rumors of future ones.

Like the Mexican and Italian gangs, the black gangs were relatively stable in their membership and, once established, tended to endure for several years. By the time the members of the black gangs reached late adolescence or as some of their members began to get past high school age, however, their gangs began to break up. Both the Mexican and the Italian gangs showed greater durability, sometimes surviving into the early adulthood of the members or providing the source of recruitment into adult groups. With the decline and disappearance of one of the black gangs, however, others seemed to be emerging to take its place.[13]

The Puerto Rican boys represented a considerable exception because they lacked any street-corner group during the period 1962–64 before acquiring one in 1965. The way this occurred,

13. Ibid., see pages 131–37 for further discussion.

however, was especially instructive because it seemed to illustrate the generic basis for all the other gangs. Until 1965 the Puerto Ricans were a small, isolated enclave numbering no more than eleven hundred people. From the point of view of the local Mexicans, blacks, and Italians, the Puerto Rican boys were simply too small in number to present any kind of threat. Similarly, the Puerto Rican community itself was so small that practically everyone was on a first-name basis with everyone else, and group identities were simply useless as a way of referring to anyone. This was clearly evident on several occasions when a number of Puerto Rican boys proclaimed themselves a gang and, in succession, took up a series of ferocious names (for example, the Young Savages). None of these names stuck because the other residents simply laughed them off as pretentious fantasies on the part of children they already knew. In 1965, however, many of the local Puerto Rican youngsters came into conflict with others in the same age group in an adjacent Puerto Rican neighborhood. The main bone of contention was access to a YMCA located in the nearby neighborhood and previously claimed almost exclusively by Puerto Ricans from that area. At the time, social workers attempted to encourage broader usage of the YMCA by drawing in the youngsters from the second Puerto Rican neighborhood. This resulted in a great number of threats and an occasional fight, although nothing quite comparable to the movie version of a gang fight. It also resulted in the local Puerto Rican boys taking on a name and gaining considerable notoriety. This name stuck and the group retained a stable membership. It also continued an unremitting verbal war with gangs from adjacent neighborhoods. As in the Mexican, Italian, and black gangs, there was more talk than action, but an occasional boy got jumped to give credence to the new structure which had developed.

With the emergence of the first Puerto Rican gang, it became even more evident to me that the most important function of the local adolescent gangs was that of territorial defense. Gang fights and the language of group conflict was used exclusively to represent altercations between neighborhoods. Fights among boys within each ethnic neighborhood occurred, but they were perceived as individualized contests between two boys who were left to settle the matter among themselves while their fellow peers looked on as unintended referees. The merciless pattern of jumping boys and using almost any means to retaliate against them was restricted primarily to conflict with boys from another neighborhood. Rivalry prevailed among the gangs within a neighborhood, but with other neighborhoods there existed a declared war of avoidance and threat. Clearly the adolescent gang and its symbolism were activated and became meaningful only in interneighborhood conflict.

This interpretation was not novel, at least to the boys who were members of each gang. They explained simply that they were bound together to protect themselves and their neighborhood from gangs in adjacent neighborhoods. They saw this as a necessity because of the assumed unity of adjacent residential groups and the well-publicized disrepute of each of these neighborhoods. In this judgment they were well supported by corroborating opinion as well as the available evidence. Invariably the mass media portrayed the entire section of town as ridden with crime, violence, and danger. Popular stereotypes were only a little more specific, and each neighborhood as well as all those nearby was known to include at least one prominent gang with a reputation for violence and exploitation. The people in each of these neighborhoods bore all the usual signs of poverty or low income: cheap clothing, aging homes, and uncleaned streets. So far as the boys were concerned they stood as a sort of permanent posse sworn to defend and avenge themselves against nearby groups obviously untrustworthy.

In this respect the boys were not altogether unsuccessful. As the boys gathered together, they barricaded the roads from adjacent neighborhoods and created an island of relative peace. This was achieved as much by their own avoidance and fear of other neighborhoods as by their active retribution against "invaders." The security of each neighborhood was also achieved by the circumspection which outsiders, adult and adolescent, felt necessary to observe in moving from one neighborhood to another. Pedestrian traffic was almost totally limited to the daylight hours

or the better-patrolled and lighted streets. Within each neighborhood, then, the problem of anonymity was lessened, and those
who met on the streets frequently knew or knew of one another.
To a large extent, the residents' fears centered on young males
from adjacent neighborhoods who were directly opposed by the
local gangs.

The surveillance provided by the gangs was of course limited.
It excluded adults considered dangerous to the neighborhood, but
indeed the area was relatively free of burglaries and robberies as
compared to some other areas of the city with a less structured
pattern of turfs and long-term claimants. The Italian adults, noted
for their connections with the Mafia, or as it was known locally,
the Outfit, provided an additional level of control and surveillance.
The protection the local gangs provided, then, was widely distributed among the adults and youths. It was not entirely orderly
and it diverged highly from what we would consider fair or hu-
mane methods of protecting life and property. Certainly their
tactics fell short of what we would support as an ideal for the
police force. The young gangs and their adult counterparts,
however, were comparatively effective, although their long-range
consequence may have been to help perpetuate the ethnic opposition and mutual mistrust that prevailed.

By contrast, the city police seemed relatively helpless in dealing
with the vast potential for deviance which existed throughout the
West Side of Chicago. Subsequent riots in large parts of the area
have dramatically demonstrated this, but in 1962–65, it was
already evident. A relatively large volume of unsolved property
crimes has long characterized the area, and in many instances
people did not even call the police in an effort to recover stolen
articles. The police were obviously undermanned and could
scarcely provide the level of surveillance necessary. As a result
the police tended to compromise due process by harrassing
suspected offenders and by sweeps aimed to intimidate potential
offenders. Resentment of the courts was common among the
police and some of them settled for "sidewalk justice," especially
when dealing with juveniles. In the time available to police, attention to the complaints of victims was sacrificed in order to pursue

the immediate problem of patrol work. In addition, the presence of organized crime in sections of the area had resulted in the corruption of some policemen and a general lack of confidence in their integrity.

Taken together, the inadequacies of the police were so great that one might almost expect the residents to appreciate the social control provided by the gangs. In fact, some of the adult residents did voice this judgment, especially the Italians. When asked about the dangers posed by other neighborhoods, many of the Italians would point out that "the kids around here can handle any trouble makers."[14] Furthermore, the Italian adults seldom voiced unequivocal condemnation of the local Italian gangs but in general saw them as a natural and reasonable form of adolescent association. As I shall stress later, this was probably due to the long-term development of the Italian neighborhood and the personal experience of many of the Italian men who had belonged to similar groups in the past. But the Mexicans and Puerto Ricans were also reserved and equivocal in their evaluation of their local gangs. Although I never heard of one of them encouraging membership on the part of their children, they generally did not discourage it either. Only some black mothers were very strongly opposed to their sons' belonging to street-corner gangs, and they were also the most consistent in referring to these groups as gangs. The Mexican, Italian, and Puerto Rican adults generally spoke of clubs or SAC's (Social Athletic Clubs), although they continued to use the term *gangs* to describe groups from neighborhoods other than their own. Some of the reasons for these differences between ethnic groups should be clearer after we look at intergenerational relations.

14. A humorous example of how some adults are aware of adolescents' responsibilities for territorial defense occurred when the recent Democratic convention was held in Bridgeport, an old inner city neighborhood in Chicago. A newspaper reporter asked some of the residents if they were afraid that the Yippies would come into the neighborhood and endanger it. The residents said, "No," and explained, "the kids around here are pretty tough. They'll keep them out." (*Sun Times*, 25 August 1968). Several thousand federal and state troops had been brought into the area to protect it, but the residents were still depending on their kids.

Intergenerational Relations

Originally the area occupied by all four of these ethnic groups had been settled primarily by Italians. Their dominance in the area dated from at least the late 1920s, and only gradually had the Mexicans, Puerto Ricans, and blacks come to take over about two-thirds of the area. As a result, many of the older Italian men had grown up in the area or one very much like it. In the course of this time, quite a few had belonged to street-corner gangs similar to those to which their sons currently belonged. Among the adults, the residue of these old street-corner gang memberships was preserved in several (fourteen) store-front SAC's. In many respects these groups were like those of Italian youngsters except that the adult males had retreated from the streets and made no overt or pronounced claims for their fighting powers. In my observation, most of the time of these adult groups was spent in talking, playing cards, gambling, or drinking beer.

In addition to their membership in these Social Athletic Clubs, many of the Italian males were reputed to belong to the Outfit. A few of the local Italian adults were connected with organized crime, and this gave to their groups as well as to adult males in general an image of subterranean power which few people were willing to question or contest. Accordingly, the Italian boys, as well as the Mexican, Puerto Rican, and black ones, tended to behave rather gingerly when in the presence of their Italian male elders. Rumor had it that many of the Italian males had ready access to professional "skullers" and could carry out heavy-handed retaliation against anyone who challenged their authority or dignity. This was not altogether untrue, and I recall one black teenage boy who, after trying to extort some money from an Italian shopkeeper, went into hiding following the appearance of two "Italian looking men in dark hats and suits" asking about him in the neighborhood. It is doubtful that many of the local Italian males had connections equivalent to those of the shop-keeper, but this was not a question that many of the local gangs or adolescents cared to pursue to any great length. Instead, the usual practice was to show deference to the Italian male adults, and on the streets it was not uncommon to see individual Italian men upbraid an Italian boy without any hesitation or fear.

The reputation of the Italian males for power and prestige was enhanced by the widespread assumption that any one of them was likely to have important political connections with the West Side Bloc. The West Side Bloc was a group of elected politicians, mostly Italian, who controlled considerable patronage and were reputed to have direct ties with the Outfit. Whatever the veracity of this imagery, the local Italian males were able to stand in the shadow of the West Side Bloc, and it gave to each of them a hint of being someone able to do a favor or help find one's way into "high places." For this reason, as well as the others already mentioned, they were shown due respect not only by the local teenagers but by other adults.

The adults in the remaining ethnic neighborhoods possessed nothing like the Italians' SAC's, Outfit, or West Side Bloc, and this difference was apparent in the deference youngsters showed in their encounters with adults. What was most evident was a fine gradation in intergenerational respect relations depending on how nearly the adult males in each ethnic neighborhood had approximated the status achieved by the Italian males. Next to the Italians, the Mexicans were the oldest settlers in the area, having first started to invade it in the 1930s. Many of the adults had belonged to adolescent gangs when they were young, and by the 1960s the Mexican men had established one adult SAC—although this was soon disrupted by urban renewal which tore down their storefront. Nonetheless, a few of the Mexican adult males had outstanding reputations as veteran street fighters, and several were able to claim close association with some of the Italian SAC's and the Outfit. A very few were members of the Italian SAC's. In addition, some Mexican adults were reputed to be lower-echelon members in the Outfit, and by 1965 the local political organization picked an Italian candidate for alderman who had a name which sounded very Mexican. Over time, the Mexican men had established themselves as regular patrons in a few local taverns and, even without the benefit of a corporate identity, had managed to give an impression of considerable unity and a capacity to enlist their peers in any assault on their dignity or authority.

If the adolescent Mexican boys did not show strong respect for their male elders, they certainly avoided any contest over whether or not respect was due. The Mexican men followed a similar pattern, and it was not uncommon to see even sons and fathers pass each other on the streets without acknowledging each other's presence. This pattern seemed to follow traditional Mexican intergenerational norms, but it was also buttressed by a self-consciousness of the dangers of taking liberties with one another. As the Mexican boys put it, "We just don't fuck with them older studs."

The Puerto Ricans were relative newcomers to the area, having first come there in the early 1950s. They remained a very small community, concentrated for the most part on two streets. Within this rather confined population and area, intragenerational relations achieved a sort of high-decible familiarity. In turn, intergenerational relations were often bridged by an awareness of one another's first name or parallel acquaintanceship between two generations within the same family. Thus, whereas age groups and generations were sharply distinguished, indirect knowledge through a parent or through a child was almost universal. Intergenerational relations then tended to be less conflictual and more individualistic than in some of the other ethnic neighborhoods, and it was easy for adults to "get to" adolescents through a parent or relative. Accordingly, adolescents tended to be rather respectful of their elders lest word of their ill behavior reach their parents' ears.

Like the Puerto Ricans, the blacks had entered the area in the early 1950s and were relative newcomers. Doubtless some of the older black men had belonged to street-corner groups, but no vestige of this remained either in neighborhood gossip or in the claims of the casual gatherings of black men on the streets. The prevailing stereotype among the black adolescent boys was that the black men were all "country," rustics who were unfamiliar with urban ways and lacking in "street knowledge." The local black men were in no position to alter this stereotype. The discriminatory practices of local landlords was so effective that none of the black groups, adolescent or adult, was able to rent a storefront after the manner of the Italian SAC's. The local blacks could comfortably frequent only one local bar, and this had the character of a night club which attracted people from all over town. According to local assumption, the blacks were totally excluded from the Outfit and the West Side Bloc. Although this was not quite true, it was certainly as true as the broader assumption that all the Italians had first-hand connections in these groups. The general tendency was for the adolescent males simply to dismiss their male elders as inconsequential and refer to them as "nothing" or "nobodies." In turn, black men and women showed every sign of being frightened and intimidated by the local adolescent gangs. Many of the adult blacks, especially the women, were quick to condemn the adolescent groups as gangs and complained of their aggressiveness. Adults not only hesitated to try to control the behavior of these adolescent gangs but also would occasionally go so far as to cross the street when they saw them on the sidewalk.

Intergenerational relations in all four neighborhoods can be seen as an expression of the actual and assumed capacities for corporate action on the part of age grades. At one extreme, the Italian men had assumed numerous claims to power and status and clearly dominated the age grades younger than themselves. Just the reverse was true of the blacks. The Mexican adult males were intermediate, and the Puerto Rican community was so small that personal relations precluded the development of corporate age groups. This pattern of intergenerational relations was paralleled by a similar gradation in the power expressed in adolescent cross-sex relations.

Cross-Sex Relations

In all four of these ethnic neighborhoods, adolescent cross-sex relations differed from the stereotypic pattern attributed to American youth. The most general pattern was one where associations were restricted primarily to the members of one's own sex group. This tended to preclude individualized dating, and both boys and girls tended to move about their neighborhood in groups of the same sex rather than individually. Ordinarily, parents thought their daughters loose if they deviated from this pattern, and the local boys were quick to interpret individualized attention on the part of a girl as "getting serious" or being an "easy lay."

Beyond this very general pattern, cross-sex relations were quite different in each ethnic neighborhood. Among the Italians there were no named girls' groups, and in general young girls steered clear of the boys lest they be compromised.[15] The boys practiced equal avoidance lest they be taken as having overly serious intentions, unless the girl had gone so far as to be considered an "easy lay." Italian parental guidance on this issue was quite firm. Before leaving the house, girls were asked which girl friend they were going with, and if a girl showed much attention to a particular boy, relatives were quick to tease her. In the view of both the local Italian boys and their parents, girls who joined named (debette) groups were being so forward as to invite sexual attention. The local Italian gangs themselves regarded the girls as so inferior to them that they ridiculed any attempt of the girls to claim a corporate identity. In turn, girls who attempted to join groups or associate themselves with some of the boys' gangs were subject not only to ridicule but to outright physical abuse. In the eyes of the local Italians, this sort of treatment was inevitable if not altogether desirable, and it seemed the appropriate reaction in a community where men were noted for their exercise of unvarnished power.

Among the Mexicans, cross-sex relations were somewhat more equalitarian, and the Mexican girls possessed four named street-corner groups of their own. Each of these groups, however, was explicitly affiliated with a boys' group and expressed this in joint names with feminine suffixes. The girls regarded the boys' group as their protector, and in turn the boys referred to them quite explicitly as "our girls." Although the association between

15. For a similar observation see William Foote Whyte, *Street Corner Society* (Chicago: University of Chicago Press, 1943).

these male and female groupings was quite firm and durable, it did
not necessarily extend to a pairing off of couples. The girls seemed
quite ready to hover in the protective shadow of the boys' groups,
and although they were not as confined to the home or to all-
female company as were the Italian girls, there was little doubt
of their subordinate status.

For reasons which may already be obvious, the teenage Puerto
Rican girls possessed no named groups of their own. There
were, of course, no boys' groups to attach themselves to until 1965,
and then only one such group was available at the time of this
study. Also, like the Puerto Rican residents in general, the local
girls shared in the easy informality through which they were
widely known by name and reputation. Like the Italian and
Mexican girls, they usually traveled with girl companions who
acted as mutual chaperons and avoided being forward with boys.
In turn, the Puerto Rican boys were likely to speak of "our girls,"
meaning all the local girls, for whom they seemed to take on a
certain paternalistic responsibility. Nonetheless, the girls did not
seem to actively seek the boys' protective presence, and once again
personal relations in the Puerto Rican neighborhood seemed to
have precluded a pervasive corporate definition of their relative
status. Boys and males in general were considered dangerous to
one's virtue and expected to play some minimal protective role.
Beyond this, the males neither asked for nor received further signs
of deference.

Not only did the black teenage girls possess two street-corner
groups of their own, but these girls' groups were totally detached
from the boys' groups. Their names bore no resemblance to that
of the boys' groups, and the girls themselves derided the idea that
there was any connection with the boys. In fact, the two girls'
groups tended to be more durable than those of the boys and, as
the girls reached young adulthood, their groups outlasted the two
oldest boys' groups by a year or so. The independent stance of the
girls was reflected in broader areas of behavior and by girls other
than those belonging to the two groups. The girls often feared the
boys because of their reputation for sexual opportunism, and they
often spoke of the boys as derisively as the boys spoke of them. It

was not unusual, for instance, to see a collection of black teenage girls and boys on the street despite parental discouragement. The black boys practically never spoke of "our girls" in a paternalistic sense, but sometimes a black boy and girl would couple off and refer to one another as "my girl" or "my boy." All in all, then, cross-sex relations were quite equalitarian with two exceptions. First, the black boys, like their peers in the other ethnic neighborhoods, were assumed to be unrepentent sexual predators for which the girls were no match. Second, toward the spring of 1964 a new boys' and a new girls' group (the Gutter Guys and the Gutter Gals) with an explicit alliance between them developed simultaneously. This was the first alliance of this type in anyone's memory and may have signaled the first steps toward less equalitarian relations among the teenage male and females in the black neighborhood. Except for this particular instance, however, cross-sex equalitarianism was the rule, and other black males showed little protectionist or proprietorial interest in the local girls.

It seems clear from this account that gradations in the deference and respect shown males by the female teenagers was a reaction to male dominance in general rather than a specific reaction to particular boys or particular groups. The Italian males, including the adults, had established themselves as unchallenged authorities, and the Italian girls were very restricted in their movements and claims to a corporate identity. In the Mexican community, male authority was more questionable, but girls still sought their protective association. Relationships in the Puerto Rican neighborhood were the most individuated, and this general principle was extended to cross-sex relations as well. The lack of authority attributable to the black adult males had the general effect of extending to the claims of adolescent males, and the deference girls showed the latter was as little as that shown the former.

Voluntary Community Groups

As in most other inner city low income areas, local voluntary associations in these four neighborhoods were notable for their scarcity. A number of people belonged to labor unions and nationwide groups (such as the Knights of Columbus), but the development of local voluntary associations was truly rudimentary. In all, there were eleven voluntary associations which were local to the area, but most of these had been initiated by social workers, and oddly enough, the area lacked the local block clubs which are so common in some black neighborhoods of Chicago. Among the Italians there were four groups, two of which were mothers' clubs organized by the local Catholic churches. These women met to talk with one another and carry out minor charitable activities; otherwise they scarcely came to anyone's attention. Another association was a store front organization which had one full-time employee who was supposed to work with youngsters in the area. Originally the organization was established by the old Chicago Areas Foundation, but financing had since been provided by the United Charities. In 1964 this financial aid was refused because it was decided that the organization was not doing anything. This organization never attracted any members other than its hired director, and it is questionable that it should be called a community organization.

The most widely known group to which a number of Italian women belonged was a temporary group formed to defend the entire area from urban renewal and clearance for a local university. Although the group's leader was Italian and the group itself was identified with the Italian neighborhood, a number of Mexican women also belonged to it. The group failed to attract any male members. In fact, the males seemed openly to boycott the group, referring to it cynically as a useless exercise. In barroom conversations the men said they knew you could not fight City Hall and sometimes accused the female leader of trying to get attention. Some of them felt their suspicions justified when she later ran for public office.[16] It should be added that the males could say little else without belittling the power of their own reputed ties to "downtown" through the Outfit and the West Side Bloc. Indeed, this seemed to be a general barrier to further adult male organization in the Italian neighborhood, and some men confided to me that

16. Incidentally, she obtained a lower proportion of the votes from the local Italian precincts than from the local black precincts.

they "hoped R———— would win" but did not intend to openly support her. Such considerations seem to have been pervasive among the Italian men, for they lacked any organizations which were explicitly addressed to the problem of community betterment or improvement.

The group organized by this Italian woman soon declined after the decision to locate the university in the area. This left the Italian area without any local voluntary associations other than the two mothers' clubs. The Italians' dependency on the Outfit and the West Side Bloc and the men reputed to have connections with them was so great that it precluded the development of organizations aimed to negotiate for city services and serve local residents in a more direct way. Italian informants assured me that this situation had been typical for more than twenty years and recollected the early failures of the White Hand[17] as an archetypal example of how straightforward and honest attempts to deal with community problems and city services had languished. As an elderly, one-time member of the White Hand put it, "If you can't get City Hall to help you fight the Outfit, what's the use of organizing?" Apparently the Italians' retreat to the Outfit and the West Side Bloc had been strewn with the failures of other alternatives.

Local community organization in the Mexican neighborhood was somewhat different in form but similar in orientation to that found in the Italian area. Of the two local community groups which existed among them, one was quite formidable. It called itself the Club Hispaño and claimed to represent all the local Mexicans. This group included among its members some of the most reputable and widely known adult Mexican males in the area. Indeed, the group included specifically those Mexican males who were said to have connections with the Outfit, the West Side Bloc, and prominent members of the Italian neighborhood. Its connection with this subterranean avenue of power were evident in other ways.

17. A group originally formed to oppose the Black Hand and to protect the victims of organized crime. The group failed primarily because the local Italian population doubted its ability to oppose already established "official corruption or tolerance of corruption." Humbert S. Nelli, *The Italians in Chicago* (New York: Oxford University Press, 1970), p. 136.

Public entertainment provided by this group was often held in an Italian church, and Italian precinct captains and ward heelers always took the opportunity to make appearances. The group had an acknowledged and warranted reputation for being able to settle difficulties between the Italian and Mexican neighborhoods. It settled some feuds, distributed some patronage, and, among politicians, had the esteemed reputation of being able to get large crowds of Mexicans to come to its dances and dinners. The leaders of this group, however, had no interest in protest politics or any other public methods of securing city services and funds. As among the Italians, there was a tendency to deride public hearings, regular channels of protest, or the ordinary channels for making a request for public service. The leaders of the group saw it as a way of circumventing these regular channels and gaining access to levels of discretion where "real" decisions and "real" benefits could be obtained. There was every indication that the group had made strong headway in this direction, and members of the Outfit and the West Side Bloc sometimes favored the group with appearances at its public events and its private councils. Within this group the Mexicans seemed to be searching for an avenue of power which, like that of the Italians, would reduce the importance of community organizations devoted to an ostensive and legitimate approach to procuring city services and benefits.

The second local community group among the Mexicans was a group of Mexican women who had been brought together by a social worker who had come there in the employ of a youth organization which ran a program in the area. The group was supposed to provide volunteer services in the neighborhood and help to sponsor get-togethers for the local adults interested in community problems. In practice, the group usually met to decide what activity it was to create and, in the absence of obvious alternatives, ended by deciding on some entertainment for its members. On a few occasions the group chaperoned public entertainment for juveniles. The social worker who organized this group was himself a Mexican with previous ties in the neighborhood. Apparently he did not view the group as a terribly important way of serving the community, for he soon joined the Club Hispaño and devoted most of his time to it. The importance of the group he organized could be judged from the rather minor leadership role this social worker was allowed to play in the Club Hispaño.

The type of group organized by this Mexican social worker was characteristic of those found among the Puerto Ricans and blacks. The Puerto Ricans possessed one of those community groups which had been organized by a Puerto Rican social worker from outside the area. The group spent most of its time chaperoning teenage entertainment, socializing among its own members, and sponsoring a training program for leadership. The members were mainly women, but a few relatively unknown men attended its meetings on occasion. The group was not widely known, and no one resorted to it as a way of getting favors or asking for help in getting city services and the like. The Puerto Rican men tended to ignore the group rather than deride it as would have the Italian or Mexican men.

Social workers who had come into the area had been most effective among the blacks and were successful in founding five community groups devoted to volunteer service. These groups consisted almost entirely of adult women, although a sprinkling of men sometimes would attend a meeting. One exception to this was a young men's organization formed from the membership of two of the oldest black gangs in the neighborhood. This group met for about nine months before dissolving. Like the other groups organized in the community, it was charged with the responsibility of chaperoning teenage entertainment and seeing to its own social gatherings. This group was the most widely known of its type in the neighborhood and toward the end of its existence became co-ed. Shortly afterward, however, the group broke up, apparently because some members failed to attend, but also because the group seemed to lack any certainty about what it was supposed to do. The four groups of women continued their volunteer work occasionally and met periodically. They were reasonably well known in the neighborhood, but people thought of them mainly as someone to call on to help manage a dance or work at a social event.

On the whole, there appear to have been two main patterns of community organization in the four neighborhoods. In the Italian neighborhood, and to a lesser degree the Mexican neighborhood, the men were drawn into a subterranean network of exchanges which extended into the West Side Bloc and the Outfit. Volunteer groups, protest groups, and regular channels of political influence were derided for their ineffectiveness and naïveté. Among both the Italians and the Mexicans, the adult males were the gatekeepers to this subterranean network and, by contrast, the women were placed in a very secondary role. In the Puerto Rican neighborhood and especially the black neighborhood, community organization was sponsored by professional social workers. The organizations sought explicitly to help their community, but they could do little beyond keep order at local gatherings. The members of these groups were mainly women who became reasonably well known but were not considered influential outside the community. Except for one group in their late teens and early twenties, men did not participate in the groups, or they played a secondary role.

Family Variants

Within all four of these ethnic residential groups, the families I observed were more alike than different. The most frequent arrangement was an intact nuclear family with the husband-father assigned the major role as breadwinner and authority. Most of the families, of course, were relatively poor, and the income of the men was drawn from low status occupations. People were mindful that they lived in a "tough" neighborhood and that there was a wide disparity between national ideals and some of the practices of their own men. The residents took this disparity in their stride, however, for the lines of continuity were greater than those of discontinuity.

Nevertheless, within each ethnic group there were variants of this main family type which were frequent and which also caused comment among the residents themselves. At one extreme were the Italians. Generally the family was intact, and great deference was shown the male head of the household. On inspection, however, this position proved to be mostly honorific or ceremonial in practice. Fathers were to be admired and respected but not touched.

This was most apparent when a boy came into contact with the police because of misconduct. There being a few Italian policemen in the area, their usual practice was to take the child to his mother, and both the policeman and the mother would threaten to tell the father. Actually this seldom took place and usually discipline stayed in the hands of the mother, whereas the father remained a remote figure occasionally used to threaten children rather than instruct them. When made aware of his son's mischief, the Italian father threw something of a temper tantrum that ended in a beating without further discussion between father and son.

This basic pattern was not only common among the Italians, some elements of it were spoken of as an ideal objective, particularly the emphasis on male authority. The less official but more substantively important role played by the mother was not held up as an explicit aim of family life but regarded as an inevitability based on the weakness of motherly love. Otherwise, the more important role of the mother in the day-to-day management of the household was treated as a sort of subcontractual arrangement which in no way reduced the authority of the father. In fact, heavy involvement in the day-to-day details of household management and disciplining of children was regarded as onerous and beneath the dignity of men.

The extent to which the Italian family was a detached and self-contained unit with the exclusive responsibility for child-rearing should not be overemphasized. The Italian family, like that of the other ethnic groups in this area, was cross-cut with strong peer group loyalties and a sharp separation between the sexes. In day-to-day behavior the family was together during mealtime, but for the remainder of the day, the family members tended to separate out into peer groups of boys and girls and men and women. After about the age of five, children spent the vast majority of their time with their peers, often close by the home but not under the direct supervision of either parent. Similarly, the parents had their own peer groups, and these associations also weighed most heavily except during times (such as funerals, weddings, meals) explicitly set aside as family gatherings. Even during those times when all the members of the family were at home, they tended to be sorted out according to age and sex. Husbands would be off with male friends and visitors. The same was likely to be true of wives and children. Effectively then, the peer group was a more continuous and time-consuming form of association than the family.[18]

There were, of course, some Italian families in which the spouses were divorced or separated. Judging from my own field observations and from the 1960 census, these families were few in number (see following table). The Italians, unlike the remaining ethnic groups, simply had no stereotypic imagery for these dissolved families and when asked about them began to describe the circumstances surrounding each particular case. In my observations, one-parent families tended to be grafted onto one of the spouses' family of procreation, through either joint residence or a visiting pattern wherein the mother and her children came to her parents' home practically every day.[19] In many instances this visiting pattern was especially convenient because of residency in the same neighborhood. Although this visiting pattern had often settled into a fixed routine, it was not commented on, and the Italians were secretive about the reasons for it. In fact, it was possible to spend many long afternoons and evenings sitting on the front stoop of an Italian household without learning that the recurrent visits of a daughter and her children were due to a separation or divorce.

In recounting the ideal role of the father, Mexican and Puerto Rican informants usually reported an image that roughly coincided with the Italian practice. Typically, they assigned great authority to the male head of household and expected him to behave rather arbitrarily, although they also excluded him from any detailed participation in the rearing and instructing of children. Unlike the Italians, however, there was no pretense that all husband-fathers subscribed to this pattern. As many women were likely to point

18. For a similar observation see Herbert Gans, *The Urban Villagers* (New York: The Free Press of Glencoe, 1962), pp. 45–103.
19. This pattern was not readily evident because it was also observed by daughters who were still married. Also, after an Italian woman's children reached adulthood, she sometimes seemed to experience a sort of emotional crisis which was so great that she might return to live with her mother for a few months.

Marital Status of White and Nonwhite Females among Those Ever Married (1960)

| | White | | Nonwhite | |
	Number	Percentage	Number	Percentage
Married	3678	75.7	500	50.3
Widowed	755	15.5	206	20.7
Separated	216	4.4	223	22.4
Divorced	212	4.4	65	6.5

Note: Data are from *United States Census of Population,* 1960. The period of my field study was 1963-65, and so the figures given in this table may vary slightly from those occurring in this later period.

out, many of the husbands and fathers they knew (usually they exempted their own husbands, except when they were temporarily on bad terms with them) did not help support the family, did not make the children behave, and failed to come home at night. These discrepancies in male performance were elaborated into a broadly understood stereotype of the husband who was "just no good." Some women spoke of him as they might a bad apple they had bought at the supermarket: a man who was just faulty and not worth keeping. Even when a woman could not quite identify a specific man who fulfilled this stereotype, she was able to verbalize his character: disloyal, undependable, a poor provider, and someone whose whereabouts were hard to determine or assume.

As a counterpart to this stereotype of the "no good" husband, the Mexican and Puerto Rican women possessed a stereotype of the abandoned mother who felt free to diverge from the modest and subordinate role of a woman and take control of her family's fate. In truth, there were several such families among the Puerto Ricans and Mexicans which were broken by separation or in which formal alliances remained only as a fiction to appease their Catholic conscience. In these families the mother unhesitatingly stepped forward to take control of her family without necessarily relying on other relatives. This was done in a forthright manner without much attempt at pretending otherwise. Moreover, it was taken as a justifiable type of action in which the image of the "no good" husband provided the grounds for a sharp departure from traditional ideas of what was a good woman or a good wife. The frequent availability of welfare funds (particularly through Aid to Dependent Children, or ADC) given directly to the female head of household provided an additional argument for her exceptional independence and authority. Among the Puerto Ricans and Mexicans, then, the matrifocal family was not only a structural variant but a normative one as well. Lest this be misinterpreted, it should be emphasized that an intact family with jural authority in male hands was still the dominant normative and structural type. The family with a female head was a less preferred alternative justified on the grounds of presumed male inadequacy. Sometimes, of course, this presumption was wrong, but, unlike the Italians, the Puerto Ricans and Mexicans did not press to inquire beyond the stereotype.[20]

Domestic arrangements among the blacks were similar in many respects to those among the Puerto Ricans and Mexicans, except the blacks seemed to have a different starting point. Among the blacks the ideal image of the father-husband role was very much that publicized in the mass media of this country. A father should not only provide for his children and wife, but be chummy with them, instruct them, sympathize with them, take an interest in their movements outside the family, and all and all, spend a great deal of time in the detailed management of domestic life.[21] Like the Mexican and Puerto Rican women, however, the black women were adamant in their conviction that a great number of local mates failed to fulfill this imagery. Several men had abandoned their families without so much as a divorce and others carried on an episodic relationship with their families. Some were only

20. I am here trying to avoid the overgeneralizations in U.S., Department of Labor, *Negro Family*, and Miller, "Lower Class Culture." For a similar attempt, see Lee Rainwater, "The Problem of Lower Class Culture," Paper prepared for the Department of Sociology Colloquium, University of Wisconsin, 23 September 1966.

21. For further discussion of the preferred family type among blacks, see James F. Short and Fred L. Strodtbeck, *Group Process and Gang Delinquency* (Chicago: University of Chicago Press, 1965).

stand-in husband-fathers after the original had "gone ADC."[22]
A few were said to be total opportunists who gained sexual privileges without any apparent reciprocation.

There is little doubt of the force of the blacks' ideal of the
husband-father role, for there were occasional and rather tragic
attempts on the part of the male to "show who's boss" only to be
put down by child and wife because of his inability to support the
family or regularly participate in its domestic life. Some of the
most poignant examples of this type were observed among young
couples, sometimes no more than eighteen or nineteen years old,
when the husband would try mightily to be a good companion to
his wife and young child only to fail a few days later when he was
out of money, stayed out late with old friends, or "got busted."[23]
Such lapses of husbandly conduct were not unexpected by wives,
for they too had a stereotype of the "no good" husband and the
justifiable measures a woman should take to regulate her own
family. Basically she assumed jural and actual responsibility while
either disowning her husband or treating him as a dependent. The
husband, ex-husband, or boyfriend did not always willingly accede
to this treatment, and sometimes this led to vehement attempts to
reclaim male authority. In these contests the man was in a poor
bargaining position, not only because of his actual lapses from
proper husbandly conduct, but also because of a more general
assumption on the part of observers, children, relatives, and
neighbors that he was in the wrong. The broad stereotype of the
"no good" husband was widely accepted, and the burden of dis-
proof was a male responsibility.

Judging from my own observations, this shift of domestic
authority from male to female hands was certainly more common
within the black neighborhood than in the Puerto Rican and
Mexican ones. The 1960 United States census figures as well as
other studies would seem to bear this out. A number of com-

22. Literally, Aid to Dependent Children, but also understood to mean
"after Daddy cut out." The point is that welfare funds seem to serve as a
critical increment to the woman's contribution and make the male in the
household appear as a "kept man."
23. For similar observations see Elliot Liebow, *Tally's Corner: A Study
of Negro Streetcorner Men* (Boston: Little, Brown and Co., 1967).

ments are in order, however, to avoid a careless and uninformative application of the matrifocal family literature to these cases. First, in none of these ethnic neighborhoods is the matrifocal family a dominant structural form or normative ideal. Most of the families are intact, and in not all of the ethnic groups is there a commonly understood normative set of justifications for deviations from the intact family as a secondary alternative.[24]

Second, much of the literature on the matrifocal family makes an implicit contrast between it and the companionate family to argue that the lower class subculture or the culture of poverty would disappear if lower income people would only model their own families on those of middle class Americans.[25] Neither the intact nor the broken families discussed here tend to bear out this inference. The stable families among the Italians, Mexicans, and Puerto Ricans are patricentric in their allocation of jural authority and matricentric in the enforcement of that authority. The stable families among the blacks tend to be more companionate, and the blacks hold up the companionate family as an ideal. If normative prescriptions were the main bulwark against the development of a matrifocal family, the blacks ought to be the least likely to develop such a structure.[26] Just the reverse seems to be true, and one suspects that the inappropriateness of the companionate family model is one of the reasons why black men have such a difficult time fulfilling their wives' and children's expectations. A stable low income community may require a stable family structure, but the companionate family is a doubtful model and, in any case, normative preferences are not alone a sufficient condition for the development of a stable family.

Finally, what the findings do seem to show is the importance of the corporate or collective reputation of men in each neighborhood as against the separate and idiosyncratic behavior of each husband. In the Italian community, men had a reputation for power and for

24. See also Rainwater, "Lower Class Culture."
25. For an extensive and critical review of this question see Charles Valentine, *Culture and Poverty* (Chicago: University of Chicago Press, 1968).
26. See Ibid., and Short and Strodtbeck, *Group Process*.

achievement. In turn, the burden of proof seemed to be on women to demonstrate that their husbands were "no good" and that their right to transfer domestic authority was justifiable. In the face of such counter-assumptions, women disguised their husbands' absence, and other relatives and neighbors went into collusion with them to maintain appearances. In the Puerto Rican, Mexican, and black neighborhoods, the burden of proof was on the males to establish their adequacy as a parent and husband. The stereotypes developed in each ethnic neighborhood were not groundless, but they were based on the general behavior of men rather than that of any single one. For this reason, the Puerto Ricans and Mexicans may have held the stereotype of the "no good" husband with a little less assurance than did the black women. It is my impression that this was true—although I cannot call forth from my field notes strong evidence on the point. In any case, the normative acceptance of variants of the intact family is graduated, as we would expect, based on the corporate standing of males in each ethnic neighborhood.

Child-Parent Relations

It should already be evident that child-parent relations in these four neighborhoods were very reduced owing to the demands of peer-group relationships. Adults and juveniles, males and females tended to go their separate ways or to confront each other in the companionship of their respective peer groups. This was least true of the Puerto Ricans, whose small population made informality and familiarity easier to achieve between generations. Even in this population, however, peers were the most common associates, and individualistic and personal information was just more generally shared. Even when families of any of the four ethnic groups were together, they were cross-cut by age and sex segregation, which was as apparent in a room in the home as on the streets.

The easy familiarity observable within each peer group was counterbalanced by an uncomfortable awkwardness in intergenerational or cross-sex relations. After a few pleasantries, youths and adults or unmarried men and women seemed just to run out of

anything to say to one another. One of the main reasons for this
was that the intimacy of peer groups was so great that the conversational content shared among them was quite improper for sharing with different age and sex groups. Within peer groups,
conversation was a ribald mixture of personal betrayal and iconoclasm. After sitting in on the daily conversations of these groups,
one began to wonder how such honored institutions as the church,
the state, the family, and the school can survive, considering the
low opinion expressed of them or, more particularly, of their
members. Such conversational liberties, however, were taboo in
mixed company, which in this case refers to age levels as well as
sex groups. In this sort of mixed company, conversation either
languished altogether or became very proper. Thus people lived
in a perculiarly dualistic world, one which was frank, critical, and
iconoclastic and another which was proper, traditional, and muted.

This style of interaction was limited by age and sex differences
within the family, although it was more noticeable between children and parents than between spouses. Until their marriage, some
women confided to me, they had always suspected that men "talked
like that," but it was not until after marriage that they ever shared
in similar conversations with their husbands. As a woman became
older, especially after she had gone past the point where she was
commonly regarded as a potential sexual partner, she could sometimes enter genuine conversations which included her husband and
his peers. With young unmarried males and females, however,
discussions of this type were always taboo for the parental
generation.

The result was that very little was said between generations or
between parent and child. The extreme to which this could go was
illustrated in some familites where the parents spoke Spanish and
the children spoke English without any apparent feeling that they
should learn each other's language beyond a few commands and
questions. When conversations between parents and children went
beyond this rather rudimentary point, they tended to consist of
mechanical repetitions of moral dictates which were extremely
"safe" as far as the parent was concerned. Among the Italians,
Puerto Ricans, and Mexicans, this often meant an appeal to Catho-

lic notions of saintliness and morality. Dating might be proscribed altogether; children should always be obedient to priests and teachers; boys should always be quiet; one should work hard, not be a bum, and respect one's elders. Among the blacks, certain tenets of Protestant fundamentalism were invoked to give somewhat the same advice except that greater emphasis was put on not wasting money, and on abstaining from material things such as automobiles, candy, and clothing.

Often the parents themselves delivered this advice half-heartedly and explained later, "You can't tell these kids anything." The children seemed to be enduring only a sort of lecture as if it were punishment in its own right quite apart from parental warnings or more general threats. Most typically, however, such lectures were delivered with some heat when a young boy or girl was already in trouble. Thus the moral lecture tended to have the obvious aim of punishment, as if the parent were purposefully shaming the child by contrasting his behavior to an enduring ideal. In any case, children seemed to take such talkings to as just another penalty entirely comparable to a spanking except that it was shame rather than pain they felt.

Certainly such moralism had little immediate appeal as either a guideline for their own behavior or as a basis for insuring equitable exchanges in their daily life. This moralism did not describe the practices of their parents, that of their peers, or that of the few public officials present in the area. The heroes of the mass media and the respected individuals in the neighborhood were immoral by these criteria. Accordingly, there had developed a kind of moral frontier,[27] and, like their parents, the children turned to their peers for consultation. Within the confines of their peer groups, discussion was open, familiar, and personal. Advice of a general sort was seldom sought and seldom given. Instead, instruction was carried out by example and through a body of

27. For a general discussion of this moral frontier see Thrasher, *The Gang*. Perhaps the best portrayal of this moral frontier between generations is delivered by Claude Brown, who refers to the preachments of his parents as "all that shit" they brought from "down South" (Claude Brown, *Manchild in the Promised Land* [New York: Macmillan, 1965]).

stereotypes about men, women, girls, shop owners, police, teachers, priests, and the like. It is impossible here to detail the specifics of these stereotypes except to say that they produced a kind of personalistic morality in which each place and person went by reputation. In this sense moral norms were not generalized but conditional on the basis of whom one was dealing with.

Such a morality has some obvious limits, particularly in the absence of general guidelines for conducting oneself outside of the local world of the neighborhood, peer group, family, and relatives. In fact, many of the youngsters were very reluctant to go out of the local neighborhood, and when they did, they often showed acute signs of awkwardness, embarrassment, and general confusion. One tendency on the part of boys was to regard the outside world as a sort of Hobbesian jungle where there was an ongoing war of all against all. Others simply relapsed into mute apprehension as if they were sure some kind of failure or victimization was imminent.[28] Doubtless this restricted the boys' opportunities for certain kinds of employment and rendered them rather ineffective in presenting themselves to strangers. Since success and one's sense of personal well-being in the wider urban community are very dependent on one's being able to handle social relations with strangers comfortably, the boys in these four neighborhoods were rather limited in their social world. I do not mean to suggest that they suffered much anxiety or personal stress over this. In fact, they seemed like reasonably satisfied individuals. What they had to be satisfied with, however, was a sort of provincial urban village that further confined them to their peer groups and the narrow basis of trust which is so productive of violence and vigilantism in our cities. The peer group provided a moral basis for behavior, but it was a narrow one that seemed calculated to reproduce rather than reduce the importance of the vigilante gang and the defended neighborhood.

Within this general situation the schools and other public institutions seemed singularly unable to provide an alternative moral-

---

28. For a discussion of the conditions under which these responses prevail, see Suttles, *Social Order.*

ity. Their general tendency seemed to be to treat ethics as a sort of intact and permanent body of principles which the individual was to adopt irrespective of what other people were doing. Ethical principles, then, took on the character of abstractions rather than interpersonal agreements and understandings which people sought among themselves in a search for their collective welfare. Indeed, people who adhered to moral or ethical principles were regarded as sacrificing their personal interests rather than seeking the conditions under which they could safely pursue their interests. This point of view was quite evident among the teenagers, who regarded someone considered moral as a sort of saint who had simply given up worldly enterprises and interests. Morality then was seen as lacking practicality and served only as a kind of adornment for peculiar and unearthly people.

The family itself, of course, promoted this view of ethics and morality. The schools and other public institutions, however, reaffirmed it and reduced it to a monotonous formula. This was most evident in some of the parochial schools where traditional saints were held up as examples of morality and where well-behaved boys and girls were automatically seen as members of some select group who should be encouraged to join the priesthood or retire to a nunnery. The children also spent hours writing sentences which ran on: "God is good," "God is generous," and the like. The public schools spent less time on religious imagery, but the moralism they represented was equally remote from the practical ethical considerations of an inner city neighborhood. Children were told that they should always be honest, never fight, always be fair, always be quiet, and so forth. Such persistent and unremitting virtue could find few followers in a neighborhood where it sometimes took teenagers two years of close acquaintanceship before they were willing to lend one another money. In fairness to the public schools, it must be said that they did not try hard to enforce this morality, and certainly they did not presume it on the part of their students. Instead, a great deal of time went into the enforcement of rules to extirpate smoking, noise making, and fighting.

No doubt many of the virtues taught by the schools were publicly commendable and might even have served well some of the youngsters in these four neighborhoods. But they were not taught as persuasive examples of enlightened self-interest, and above all, such precepts lacked any consideration of the conditions under which they might be profitably followed. On the other hand, the peer group possessed a rich lore exactly on these conditions under which one could assume the reciprocity of ethical standards. It was the peer group that could tell one when it was necessary to fight or not necessary to fight, when to lie or not lie, to be quiet or demanding, and the like. Unfortunately, the peer group's lore tended to stop at the boundaries of its neighborhood and left its members in the lurch once their life took them into the wider community.

Conclusion

In the four inner city slum neighborhoods discussed here, the territorially defined single-sex peer group was a dominant form of social organization, and its demands required considerable adjustment in such other institutions as the family, intergenerational relations, cross-sex relations, and voluntary associations. The basic functions of the peer group seemed to be territorial defense and the moral enlightenment of its members. In this sense, such peer groups are vigilante gangs which develop out of the inadequacy of formal institutions that have authorized responsibility for the protection of property and lives and for moral education. The failure of the police, courts, and public schools is a central stimulus to vigilante groups everywhere, but the persistence of this failure in inner city areas is what forces such long-term solutions on slum residents.

The foremost adjustment required in the area was a specialization of the male-adolescent peer group into a sort of informal police power which barricaded its neighborhood for selected hours of the day and on conditions of the entrant's personal deportment. Not all the youngsters were impressed into this kind of duty, and the ones drawn into such activity may have come from the poorer families or have been the least able in their school work. Personally, I doubt that such differences existed between gang and non-gang boys in these four neighborhoods. In any case, such background characteristics are an insufficient explanation for the presence of named gangs with a continuing reputation and ability for territorial defense.

The importance placed on the vigilante gang and peer groups in general had ramifications throughout several institutional sectors. In the short run, the adolescent vigilante gang tended to undermine the claims of adult authorities, particularly those of the adult males, although eventually these adolescent groups might form the nucleus of adult groups with considerable authority. In turn, the reduction of adult male authority extended to the family and to intergenerational relations. In the long run, of course, the vigilante gang might advance into adulthood itself, restoring male authority and a more male-centered community than is common or expected in the United States. Along with this restoration of male authority goes a less equalitarian relationship across sex lines and between generations. The slum neighborhood, then, seems to shift between extremes in the authority of adult males. Initially, male adolescents may overshadow their elders, but as they grow into adulthood, they reassert adult male dominance with a vengence.

The importance of the all-male peer group acting as an unauthorized police power placed emphasis on irregular and illegitimate channels of influence, favoritism, and patronage. Regular channels of achieving community services and public benefits are always scarce in inner city slum areas, and often voluntary community groups find it futile to bother with such bureaucratic procedures as are available. The adult-male peer group was a further obstruction to the use of these citizen associations and those proper channels which do exist. On the one hand, members belittled the use of these avenues of community betterment because the men wished to emphasize instead the effectiveness of their own subterranean methods. On the other hand, they demonstrated by their own activities the greater success of illegal and irregular methods.

Within the family itself, the peer group tended to be an obstruction to communication across generations and to foreclose the family's obligation to be a strong moral force in the life of its children. In turn, the corporate reputation of adult-male peer groups tended to provide a collective identity for males which justified either a sort of jural patricentric family or a practicing matricentric family.

This pattern of institutional adjustments is above all an American pattern and more generally a New World pattern to be found in those cities undergoing rapid growth and throwing together populations with peasant backgrounds and different primordial identities. And despite the generally functional character of such institutional adjustments, they have involved enormous social costs. In the neighborhood discussed here, a large number of its younger males spent a portion of their lives in jail or prison. The community formed a haven for organized crime and gave support to a political bloc notorious for its corruption and the narrow interests it served. Most often the gangs found threats sufficient to defend their area, but over the years some lives had been lost. People with connections got jobs, supported their families, and looked forward to something better. But the debts and favors they owed often demeaned them, and many people were hardened to the point that they took a cynical and opportunistic view of all social contacts beyond kith and kin.

Nonetheless, the adolescent and adult peer group functioned as educator, vigilante policeman, and political jobber. The costs they entailed could have been avoided only if other institutions had stepped in to fill equally vital roles. Above all, this would have meant a respected and capable police force as able to insure the residents' safety as the local gangs. Such a move would involve heavy costs for Americans both in economic and ideological sacrifices. A service-oriented and professionalized police force, such as that described by Ramsey Clark, is undoubtedly an expensive public agency, although it might eventually pay for itself through the reduction of crime and vigilantism.[29] More important, perhaps, it would probably mean sacrificing some of our beliefs that the individual is ultimately and fully responsible for his legal conduct whatever his socioeconomic or ethnic status. The explicit recognition that a constabulary body is necessary to maintain order in our large cities is under current assumptions a denial of the full self-reliance and personal responsibility expected within our doctrines of individualism. These doctrines of individualism have given rise to a limited role for policemen: they are to catch wrongdoers rather than to insure such a high standard of order or serve to reduce conflict to the point that citizens do not take the law into their own hands. Revisions of the sort that Ramsey Clark is calling for require not only a greater financial outlay but also an alteration in some of our basic ideas about the limits of how nearly laymen can preserve order in society.

Similar costs are involved in a publicly sponsored employment and welfare organization which is competitive with organized crime, "clout," and the loose system of connections with the right parties which are present in most inner city areas. The financial costs are evident.[30] The questioning of some of our notions of self-reliance are more subtle but nonetheless a source of resistance. Indeed, almost any attempt to bring legitimate order to slum neighborhoods is going to be expensive and give government a larger hand in our public life.[31] In turn, this large a role for government may require a reversal in the contempt that Americans seem to feel free to shower on politicians and government bureaucrats.[32] An effective police force and welfare bureaucracy must be lodged in a larger structure of civil service and representative politics from which each receives its prestige and legitimacy. As Rose points out, however, American notions of

29. Ramsey Clark, *Crime in America* (New York: Simon and Schuster, 1970).

30. For estimates see Edward E. Schwartz, "A Way to End the Means Test," *Social Work* 9 (July 1964): 3–13.

31. Above all it may force us to distinguish between public and private realms of life, which is a legal issue that has not received much attention in the United States.

32. Rose, *Power Structure*, pp. 456–82.

the ideal political leader or civil servant are so unreal that they
cannot help but lead to disenchantment and the discouragement
of potentially honorable public servants.[33] The Dick and Jane
morality of the public schools is no corrective to this lack of
realism. But the basic obstacle seems to be a wider cultural
assumption that honorable conduct is solely an individual responsibility and that people can and should persevere under any
and all conditions. This point of view evades the problem of how
one creates a social environment within which people can be
honorable, trusting, and peaceable. But these extreme notions of
individualism are cherished beliefs, and for those who have obtained comfortable incomes and live in safe communities, these
beliefs make their circumstances seem unqualified, individual
accomplishments.

It is understandably difficult for those who are successful to
give up the view that they are solely responsible for their comfortable and secure position. Heretofore, prosperous Americans have
been unwilling to relinquish this cherished portrait of themselves
and develop the high quality of public services which would be
necessary to diminish the extralegal patterns which are so common
to slum neighborhoods. Thus, many vital social functions have
been left to vigilante social groups. An overstated pride in the
ability of grass roots volunteerism dating from de Tocqueville
tended to overlook other grass roots social functionaries like the
street-corner group. This imbalance in reporting seemed to leave
uncontested the virtues of citizen and lay participation in every
realm of life. There are limits and costs to this doctrine of individualism, and the street-corner gang is one of them.

33. Ibid.

Part 4

The Social Construction of Communities

Chapter 4

The Social Construction of Communities?

9. Potentials in Community Differentiation

One of the aims of this volume has been to approach the local residential urban community as a response of territorial populations to their environment rather than to look at it as a vestigial remnant of a more fragmented and localized society. This approach takes us in a number of directions, three of which seem most promising: the community as a territorial basis for associational selection; the community as an identity which distinguishes it from other territorial and nonterritorial populations; and the community as an object of administration. I will first discuss briefly each of these aspects of the local community and then to turn to the problem of classification. My hope, however, is not to construct some sharply delineated urban communities but to center on the processes of community differentiation which do not always yield well-defined territorial units. It will be obvious that I have relied heavily on Warren's distinction between the horizontal and vertical patterns of community structure, although it will also be obvious that I do not pause often enough to acknowledge him or my differences from him.[1]

The Community as a Territorial Basis for Associational Selection

It is probably self-evident that residential proximity creates its own dangers and difficulties of social control. People who are close at hand are impossible to avoid; they can teach your children dirty habits, abuse your daughter, throw cigarette butts in your doorway, or snatch your wife's purse on her way home from downtown. Understandably, people want to live in a "good area" where they feel reasonably safe and are a known distance from those people they distrust. They also want to know something

1. Roland Warren, *The Community in America* (Chicago: Rand McNally, 1963), pp. 237–302.

about how far the "good area" extends so that they can say something definite about how far their children can go when they play, how far away to park the car for the night, and a multitude of petty day-to-day decisions which require that we break the city up into more or less trustworthy areas.

To arrive at such discrete areas, residents may consult with their neighbors, rely on stereotypes conveyed in the newspapers, or individually foresee the dangers to passage as they cross impersonal domains or no-man's-lands.[2] It does not take a highly imaginative person to invent such boundaries, for they derive from his most primitive notions of how space, distance, and movement have inevitable and universal meanings. Individuals who share an arm's length of space are vulnerable to one another, and this is a lesson learned early and widely. Movement away from or toward one another must be endowed with intent and motive, or else the individual will not survive long in the traffic of life. To openly move closer to one individual than another conveys affect and sentiment, and the person who fails to find this out will certainly fail to express one form of affect which is essential to all societies. It is out of such primitive conceptions of space, distance, and movement that the community—and other spatial groupings—is constructed. We are not speaking here of native or inborn conceptions but of universal cultural forms which are required by the mechanics of life itself. The quest for a good community is, among other things, a quest for a neighborhood where one does not fear standing an arm's length from his neighbor, where one can divine the intent of someone heading down the sidewalk, or where one can share expressions of affect by the way adjacent residences dress up for mutual impression management.[3]

Decisions like this about an area require us to draw distinctions among areas and ultimately boundaries between them. The ideal boundary is the physical obstruction across which danger and

2. Gerald D. Suttles, *The Social Order of the Slum* (Chicago: University of Chicago Press, 1968), pp. 35–38.
3. For further discussion of this type of mute impression management among coresidents see Suttles's "Deviant Behavior as an Unanticipated Consequence of Public Housing," in D. Glaser, ed., *Crime in the City* (New York: Harper and Row, 1970), pp. 162–76.

traffic cannot advance at all. There are, of course, no such boundaries in a modern city, but there are fair approximations in some of our expressways, elevated lines, blocks of industry, rivers, and so on. An alternative is to select strips such as vacant land or rail lines where people "have no business" and, since they are inhabited only by trespassers, are dangerous places to cross. Obviously such obstructions are not always available nor do they always draw a significant boundary between noticeably different populations. What often happens, then, is that rather arbitrary streets, passageways, or some kind of physical marker are hit upon as a point beyond which the gradation in what people are like is said to make a qualitative change. The problem is not too much unlike that of a teacher who must take a continuous sequence of exam scores and decide on a cutting point between those who pass and those who fail. The choice is a familiar one, somewhat arbitrary, but necessary.

Individual Strategies in the Defended Neighborhood

Naturally, this need not mean that there will be much consensus on such boundaries, although the reasonable tendency to consult other residents on this matter is a powerful move in that direction. Often, however, the new resident will have only an ill-formed notion of the boundaries of the area he is moving into and the character of his fellow residents beyond what is conveyed by the appearance of their houses. For such a new resident there seem to be two separable strategies, not mutually exclusive, but likely to receive greater or lesser emphasis depending on his capacity for residential mobility. One emphasis may be on selecting a residential area where the character of fellow residents is assured by the costs of living there and the presumed reputability of people so heavily rewarded by society. Another emphasis is to cultivate one's neighbors once one is in an area to the point that they come to share a personal covenant, look out for one another, and exempt each other from the general suspicions and defensive provocations which are so productive of the violence, insult, or damage that neighbors fear in the first place. The first type of strategy is most available to people with high incomes and transferable skills.

Where this first strategy is pursued to the exclusion of the second, it is apt to produce what Morris Janowitz has called the community of limited liability: a community where the resident invests neither himself nor his capital so deeply that he cannot pull out when housing values and the character of his neighbors begin to decline.[4] The practice of cultivating one's neighbors is apt to be more common among people who are disbarred by color or who cannot afford to live in a wide range of neighborhoods or are more sessile because of their jobs, local investments, or family traditions which give them a large place in a small pool.[5]

Naturally, both strategies can be combined and this frequently occurs in elite communities where a personal referral is as necessary as cash to assure one the right of purchase. Similarly, there are people who can follow neither strategy because they cannot afford to move and they so thoroughly and reasonably distrust their disreputable neighbors that they are unable or unwilling to try to cultivate them.[6] Such communities are apt to be very fragmented, composed of isolated families, and especially among adults, to form a kind of dormitory community where people try to reach their dwelling units before dark. Some of our public housing developments take this tendency to an extreme.[7] As with

4. Morris Janowitz, *The Community Press in an Urban Setting: The Social Elements of Urbanism,* 2d ed. (Chicago: University of Chicago Press, 1967).

5. E. Digby Baltzell, *Philadelphia Gentlemen* (New York: The Free Press of Glencoe, 1958), pp. 173–222; and Lee Rainwater, *Behind Ghetto Walls* (Chicago: Aldine Press, 1970). Both works show how the top and the bottom of a stratification system may have limited choices in their residences, although for different reasons.

6. The reader might note that these two strategies can be combined to produce a two-fold table or "property space." I have mercifully abstained from this, not because such a table would add little which is new to the discussion, but because it would add too much. Such individual strategies do not produce communities because they need not be uniformly followed within any particular area. For this type of uniformity to prevail, a host of other institutional conditions must be present in the community as well as outside it. I intend to get to these institutional conditions, and in the two preceding paragraphs my only purpose was to show that these strategies and their combination form the first step which works hand-in-hand with further processes of community differentiation.

7. Rainwater, *Behind Ghetto Walls.*

other "dumping grounds," however, they seldom lack a residential identity. People in other areas are only too eager to disown them. More affluent and comfortable dormitory communities may remain more anonymous, especially where the automobile and extensive traffic arteries offer quick means by which people can lose an accountable residential identity and pass as something else.[8]

Institutional Collaboration

However these strategies combine, they lead to another strategic decision about whether or not to defend the area and stabilize its boundaries so that they are more than arbitrary markers and become real walls and barriers against the incursion of outsiders. For the individual who has only bought a negotiable stock and wishes to avoid the provincialism of the local area, his interests are served best by specialists at this business. Since he can usally afford them, the restrictive covenant, similar informal practices, home improvement associations, and "reputable" real estate agents are to be sponsored and supported at least to the extent of favoring them with one's trade and contributions. These efforts may be supplemented by that of night watchmen, private policemen, and doormen. Even more important, however, may be the protective shield provided by city administrators, highly placed politicians, and the leaders in certain businesses, particularly those in construction and real estate. Some of the tools available here are obvious: zoning regulations, the permissible size of lots, the enforcement of building and fire regulations, the location of desirable or undesirable public facilities, and so on. Other ways of doing the same thing may be less apparent: police policy toward "trespassers" and the vague way in which administrative decisions and plans on land usage cumulate as an omen of the future for renters, home owners, local businessmen, and prospective residents.

It is evident that the defensive system of such a neighborhood

8. Leo Schnore, *The Urban Scene* (New York: The Free Press of Glencoe, 1965), pp. 137–252, 330–43.

is only partially a local responsibility and not a duty which falls altogether on the local residents. Instead, this defense system represents a combination of political, administrative, and business institutions in the service of local populations. What imperils such communities, then, is not so much a decline in their own interpersonal loyalties and attachment to place as a breakup in the precarious collusion of several governmental and private organizations. Recently the federal government has partially retreated from this combine by passing and enforcing open housing legislation, by funding low and moderate income housing or rental subsidies, and by the broader and more equitable enforcement of building and zoning standards.[9] Certainly the federal government has not wholly withdrawn from this combine, but even its limited changes in policy have been enough to panic the residents in many communities who seem to fear an invasion by the "dangerous classes."

Neighborhood defense is not so precarious but it is more onerous in many communities where the residents cannot depend on the protective shield of external organizations and must engage in a sort of grass roots vigilantism. This type of defended neighborhood is most flagrant in slum areas where street-corner gangs, open bigotry, and physical abuse are the first line of defense against people from other ethnic or racial groups or, more recently, the incursion of off-beat social types like the hippies and beatniks. But affluent and refined communities may find the problem of neighborhood defense their own when they try to draw the line between those with respectable wealth and the parvenu or "shady rich." Their tactics may also become flagrant when a notorious but wealthy gangster must be excluded by harrassment and ostracism after attempts to buy him out have failed. As a rule, however, such communities use the quiet and expensive tactics of circulating homes by referral and selling their property to something less than the full pool of possible bidders. Additional burdens may require a clubhouse, participation in its affairs, the support of a private school, and the actual construction of a wall

9. For an evaluation of how fully federal guidelines affect areas receiving federal funds, see David Nelson, "Black Reform and Federal Resources" (Ph.D. dissertation, University of Chicago, in preparation).

with guards and dogs. Defending oneself against those who have only money can be genteel, but it is expensive in both time and money.

Naturally there are areas in most cities which are left undefended and open to invasion by almost any sort of resident. The entrepôts of our large cities are a prime example. Properly speaking, however, it is not that the residents of such areas lack the impulse to defend their areas but that they lack the wherewithal to do so. They might better be called defeated neighborhoods than undefended ones. The defeated neighborhood is in some ways the reverse of that which is defended by a combine of political, administrative, and business interests. It is subject to insufficient or quixotic enforcement of building standards, zoning rules, police protection, and wide disparities in the delivery of all the available community services. Above all it is a community which citywide, regional, and federal agencies treat as an object without much fear of retaliation from a local constituency. Typically, then, the defeated community suffers from two sources of weakness in its defense. First, it is unable to participate fully in its own governance. Sometimes this is because it is so heavily populated by new residents, ex-felons, aliens, and transients that even the ballot box is not a significant avenue of influence.[10] At other times it is a community so heavily stigmatized and outcast that its residents retreat from most forms of public participation out of shame, mutual fear, and an absence of faith in each other's collective concern. Skid rows illustrate the former weakness of the residents, and some of our worst public housing projects illustrate the latter.[11]

A second source of weakness in the defenses of the defeated neighborhood is its choice as a site for businesses and industries which have powerful interests that are simply antithetical to the aims of any residential group. Some of these businesses are outright illegal, whereas others seek out special exemptions from

10. Claude Brown has pointed out that so many males in Harlem are ex-felons that they are practically a disenfranchised group in the city (*Manchild in the Promised Land* [New York: Macmillan, 1965]).
11. Rainwater, *Behind Ghetto Walls*.

civic standards: cheap bars, pick-up joints, day-labor offices, flop-houses, polluting industries, unseemly restaurants, brothels, and hock shops. All these businesses have an interest in the corruptibility of city agencies and are apt to go into alliance to see that their interests rather than those of the local residents are served. Such powerful adversaries tend to cancel out the efforts of the residents, to drive out from among them those who might be outspoken adversaries, and generally to make the area available to residents who are powerless and outcast from other areas of the city. In such areas neighborhood defense tends to descend to mere violence, often that of young predators or that of individuals looking out solely for themselves.[12] Although this sort of pattern is most evident in skid rows, it can also become full-blown in some company towns where the powerful interests of the firm run counter to those of the residents. This was certainly true in many mining and lumbering communities where strikebreakers and other alien elements were drawn into the community in the interests of the firm and counter to the desires of the previous residents.[13] The company town has not, however, always found the firm unwilling to play a paternalistic role and to defend the community as it would defend itself.[14]

Boundary Selection

Most neighborhoods are intermediate among these various extremes, and most residents spend some time defending their own community while they also get some help from political, administrative, and private organizations. The clarity with which they can define their boundaries and defend them is always dependent on more than one consideration, and it is possible to identify some of the major ones. First, some communities have well-defined boundaries because all the adjacent communities disclaim their

12. Clifford Shaw, *The Jack Roller* (Chicago: University of Chicago Press, 1966) includes descriptions of such "victim prone" areas.
13. John Kenneth Moreland, *The Millways of Kent* (New Haven: College and University Press, 1965).
14. William Manchester, *The Arms of Krupp* (Boston: Little, Brown and Co., 1968) describes a large-scale example in the Krupp's paternalistic treatment of the workers in Essen.

residents. These residential enclaves acquire an identity and a set of boundaries simply because they are left out of others. Although it may be unusual for an area to be disclaimed from all sides, this does point up the extent to which such a boundary line is the work of more than one spatial grouping; it does not simply well up out of the desires and sentiments of one group.

A second determinate of defended boundaries is the presence of conveniently available physical barriers. Railroad tracks, expressways, parks, and blocks of industry are real obstructions to casual foot traffic, and people are only reasonable in selecting them because they are plausible limits to heavy cross-traffic, especially that of pedestrians. Since the defended neighborhood grows partly out of fear for personal security, residents are only showing wisdom when they select barriers which give them some assurance of physical segregation. Thus, the presence of such boundaries may not create a community, but certainly people may select them as a reasonable starting point to help create one.

A closely allied candidate for neighborhood boundaries is the gradient of prices which are attached to residential land usage. These price gradients are a form of assurance about the peaceableness of the people one can expect to move into a neighborhood, and therefore they create additional plausible boundaries for people to select in starting to create a durable community. After all, social class or income is not merely a matter of snobbery or an arbitrary taste for a particular style of life. There is a very real sense in which social class and income do distinguish between people more or less prone to violence and physical abuse.[15] For whatever reasons, income is a reliable sign of a neighbor's tendency to have children who fight, resist school authorities, and meet in unsupervised settings. In addition, class conflict itself is a real possibility in a society which has difficulty in justifying its contemporary income differences. Thus, on either hand, the individual has reasons for avoiding socioeconomic groups poorer than his own. He also has reasons for seizing on some of the gradients in

15. Rolf Dahrendorf, "On the Origin of Inequality among Men," *Essays in the Theory of Society* (Stanford: Stanford University Press, 1968), pp. 151–78.

rental, land, and house prices as a boundary line behind which he will exert himself to see to it that land values are kept up and that not just anyone can live there. Happily, such cost gradients often coincide with a change in altitude, the location of natural attractions such as a river or lake, or some other physical obstruction or marker which renders them legible as well as effective.[16] But this is not always true, and I will return to this question shortly.

What seems to me by far the most effective and frequent barrier between residential groups is what we might call enacted boundary lines.[17] Enacted limits to a community are simply those imposed on the urban landscape as an arbitrary line marked off on a map by organizational proclamations. A vast number of our local urban communities are a historical debris left over from the previous proclamations of developers, planners, boosters, map makers, sociologists, newspapers, and businesses in search of a clientele. To a large extent these localized settlements have been brought into the urban mix by annexation and have persisted on the faithful grounds that extracommunity institutions would continue to warrant their security from invasion. No doubt many residents have been disappointed, but once started, such a previously incorporated area is a rallying cry around which residents can agree and press their claims to a set of boundaries which have presumed consensual support. And there are grounds for their faith, for the proclamation of community boundaries is supposed to represent popular demand as well as to enlist the aid of external organizations as allies on behalf of a natural group. Frequently this aid is enlisted, and both legal and political forces have been harnessed to serve the defensive interests of such communities long after their original residents have been replaced. As with cost gradients, physical obstructions, and residual areas, these boundaries seem reliable fixtures to seize on and to defend, whether it means going into collusion with the neighbors or seeking allies outside the

16. Kevin Lynch, *The Image of the City* (Cambridge, Mass.: The M.I.T. Press, 1960).

17. Here the term *enacted* follows the meaning given it by William Graham Sumner, *Folkways* (New York: Dover, 1959).

community. In the absence of other boundaries which are self-enforcing, those endorsed by powerful groups and historical precedent are the best which can be chosen.

An interesting and now frequent example of enacted community boundaries is the suburban development, uniform in its placement within cost gradients, isolated from cross traffic, furnished with its own convenience shopping and business district, and named and bounded by the choices of a showman anxious to lure buyers susceptible to such labels as Enchanted Forest and Wilderness Lane.[18] These suburban creations represent a historic demarcation with which we and the residents must live for a long time. The temporal, architectural, and dimensional uniformity of such residential areas is apt to preserve them as distinct and legible entities which can lay claim to uniformity in their treatment and the homogeneity of their interests. At the outset, of course, such communities are protected by their developers, whose interests in defending the neighborhood are just good business. Chances are that the developer will preserve some interest in the area until first mortgages are paid off, written off, or renewed. Afterward the residents will probably expect a similar kind of paternalism which acknowledges their common past and will turn to public officials, politicians, and other allies to insure their invulnerability to widespread invasion. Most likely this will involve some effort, cohesion, and organization on the part of residents. But in the main, they will have to look for allies outside the suburban development to protect themselves, because the suburban development is usually so lacking in local institutions and individuals prominently known in the suburb that it must depend on the protective shield provided by the wider community. In this respect the defensive arrangements of an increasingly frequent type of residential group are likely to become a shifting balance between ism. As the corporate city continues to be a place of outmigration and expansion, the outmigrants will encroach on the nearby grass roots vigilantism and organizationally sponsored protection-

18. For a brief discussion of how these stereotypes fit into residential planning and marketing see Herbert Gans, *The Levittowners* (New York: Pantheon, 1967), pp. v–viii, 3–19.

suburbs and arouse administrative, legal, and vigilante efforts to
ward off the invasion and protect what is regarded as an identity
already agreed on and popularly supported. All of these attempts
are likely to arouse the established residents to clarify their identities and to concert their opinions, attitudes, and definition of
boundaries. This is simply an expansion to the outer limits of the
city of the conflicts, competition, and process of succession which
has been characteristic of the inner city as a result of urbanization and population growth. The suburb, unlike the inner city,
often lacks many important institutions and administrative arrangement (for example, its own police department, water supply,
higher educational institutions, museums, and so forth) which
can help to exclude or control these invaders without arousing the
residents themselves. Since the suburb adjacent to the city limits
is so vulnerable, it may have to resort to a good deal of vigilantism
especially now that restrictive covenants have been legally proscribed.

What all this seems to indicate is that residential groups do not
have too few boundaries to defend but too many. This is one of
the reasons there is often little consensus on community boundaries; the likely physical obstructions, cost gradients, and enacted
enclosures do not coincide to give a single limit at which residents
can be sure they are secure from encroachment. Thus some residents may pick a rail line to define their neighborhood, whereas
others may settle on a definition which depends more on the expense of housing or authoritative mappings. This confusion is
partially due to the independence of organizations outside the
community which do not choose their own boundaries by consulting one another or the local community but simply draw lines on
a map to suit their own requirements. This type of external gerrymandering is not just the habit of politicians but also that of
business and public administration. Especially in the United States,
we have no reliable prefectures but a frequently changing mosaic
of administrative districts and client communities which seldom
coincide.

These seeds of confusion, however, are not sown only by ignorant and inattentive outsiders. The residents must communicate

about where they stand relative to other locality groups, and some residential groups lack even this primitive capacity to be sensitive to public images of themselves and the physical and economic walls and moats which surround them. In this sense it is possible to say that many communities do have a communication problem, and some residential areas are so fragmented that they cannot come to agreement on much of anything. Some of these residential areas are composed of transients who have no long-term stake in the local community: hucksters, students, drummers, assistant professors, and tourists. Others are warned away from one another by public stereotypes which forbid communication at the risk of total victimization: the disreputable poor, the psychotic, the notoriously perverted, and the physically damaged.[19] What is most noteworthy about these groups is not their internal fragmentation but the rarity of communities composed of them alone.[20] Most residential groups can at least take the risk of talking and planning with one another.

The Alliance on Behalf of Communities

Without external allies the local community and its defended boundaries are in a precarious position. Not only are such allies essential to its defense, but their opposition or realignment may be fatal to the neighborhood's sense of integrity and self-determination. In recent years there is reason to believe that it is the changing posture of these external allies rather than any marked decline in their own internal defensiveness and solidarity which has so panicked many communities. With the passage of federal and state open housing laws and the desegregation of some local schools, a number of community groups righteously felt themselves betrayed. The growing role of the federal government in constructing housing and in providing mortgage money threatened to be another blow to a long-term alliance in which the construction

19. That is, outcast groups such as those pointed to by Erving Goffman, *Stigma* (Englewood Cliffs, N. J.: Prentice-Hall, 1963).

20. See Robert B. Edgerton, *The Cloak of Competence* (Berkeley and Los Angeles: University of California Press, 1967) for information on one such group that seldom makes up a residential group.

industry, real estate men, local government, and the federal authorities had implicitly endorsed the existing composition of local
communities. In the main, this was a source of alarm to most white
neighborhoods and to some affluent ethnic or black neighborhoods. When in addition, however, the federal government began
a number of community programs administered directly from
Washington or highly centralized agencies, somewhat the same
fears were aroused in black or relatively poor areas. On the one
hand, the discretionary authority of such federal agencies tended
to be very far removed from the local community and relatively
unavailable to local influence. On the other hand, the bureaucratic procedures of these programs represented a massive obstacle, especially to the poor and uneducated, when it came to
manipulating the administrative machinery to get the kind of
housing, police controls, public facilities, housing standards, and
zoning regulations which would help defend their neighborhood.

The inability to manipulate massive bureaucratic organizations
for collective ends made people, both affluent and poor, feel small,
not the least because they were assured that specific procedures
had been instituted for their participation. It was probably especially burdensome and embarrassing to poor blacks because their
aspirations seemed so contradictory. They could support open
housing for other communities, for example, but demanded local
control for themselves. Such a contradiction, however, was not
unique to them but is actually pervasive in the entire society. On
the one hand, there is a strong historic commitment to uniform
opportunities and standards of evaluation. On the other hand,
there is an equally strong commitment to acknowledging differen-
tial achievement and allowing people to sort themselves out
according to their accomplishments.[21] Insofar as communities differ
in their opportunities, it is difficult to allow them to differ also on
the basis of how they shape the opportunities of the residents. This
is not to say that there is no way out of this contradiction, but in

21. James Coleman, "The Concept of Equality of Educational Opportunity," *Harvard Educational Review* 38 (Winter, 1968): 7–22.

early 1970 it was clear that no obvious solution had been found. To a large extent people still thought that they could integrate the society by integrating its neighborhoods. And that was a strategy which not only threatened the defended community but left people alarmed for their safety and property. The law and order issue was basic to the defended neighborhood and, indeed, basic to the development of a community itself.

What was evident by 1970, however, was the fact that the strategies open to individuals and their own desires did not automatically make a community. In the past, a massive organizational alliance had gathered around the defended neighborhood in so quiet and crescive a way that the illusion of self-determination held fast. The weakening of that alliance has betrayed the dependency of the defended neighborhood and may open public discussion to a more explicit version of the defended neighborhood.

Community Identity

Elsewhere I have argued that the identities of local neighborhoods exist in tenuous opposition to one another and that relative rather than absolute differences give them their distinctive reputation. Obviously the main lines of differentiation are the dimensions of stratification which are pervasive to the entire society: race, ethnicity, income, education, and the like. Indeed most communities in the United States can be and are described in these terms. Ethnically and racially homogeneous neighborhoods are perhaps the most obvious examples, but far less distinctive neighborhoods find a marginal difference to emphasize and to distinguish between "us" and "them." The difficulty in establishing a neighborhood's identity, however, is not a shortage of relevant differences but a surplus of them. Even the small list given above shows that the problem is not a simple one and that almost any neighborhood is distinguished from others on more than one dimension. What I will do here is to map out what seem to be some of the governing conditions for the final determination of a local neighborhood's reputation.

Master Identities

Almost any local urban neighborhood is likely to be part of a larger sector of the wider community. Often these sectors are acknowledged by such banal labels as East Side, West Side, South Side, and so on. In any case, these are the largest acknowledged or named segments of the city, and often they are subdivided further before telescoping down to the local defended neighborhood. These broad divisions are often the creation of wide-scale public policies which assure investors and residents about the socioeconomic usage of land. Thus, in Chicago, it is fairly clear that the North Side will continue to be the major location for the city's most expensive housing and apartments. Builders, planners, investors, home buyers, and public officials have built up plans and investments to the point that this trend is almost irreversable. As a result, the basic contrast in the city's socioeconomic mapping is more or less foreclosed, and competition between these sectors ruled out as a real possibility. In Chicago it makes little sense for a South Side or West Side neighborhood to stress its affluence; it is sure to be overshadowed by some North Side Chicago neighborhood.[22] I suspect that similar patterns can be found in all sizable cities in the United States.

At the start, then, much of the importance of sheer affluence is drained off by this major contrast between urban sectors. Smaller and more local residential groups must contrast themselves within a smaller pool of communities on somewhat different criteria. For the local defended neighborhood there seem to be four prime considerations: how does it make its necessities virtues; who does it have to defend itself against; what are the competing residential areas; and what are its historic or achieved grounds for claiming a special place among other residential groups.

The broad sectorial socioeconomic divisions of the city create a special problem for those communities in sectors which fail to reach the highest rank. This is especially true for the most affluent

---

22. This situation is reversed for Chicago blacks who draw their main contrast between the poorer West Side black community and the better-off black neighborhoods on the city's South Side.

among these communities, and they stand rather like wealthy individuals who continue to live in the once elegant homes they were brought up in and around old but less successful friends. For example, Hyde Park on the South Side of Chicago is a wealthy and well-educated community clustered around the University of Chicago. Yet the community does not emphasize its sheer wealth, for that would tend to bring it into comparison with much better off neighborhoods on the North Side. These North Side neighborhoods have the further advantage of belonging to good company: an entire sector in which wealth is concentrated and likely to become more concentrated. Thus, whatever their conception of their neighborhood, Hyde Parkers cannot choose sheer wealth as a reason for their living there; on these grounds alone they would have a clearer status definition if they moved to the North Side.

Accordingly, Hyde Parkers tend to make a virtue of what is in large part the necessity of their living on the South Side. One component of this self-description is a rejection of wealth alone as a criteria for residential selection and an emphasis on counter themes: sentimental loyalties, antisnobbism, and cosmopolitanism of race and income groups. A second component is a kind of noblesse oblige by which Hyde Parkers expend much of their energies on behalf of surrounding neighborhoods in protesting the validity of employing socioeconomic evaluations of worth. Students at the University of Chicago seem especially struck with this impulse and rail mightily against the restrictive covenants which preserve the difference between the North Side and South Side as well as those which defend Hyde Park to the extent that the students themselves are not frightened away by the incursion of poor, black, and resentful residents in adjacent neighborhoods.

There are probably many neighborhoods like Hyde Park which are enough different from the sector in which they are placed that they must make a virtue of a master identity which says one thing about them and a subordinate identity which says something to the contrary.[23] In this sense neighborhood identities are very much

23. Everett C. Hughes, "Dilemmas and Contradictions of Status," *American Journal of Sociology* 50 (March 1945): 353–59.

like those of individuals: They may be more or less crystallized.[24]
Accordingly, some neighborhoods must look for an inobvious and
alternative thematic dimension to emphasize in identifying themselves. Four basic starting points seem almost self-evident: the
high income neighborhood in the highest income sector; the high
income neighborhood in a lower income sector; the low income
neighborhood in the highest income sector; and the low income
neighborhood in a lower income sector. For the first, the basic
strategy is simply holding on to what they have, since no basic
contradiction is present. The high income neighborhood in a
lower income sector is rather like Hyde Park: it must emphasize
attachment to place and sentimental loyalties which transcend
economic considerations. The low income neighborhood in a high
income sector correspondingly may emphasize its respectability
or poor but proud character in the hope of hanging on to at least
the virtues implied by the high socioeconomic standing of its
sector. The lower income neighborhood in a lower income sector
is like its counterpart in the high income sector: it can take the
implied vices of a low income sector and re-endorse them as extremes of a kind of virtue in toughness, a familiarity with sin,
and the early loss of innocence in life and politics. People in such
neighborhoods can at least claim to know their way around and
are likely to do so since they cannot claim a great deal more.

Competition among Neighborhoods

The content of a neighborhood's identity, however, is not likely to
stop here, because these are mainly citywide contrasts which do
not preempt all of an individual resident's attention. The defended
neighborhood, in particular, is apt to have a large proportion of
its attention captured by its differences from adjacent neighborhoods, especially those threatening it with invasion. It is a simple
and mechanical fact that residential encroachment in the United
States has proceeded largely in an unbroken and contiguous path,

24. I mean to use the term here without extending the analogy to
Gerhard Lenski's theory of political extremism in "Status Crystallization:
A Non-Vertical Dimension of Social Status," *American Sociological Re-
view* 19 (August 1954): 405–13.

and generally it is lower status groups which have replaced higher status ones. These local movements are likely to make defended neighborhoods especially aware of their predominant ethnicity, race, or marginal economic standing. On the West Side of Chicago, for example, ethnicity is a primordial distinction of great importance simply because there is not much else by which to distinguish people. Often, however, these neighborhoods are not nearly so ethnically homogeneous as one would think from hearing them discussed. Relative concentrations of ethnic groups are nonetheless emphasized because they say something about the past, present, and future of a defended neighborhood. Frequently this meant that an area of heavy invasion by a low status ethnic group was referred to as belonging to that group although it currently made up only a minority of the population.[25] Correspondingly, adjacent areas which had suffered less invasion were still referred to as belonging to the higher status ethnic groups. These differences were often based on small numerical quantities, but they made an important distinction to local people because they indicated which area would "go first" and which ones were better defended.

If it is at this level that contrasts of ethnicity and race are emphasized, it is also here that other differences in pedigree and ascribed background are made relevant to neighborhood identity. For example, affluent communities may not especially compare themselves on the basis of income but rather on how that income was gained. Less affluent communities may emphasize equally the type of work their residents do rather than the income they derive from it. Thus some communities in South Chicago have so many residents working in the steel mills that steel is a way of life for the community as well as the work place.[26] Such a self-description seems not only to convey a distinctive role of the community but to provide its residents with a sense of sharing in a special, even

25. Harvey Warren Zorbaugh, *The Gold Coast and the Slum* (Chicago: University of Chicago Press, 1929).
26. See a forthcoming Ph.D. dissertation by William Kornblum, "The Integration of Ethnic Groups in Modern Society: Serbian and Croatian Ethnicity in Southeast Chicago" (University of Chicago).

privileged, knowledge. The same sources of prideful exclusiveness may be present in neighborhoods which can claim an exceptional familiarity with the Mafia, Hollywood stars, political figures, and other famous and infamous people. The elements in community identity, like those of ethnicity and pedigree, become more or less relevant as they make a contrast or are threatened by change through invasion. The defended neighborhood marks itself off from adjacent ones and is most likely to emphasize those attributes it can lose; and sometimes this means deemphasizing those characteristics it shares with invaders or ignoring those which are distinctive of other residential groups that do not threaten it. Thus, some of our most elaborated community identities belong to areas which are considered very exclusive but are imperiled.

Contrasts and Competition among Neighborhoods

Except for the defeated community, all residential groups seem to make some claims for residential exclusiveness: not just anyone can live there. This sort of exclusiveness, however, is counter-balanced by the necessity of residential areas to recruit new residents and, in the modern American urban city, this means mostly residents from other communities. Thus every community has its competitors, although some are much more aware of them than others. In this country, these competitive claims are in the main farmed out to and by the realty and construction industry. The virtues and attractions of a particular community for outsiders, then, tend to fall into the hands of professional image makers. Indeed, practically every large city tends to have a city newspaper which devotes an entire Sunday section to the selling of residential images. Americans may dismiss these mercenary inspirations as only beguiling fictions. Nonetheless, prospective home buyers and renters purchase these news releases and, while they may read between the lines, they also find there a portrait or idealization of what they are seeking in the way of a family, a neighbor, and a community. Such images are not wholly fraudulent, and they are passed back to the residents as claims worth fulfilling if not entirely descriptive. "Levittown" and "New England Village" are not just merchandising labels, but really different places, and the rental and home buyers' market make them apt if not fully honest portraits. Moreover a stereotypic image presses each area into a particular league in which it vies with a special set of other communities. The rental and home buyer's market, then, projects for each residential area a selective fate, and it is out of this idealized fate that each must partially construct an identity.

In drawing on these current and exaggerated images, present-day communities are not doing something especially new or exceptional, because the mass media have recently intruded themselves into our lives so as to separate first-hand and second-hand knowledge. The United States has always had its boosters, drummers, and exuberant land sellers in search of a naïve market. Some of the earliest settlers who came to the land literally expected the streets to be paved with gold and a fountain of youth to spout from every stream. People are less naïve today, and both European immigrants and native migrants exercise some caution in reading the publicist's claims. Nonetheless, many a community has incorporated into its identity the claims and exaggerations of boosters, and our ability to brush aside the superficiality of these images makes it easy for us to forget their origin.

Residential image making is a complicated task, but at least three of its features stand out. One is the convenience aspects of a residential area in terms of its facilities, nearness to transportation lines, and sufficiency as a place of shelter and familial activities. In describing these features, a publicist is restrained to be fairly accurate because he is talking about objective facts which can be checked by a stranger. A second is its promise to provide a particular style of life once the resident steps outside his doorway to commune with neighbors. Claims about the communal qualities of a residential area are more subject to manipulation simply because they cannot easily be verified without one's first residing in the area for a time. Oddly enough, it is here that physical appearances of a neighborhood become most important and persuasive. Shady trees, large lawns, aged homes, Cape Cod fronts, sheer modern facades, and cozy backyards evoke responses because they suggest more than themselves: distinctive ways of life which people feel they can share and in which they think they can express an authentic version of themselves.[27] A third feature is the local schools, or beliefs about their effectiveness and safety. The schools provide a special problem since there are a number of indices to their effectiveness, not all of which the realtor can control or exclusively represent. The tendency here may be to emphasize selectively the physical plant of the school, its pupil-teacher ratio, or some other fairly available datum. The poor performance of these indicators[28] may not retard their continued usage, simply because they are available and little else can be used to make so fateful a decision.

What the publicists must do is make communities commensurate with one another and develop archetypes which will strike a responsive chord in the minds of prospective buyers and renters. Beyond the problems of cost and convenience, what do people want in the way of a residential area? We are dealing with uncharted ground here and can only say that these images of community are likely to be drawn from a larger inventory of fantasies which appeal to the American people. No doubt one component revolves around the rural-urban dichotomy with bucolic, leisured, and equalitarian provincialism being juxtaposed against sophisticated, artistic, and selective cosmopolitanism. Another component is likely to revolve around historic claims between those areas which can associate themselves with a special legacy as against those which strike out for something which is new, avant-garde, and unconstrained by the past. About all that we can conclude with is that these advertised Edens come in antinomies with each pole finding its counterpart and its set of more or less numerous buyers and renters. For each community these archetypes represent an element to be taken into its identity unless it is so unpopular that it is not worth advertising.

27. For further discussion of the conditions for presenting an authentic self see Suttles's "Friendship as a Social Institution," in George McCall, ed., *Social Relationships* (Chicago: Aldine Press, 1970), pp. 95–135.

28. Morris Janowitz, *Institution Building in Urban Education* (New York: Russell Sage Foundation, 1969), pp. 1–34.

Historic Claims to Fame

Aside from its comparative advantages or disadvantages, each community can also lay claim to a more or less rich historic legacy which is valued by some of its residents and incommensurate with the history of other communities. Logically it is possible for all communities to win at this game because it is like comparing apples and oranges. First, there is the new community which is unshackled by historic precedents, full of modern pioneers, and striving to find its sacred charter. People in older and more settled communities may label it crass, anomic, and "a nothing." Second, there is the community which has endured and endured without any notable accomplishments, outstanding individuals, or signal events. Their pride may have to rely on their persistent commonness, even though outsiders may express a different evaluation. Third are those communities which seek or claim a special history but end as parvenus because their assertions can be challenged as inauthentic. Finally, there are communities which do have a history and uniqueness to them which comes from a reverence for the past.

Communities of the last type are relatively scarce in the United States as compared to some areas of Europe, where local continuity has been preserved through the maintenance of special landmarks, institutions, and housing. Recency of settlement, rapid growth, and a widespread tendency to equate age with obsolescence have militated against the continued usage and restoration of local facilities in the United States. Thus, many communities have lost what could have been considered some of their most valued possessions: the homes of famous residents, public facilities belonging to the founding of the community, typical cases of an architectural period, and the scene of important events which could now make the community itself seem important. Perhaps these losses are to be expected in a nation which has grown so fast with an unplanned market economy to govern largely what is kept and what is torn down. But there is also a sense in which construction in the United States is undertaken in the first place without much expectation that a building or place will endure past a couple of generations.[29] Partly this is due to a market economy in which buildings and places are meant to be competitive on utilitarian criteria alone. It is also due to a continually changing technology and the limited vision of buyers who assume that their own usage or profits and the buildings on which they depend need not endure past their own lifetimes. Thus, most American buildings last about the average adult lifetime before they are considered deteriorated.[30]

Nonetheless, communities in the United States vary in their historical impoverishment and their ability to lay claim to themselves as a cradle for important men, events, and accomplishments. The general tendency, of course, is to emphasize newness, freedom from the past, and the promise of a future in which youngsters will respect the material constructions of their elders. A few communities not only possess an inheritance from the past but hang on to it with a tenacity which is understandable considering its scarcity, vulnerability, and most of all, the capacity of such legacies to make people proud without always making them invidious. Like apples and oranges, they are incommensurate and some of the least prestigeful communities in the United States find in their preserved histories a way in which they can associate themselves with important happenings and persons who have done important things. Their pride is not meaningless, or at least no more so than one's pride in the accomplishments of his parents, friends, the circle he associates with, or the people he is seen with at the opera. Such a community has proof that it has the capacity to produce great and unique men, events, places, and buildings.

Obviously such historic legacies are not absolutely vital to people or communities. Indeed, most Americans live without such shared pride and emphasize their individual claims to fame. These historic earmarks have only the capacity to make all communities proud of themselves; they are not a functional requisite any more than is steak or ice cream. A few United States communities pos-

29. Theodore Lowie, *The End of Liberalism* (New York: W. W. Norton and Co., 1969), pp. 101–88.
30. The President's Committee on Urban Housing, *A Decent Home* (Washington, D.C.: Government Printing Office, 1969), pp. 7–36, 39–50.

sess such riches and it is understandable that they make a great
to-do about them in their identities.

The Community as an Object of Administration

The community is a perennial referent in the rhetoric of politicians,
administrators, and sociologists. The politicians pay it eloquent
tribute and say that they represent it. Administrators say they
serve it. Some sociologists deny the veracity of the politicians and
administrators and say only that the community is declining.[31] Is
the local community declining and has it lost its raison d'être, or
has it at least lost out in the power plays which have juxtaposed
the state against the community? This is the central question which
lumbers throughout most studies of the local community.[32] Before
attempting to face the question head on, it is worthwhile to re-
state a couple of basic observations. First, total societies are not
made up from a series of communities, but communities are units
which come into being through their recognition by a wider society. Community, then, presumes some type of supracommunity
level of organization. Second, the community is not a little society
but a form of social differentiation within total societies, and the
problem is how appropriate this type of social differentiation is in
modern societies.

National Centralization

Throughout the literature on the community, the community has
been juxtaposed against the state and mass society with the latter
being seen as growing at the expense of the former. The community, then, joins a list of institutions or groups which have been
seen as declining competitors of the state and mass society: the
family, the small firm, regionalism, and so forth. An earlier forecast of the family's disappearance and its replacement by the

31. Maurice R. Stein, *The Eclipse of Community* (New York: Harper
and Row, 1960).
32. For a general overview of the question see Robert A. Nisbet, *Community and Power* (New York: Oxford University Press, 1962), pp. 75–97.

state, however, has turned out to be quite erroneous. One wonders if somewhat the same mistake is being made in studies of the community. Undoubtedly the community has been losing functions just as the family lost functions in the transformation from a rural to an urban society. Also there is a general increase in people's dependency on national levels of organization and their tendency to appeal to those organizations. Certainly the power of the state is very great as compared to that of the local community, and the limited liability of the resident does not tie him closely to the local residential group. Nonetheless, this may not mean the complete disappearance of the local community, and there are other, more interesting questions to ask about it.

First, there is the question of whether or not this zero-sum formulation in the relationship between the state and the local community is at all appropriate. Are, for example, Stockholm and its new suburbs like Farsta and Välingby less powerful and distinct because the Swedish prime minister appoints the city's mayor and the new suburbs have been totally planned and built by the central state? In fact, the direct relationship between the mayor and prime minister may establish a line of administrative authority in which power and responsibility can be joined.[33] One of the sources of community weakness in most American cities is that many mayors are responsible to local communities but have little direct recourse to the federal levels at which major power and resources are located. More direct administrative relationships between local and national levels of organization may give local residents and their representatives a louder, not a smaller, voice in determining the services which come to them. Similarly, the centralized planning and development of local communities may not be destructive of their identity and distinctiveness. On this point the Swedes provide another instructive example: most of the new, centrally planned and built suburban developments of

33. Mitchell Gordon, *Sick Cities* (Baltimore: Penguin, 1965), pp. 331–65; Lowie, *End of Liberalism,* pp. 193–206; and National Resources Committee, "The Problems of Urban America," *Our Cities: Their Role in the National Economy* (Washington, D.C.: Government Printing Office, 1937), pp. 55–70.

Stockholm are surrounded by a high cyclone-wire fence topped with barbed wire and broken at only two or three main entrances. The intent seems not to have been the creation of a defended neighborhood but the recognition of a right to collective privacy on the part of residential groups. In the United States it would be hard to justify such collective rights, since they would more often coincide with racial, ethnic, and income differences. For this same reason it has been difficult to justify any public policy which responds to the collective ends of residential groups. Yet the principle of shared usage and its importance to residential groups need not be discarded on these grounds alone.

The example of Sweden here is telling, for there are few more centralized societies with a more consolidated administrative structure. But their local communities seem extremely well served and by reputation very demanding.[34] This does not mean that Swedish communities are extremely provincial and that they are characterized by high levels of neighboring.[35] This seems to be neither expected nor achieved. But the Swedish local community is well served, and the line of authority and power which is responsible for serving it is extremely clear and consolidated.

By contrast, most attempts to preserve the local community or its autonomy in the United States have been founded on the idea of decentralization and the separation of powers. Thus, local representatives, city officials, state officials, and federal office-holders tend not to have any direct lines of authority among them. The result is often a stalemate with each level of authority disclaiming either responsibility or the power to do anything. Alternatively, the services extended to communities have been extremely inequitable and have depended very much on informal and quasi-legitimate political influence. One wonders if in the United States the state in antithetical to the influence of local groups or if the

34. City planners in other, less centralized Scandinavian countries tend to report that the Swedes are "too demanding." City planners in both Norway and Denmark have told me that they intended to put fewer convenience facilities into new communities than would have been necessary in Sweden.

35. Kell Aström, *City Planning in Sweden* (Stockholm: The Swedish Institute, n.d.).

different levels of government are simply so incoherent and poorly defined that regular channels of influence cannot be found, especially when collective ends are being sought.

A second line of support for the argument that the local community is losing significance in modern societies is that nationally based criteria of social differentiation are coming to overshadow local ones. Thus, nationally defined groups and associations are the primary sources of individual participation and avenues of power and influence. Although this may be especially true for the United States, it again could be due largely to the ineffectiveness of local government in reaching the federal levels of authority where power and responsibility can be rejoined. Within an administrative structure where local and federal authority were closely linked, the local organization might be a more effective vehicle for insuring the rights and demands of people. After all, nationally based organizations, such as labor unions, welfare rights organizations, lobbies, and what not, have only a limited effectiveness themselves, and the results are often so inequitable that they arouse constant claims of injustice which weaken governmental claims to legitimacy.[36] Interest group politics works only for some of the people some of the time. It is quite possible that a cross-cutting form of organization like the local community will produce units which are comparable to one another and which can include everyone so as to promote greater equity and help maintain the legitimacy of government. Certainly not all governmental services can be distributed in this manner, but a vast number of them are: policing, secondary education, sanitation, and so on. Since the legitimacy of government is not an insignificant functional requirement, the use of the local community as an interest group may give it greater strategic importance than is commonly associated with it.

The view of the local community being replaced by nationally based lines of social differentiation, however, contains in it a distorted perspective of what the local community is like in the first place. The local urban residential community seems always

36. Lowie, *End of Liberalism,* pp. 191–213.

to have been based on national lines of differentiation. Race, ethnicity, and socioeconomic differences are at the heart of the residential patterns giving rise to the local community and national organizations. The local rural community may have been more heterogeneous, but that does not mean that humble people living on plantations, farm communities, and industrial farms had a greater voice in determining their own affairs. Economic differentiation in such areas was only more likely to concentrate power in the hands of a small group of local elites who were manipulative to the point that they bought off dissent by charity sweetened with interpersonal familiarity.[37] The entire southeastern portion of the United States is a persistent reminder of this type of localism, and it is hardly a region where everyone has a voice which can be heard in his community.[38] Local groups with a broad constituency are probably more effective in Chicago than they are in any of the remote and unchallenged towns of the South.[39]

A more productive outlook may be to emphasize the way in which some national bases of differentiation are shifting in emphasis while socioeconomic criteria are becoming more elaborated. Race and ethnicity have been long-time criteria of social differentiation, but they are losing some of their relative emphasis as the federal government and some large businesses and higher educational institutions give them lower priority. This movement is slight and often it is only a token move toward erasing racial and ethnic criteria for the distribution of housing, education, police protection, occupational promotion, and so on. Nonetheless it is enough to panic many local residential groups and especially local elites whose monopoly on patronage and low level public offices is threatened. They are one source of the outcry against the government and centralization. Others are the relatively poor

37. Liston Pope, *Millhands and Preachers* (New Haven: Yale University Press, 1942).

38. John Dollard, *Caste and Class in a Southern Town* (New Haven: Yale University Press, 1937); and Morton Rubin, *Plantation County* (New Haven: College and University Press, 1963).

39. Compare the reports of Peter H. Rossi and Robert H. Dentler, *The Politics of Urban Renewal* (New York: The Free Press of Glencoe, 1961) with those of Theodore Lowie, *End of Liberalism*, pp. 252–66.

people and blacks who, although they have been encouraged enough to be outspoken, still find the division of powers in the United States government so great that some of them would prefer a transfer of power back to local authorities. Thus they could at least have their own patronage and minor elective offices, which is somewhat more than they can obtain in the present confusion or inadequacy of state, federal, local, and regional governments. More affluent and powerful Americans have settled for this before, and there is no reason to think that the blacks and poor have a more ambitious model.

With the decline of importance of racial and ethnic differentiation at the national level, socioeconomic criteria of occupation and education may be acquiring more significance and becoming more elaborated. But the growth of specialties, the number of people attending college, and the proliferation of tastes in a more cosmopolitan society may also bring about a finer partitioning of socioeconomic and age groups. Something like this is already evident in the growth of communes, centers of concentration for "street people," swinging sections for the young unmarrieds, retirement villages, bohemias around universities, and suburbs with a vast proportion of their residents in the process of family formation. The heavily serviced high-rise apartment house complex, the planned community with extensive recreational facilities, and the urban development fit distinct styles of life which belong predominantly to certain age and occupational groups. No doubt such groups will become progressively segregated into residential areas where they can retain an unchallenged version of their beliefs, values, and personal presentation. The problem of American communities, then, is to adapt to these more elaborated socioeconomic and age-graded bases of differentiation while relenting on the matter of race and ethnicity.

This does not mean that such local socioeconomic or age-graded communities will be formed everywhere. The United States is a large and extremely varied country. As change overtakes portions of it, other sections remain relatively stable or relocate. Thus, while new communities based on socioeconomic and age criteria are developing, immigrant communities, black belts, and very heterogeneous residential groups will remain in existence in numerous places. In addition, other communities may develop a sort of quasi-ethnic style of life which a large number of people adopt temporarily from local or historic ethnic traditions. Such communities are already partially developed in some places where a minority ethnic group provides a range of food customs, special vocabulary, and a set of tastes about furniture, clothing, and so on. Some middle class Jewish and Italian neighborhoods are Jewish or Italian only in practice; the majority of their inhabitants are neither Jewish nor Italian but simply try out a style of life which fits them into a dominant way of life. Here ethnicity has little political or economic importance but is mainly a common expressive order in which people find a sense of unity and sureness.

No doubt there will also remain areas which are atomized to the point that they have practically no identity or consensus on their boundaries and reputation. This absence of community is not only a psychic loss to most residents; it has broader functional consequences. The local community has the advantage that everyone can be a member and that it places people in relatively comparable bargaining units. Unlike labor unions, professional associations, and business councils, the constituency of the local community includes everyone and allows us to make comparisons about the equity of services, wages, building programs, and their delivery. The difficulty with interest group politics as they are presently practiced among powerful associations is that they lead to broad inequities or the appearance of inequity without any commensurate basis for settling the question.[40] This results in serious limits on the legitimacy of public institutions, government, and private businesses. Interest group politics may be able to produce equity, but it is as impossible to tell when it does as it is impossible to tell if the oil depletion allowances and ADC programs are fair redistributions of wealth. Since it is impossible to create even the illusion of equity, interest group politics seems inevitably to lay government and business open to claims of favoritism and corruption. By comparison, the local community

40. Lowie, *End of Liberalism.*

can serve as a more inclusive reference unit for evaluating the distributive justice of our society.

The Community as Communion

So far I have taken a narrow view of the local urban community by regarding it as the defended neighborhood which segregates people to avoid danger, insult, and the impairment of status claims. This is, I think, a sufficient basis for explaining community differentiation, but it is not all that communities are or become. Part of my emphasis has been a reaction to the overromanticization of the local community and the tendency to make sentiments and sentimentalism so basic to it that the community could later be dismissed as only an expressive solidarity without instrumental functions. But, like all other institutions, the local community attracts to itself additional hopes for the expression of self and sentiment. The desire to find a social setting in which one can give rein to an authentic version of oneself and see other people as they really are is not some unanalyzable human need but the most fundamental way in which people are reassured of their own reality as well as that of other people.[41] A Goffmanesque world in which people do only what is situationally suitable is ultimately a frightening world, where hypocrisy and insincerity undermine any long-term plans and the people behave as chameleons once backs are turned.[42] Every society rides on the faith that some of the people some of the time really mean what they say and do. The organization man, the other-oriented individual, and a society of labels are insufficient images if people are to trust one another long enough to get through a single day. Presentations of self, then, are not mere ways of letting off steam: they are essential expressive interludes when group members reestablish each other's

41. Suttles, "Friendship," pp. 116–20.
42. One of the bases for the broad distaste expressed for the "other directed" individual may be this fear of a social world which is uncertain because the people in it are themselves uncertain. See David Reisman, *Individualism Reconsidered* (Garden City, N. Y.: Doubleday and Co., 1955).

confidence in the coincidence between subjective and objective realities.

Within this context the local community stands out as a symbol in people's hopes for a collectivity in which they can be rather than seem.[43] Indeed this seems to be a predominant contemporary use of the symbolism of the community and the constant attempts to make other institutions into communities by labeling them as such (the community of scholars, and so forth). Among Americans this quest for community reaches almost pathetic proportions, with people falling victim to the most romantic advertisements for homes which attempt to give an imitation of a bygone age with Tudor cottages, Cape Cod fronts, and plantation porticoes attached to modest bungalows. The search for tree-lined streets, for a small community, and for a quiet place to live are in part a search for collectivities which at least have the earmarks of a place for the authentic moral expression of self. There is a certain irony in this symbolism because the original meaning which Tönnies gave community or *Gemeinschaft* emphasized its ascriptive character and independence of sentiments except as people adapted to necessity. This meaning lingers in sociology, and the freedom of people to move and be indifferent to their residential group seems almost antithetical to the traditional local community.[44] Indeed, community seems to have undergone a transformation in the minds of Americans, and what people see in it is not Tönnies's community but Schmalenbach's communion. The community is a place to share feelings and expose one's tender inner core. The freedom of people (or at least some people) to choose where they live is an essential ingredient to this meaning of the local community. Communion rests on its voluntariness, and as Schmalenbach pointed out, it was antithetical to the traditional

43. We are not speaking here of the opportunity to be merely spontaneous and licentious, for what people may feel most authentic in their expressions of self are moral convictions and statements of worth.

44. Norton E. Long, "Political Science and the City," in L. Schnore and H. Fagin, eds., *Urban Research and Policy Planning* (Beverly Hills: Sage Publications, 1967), pp. 243–62.

community which coerced membership and loyalty.[45] With the loss of the ascribed local community, the entire concept is transformed into a sort of social movement for relations which are intimate enough to be self-revealing.

Although this is a growing symbolic representation of the local community, I suspect that it is poorly realized in most actual communities. To a large extent Americans still live where they have to and, in any case, have to move so often that the community of limited liability is the most prevalent form. The coerciveness of the work place and other institutions not only creates a yearning for community but makes it difficult to realize in the residential community. Thus people seek for alternatives in other institutions: the student community, the political community, the business community, and so on. The extent to which these other institutions can offer either communion or community is limited by their institutional dependencies. They cannot be fully liberated and continue to function. The focus of the desire for community, then, will probably continue to return to the local residential community, and if people seem shallow and inauthentic elsewhere, the pressure for a community of sentiment may increase.

Whatever the condition of our residential communities, then, they are likely to have their avid defenders. They will be over-romanticized in both symbol and word. They may even be passed off as a primal and unchallengeable urge for territoriality. As Nisbet points out, the quest for community can reach absurd proportions to the point that it is self-defeating.[46] The totalistic national community is one direction in which this quest can go. Totalitarianism, however, seems rather unlikely in the United States. There are so many safeguards against centralization that government may become inaccessible while still lacking decisive power of its own. Moreover, the symbols of national communalism seem never to have been widely developed in the country. The notion of the nation as a single family, as a great unity of purpose,

45. Herman Schmalenbach, "The Sociological Category of Communion," in Parsons, et al., eds., *Theories of Society* (New York: The Free Press of Glencoe, 1961), pp. 331–47.
46. Nisbet, *Community*.

and as a geist shared by the masses has never had much credence
in this country. The American Creed remains a small businessman's creed, and it is unable to provoke people to such "noble"
and self-sacrificing utopias as the undivided, totalitarian state.[47]
The central government in the United States may get *out of* control, but it is doubtful that it will get *in* control. We can have
unpopular wars, depressions, international crises, a bad balance
of payments, urban riots, income levels which are felt to be totally
unjust, and almost total mismanagement of public life. But I doubt
the United States has even the managerial skills, much less the
symbolism, to run an authentic totalitarian government. In the
United States "the community" is likely to remain the local residential community although the height of people's expectations
for it may change.

A more likely consequence of the quest for a community of
sentiment—one where everyone can be his true moral self—is
that the utopian images evoked tend to make insignificant any
actual communities that have existed. The community, then, is
defended according to what it might become rather than for what
it is or has been. Such utopias are a powerful lure tempting us to
reconstruct history and dismiss the present. In the hands of some
defenders of the local community, these utopian images may promote a tactic of legal protectionism which has a well-worn precedent in the United States. The use of legal proscriptions to protect
the rights of certain groups and the use of the courts to enforce
them are favored practices in the United States with its weak
administrative bodies. When, however, this type of protectionism
is extended to the local community, the restrictive covenants that
have been informally practiced in the past are passed into law.
Such a procedure is unlikely to preserve existing communities and
would make it difficult for them to adjust to what is one of their
major problems today: re-sorting their membership to coincide
with a changing system of stratification in which race and ethnicity
are of less importance than they once were. Yet some of those

47. Francis X. Sutton, et al., *The American Business Creed* (New York:
Schocken Books, 1962).

who call for local control seem to fail to see this and try to preserve local groups as if their membership could be defined as a permanent legal category. The new territorialists carry this image of the local community to the point that it becomes an insurmountable obstacle to broader social collectivities.

In the context of this excessive vision of the local community, it is important to keep in mind the limited role of the local community. The local community can share some of the burden of making available to people the opportunity for communion, but this is a burden widely distributed in any society. It also has the potential to serve as a consolidated, all-purpose, administrative unit which could go far toward rejoining power and responsibility between the various levels of government and their constituencies. As a localized group of people whose placement in a national or local system of stratification warrants mutual trustworthiness, the local community can also give people a sense of security and ease. The local residential group can also be a collective identity, drawing the proofs of its members' pride from the past or the future. I suspect, however, that it is troublesome if not impossible to freeze the local residential group into its present form as dictated by contemporary restrictive residential selection. The local community must remain a partially open institution, and its rights cannot be insured as are those of racial and ethnic groups where membership is fixed and persistent. As a part or the whole of an administrative unit, the local residential community can survive, perhaps even thrive. By acknowledging its limitations, we might be able to use it for what it is: first, as a reflection of our changing system of social stratification so that strangers who are neighbors can trust one another, and second, as a small world within which people who are generally distrusted can find trust on more provincial grounds.

Index

Accountability, 162–63, 188, 228, 229
Acquaintances, network of, 55–56
Adaptability, 123–24, 133
ADC (Aid to Dependent Children), 217, 218
Administrative: pyramid, 54, 166–69, 183, 258; structure, 62, 67, 79–81
Adolescents, 189–227. *See also* Gangs; Peer groups
Adults: black, 204–5; Italian, 202–3, 205; Mexican, 203–4, 205; Puerto Rican, 204, 205. *See also* Father; Intergenerational relations; Mother
Adversaries, 50, 57, 58, 60–61, 62, 65–66
Advertising, 41, 243, 252–54, 265
Advocates, 50, 57, 58, 60–61, 62, 65–66
Affiliation, 13, 14, 163–64, 180, 183–84. *See also* Alliances
Affluence, 238–39, 248, 251
Age: grades, 163, 205, 221, 262; segregation by, 42, 220–21, 262. *See also* Intergenerational relations; Peer groups
Aggression, relation to territoriality, 121, 128–29, 140–55
Aggressive displays, 151, 152–53, 154–55; and distancing, 161, 180–81; among nonhumans, 144, 145, 149–51, 152, 155
Aid to Dependent Children, 217, 218
Alice in Wonderland, 115n
Alihan, Milla A., 23n
Alinsky, Saul, 63n
Alliances: shifting of, 166–68; of territorial groups, 57, 165, 166
Allies, external, 242, 243, 245

Ambler, Eric, 186n
American Dream, 192, 267
Amish, 172
Animals: analogy with, 118–28; territoriality among, 16–17, 119–20, 141–42, 144, 145, 149–51, 152, 155
Anonymity, 33, 163. *See also* Accountability
Arbitrariness, 17, 28, 114, 135
Ardrey, Robert, 16, 112–13, 115–39, 143, 186
Artificial neighborhoods, 15–16, 41–43. *See also* Developments
Associates, choice of, 160–62, 180, 183–84
Authority. *See* Dominance
Autonomy, local. *See* Community control
Avoidance relations, 158–60

Back of the Yards Council, 63
Banfield, Edward, 10
Barriers, physical, 53–54, 234–35, 241, 242, 244
Biological determinism, 115, 116–17, 122–23
Black Belt (Chicago), 28, 83, 171
Black Hand, 210n
Blacks: adult, 204–5; family among, 217–20; gangs among, 197, 201, 202; girls, 207–8; and schools, 98–99, 245. *See also* Segregation, racial
Block clubs, 56–57, 65, 66, 209
Boston 1915 plan, 76–77
Boulding, Kenneth E., 113n
Boundaries: confusion over, 244–45; development of, 53–54; enacted, 242–43; of household, 179; neighborhood, 22–23, 25–28, 50–51, 80–81, 161, 223, 225,